Temple Israel Library
Minneapolis, Minn.

AMERICAN JEWS:

Community in Crisis

GERALD S. STROBER

AMERICAN JEWS: Community in Crisis

GARDEN CITY, NEW YORK
DOUBLEDAY & COMPANY, INC.
1974

Excerpts from "I'd Love to See the J.D.L. Fold Up But—" by Walter Goodman, *New York Times Magazine,* November 21, 1971, copyright © 1971 by The New York Times Company. Reprinted by permission.

Excerpts from Jon Groner's "The 1973 Phenomenon: Jewish Residences" and Jon Levenson's "Life with Jews is Not Yet Jewish Life," originally appeared in the May 11, 1973, issue of *Sh'ma,* a journal of Jewish responsibility.

Library of Congress Cataloging in Publication Data

Strober, Gerald S
    American Jews: community in crisis.

    Includes bibliographical references.
    1. Jews in the United States—Political and social conditions. 2. Judaism—United States. I. Title.
E184.J5S85   301.45'19'24073
ISBN 0-385-06494-2
Library of Congress Catalog Card Number 73–22793

In loving memory of my father,

PHILIP STROBER

CONTENTS

AMERICAN JEWS:

Community in Crisis

FOREWORD

The American Jewish community is currently faced with critical problems of an international and domestic nature. In a genuine sense, the Jewish community is under siege, disturbed from without by the threat to Israel's existence, the energy crisis and the success of Arab political tactics and propaganda, as well as by the enmity and hostility of many of the same groups it once worked with in coalition; and troubled from within, by the continuing ambiguity of its relationship with Israel, and a major series of crises involving identity, the disaffection of youth, the status of religion and the diminishing effectiveness of the communal organizations. There is much evidence to suggest that these problems will deepen and intensify during the next several years. After careful study and on the basis of involvement within the Jewish communal structure, I am convinced that American Jewry is now entering the most perilous period in the three-and-one-quarter-century history of Jewish life in America.

External difficulties will cause the Jewish community to be hard pressed to maintain its position as an equal partner in the American pluralistic setting, while internal weakness and dissention will inhibit the nation's Jews from adopting the disciplined posture required to cope with the grave threat to continuity and survival. It is also likely that we are on the threshold of a major attitudinal shift in American opinion vis-à-vis the Jews, which though not resulting in overt anti-Semitic outbreaks, will nonetheless act to upset the normal patterns of Jewish communal existence while making life rather unpleasant for the individual Jew.

American reaction to the Yom Kippur war and the energy crisis, give evidence of the direction public opinion may take regarding the Jewish community. In the period immediately following the war calls to radio and television talk shows, letters to newspaper editors, editorials and communications to Congressmen, focused on the intimate relationship between Israel and the American Jewish community. American Jews were accused of supporting Israel to the detriment of United States foreign and domestic policy objectives and for exerting pressure on the Administration and the Congress. Jews were criticized for their heavy financial support of Israel and much was made of the huge contributions of specific individuals. As news reports described reductions in Arab oil production and exports and increases in the price of oil and petroleum products, Israel was charged with precipitating the energy crisis. The clear message that was directed to the American Jewish community was to either influence Israel to end her "intransigence" over the return of territories or be viewed as an accomplice with the Israelis in engendering the hostility of the Arab oil producing nations toward the United States. The events of the Yom Kippur war, including the major Soviet arms build-up of Egypt and Syria coupled with a growing Russian presence in the Mediterranean, disturbed an American public still reeling from the effects of the Vietnam experience. To many

Americans the Yom Kippur war, produced the specter of yet another military adventure in which U.S. troops would be committed to a foreign battlefield. The fact that Israel had never in the past requested such assistance had little effect in dispelling the notion that American forces would soon be stationed along the Suez front. These fears were greatly exacerbated when President Nixon suddenly ordered a world-wide American military alert in the early morning hours of October 25, 1973. This presidential action, though quickly modified, sent a shock wave through the nation.

The American Jewish community was stunned by the public reaction to the Yom Kippur war. This response was far different from the almost universal approbation placed upon Israel's decisive actions in the June 1967 conflict. The heroic and immensely competent Israelis of 1967 had become human, vulnerable and recalcitrant personages in 1973. American Jews who had basked in the reflected glory of Israel's 1967 achievements were now identified with the most negative aspects of the Yom Kippur war's causes and results. The fact that the war began as a clear case of Arab aggression and that Israel had avoided the temptation of a pre-emptive strike had little positive impact upon the war-weary American people who felt threatened by forces far beyond the control of themselves or even their government.

The American public, worried over what was interpreted as a near nuclear confrontation with the Soviet Union and troubled by the enlarging energy crunch, wanted an end to hostilities in the Middle East and expressed little sympathy for any person or government that appeared to stand in the way of a permanent settlement. Mr. and Mrs. America cannot reach out over the thousands of miles to strike the Israelis, but they can and perhaps will target the community they regard as Israel's surrogate in the United States—the same community, it should be added, that is identified in the minds of an increasing number of persons with standing in the way of *détente* through its aggressive support of the Soviet Jews.

There then appear to be factors at work in the society that make the Jewish community vulnerable to scapegoating. American Jews have served to relieve the frustrations of their fellow citizens in other periods of U.S. history—one immediately recalls the 1930s and the activities of Coughlin, Gerald L. K. Smith, et al.—and despite the relative serenity of recent years there is little reason to believe that Jews in America have become immune to manifestations of gentle hostility. Indeed, I can foresee a combination of factors related to the Middle East, the energy situation and the economy that would facilitate the formation of a WASP-white, ethnic-black anti-Jewish coalition.

As early as 1971 Norman Podhoretz, the editor of *Commentary,* described a "sharp weakening" in long-standing American taboos against anti-Semitism, while Earl Raab, a Jewish sociologist, called attention to the potential for the development of organized anti-Jewish activity in America. For these observations, Podhoretz, Raab and other prophets of gloom were labeled paranoid and hysterical by leaders of the Jewish establishment whose universalist orientation would not allow for the possibility of a decline of Jewish status in America. By "Jewish establishment" I mean that amalgam of national human relations and defense agencies such as the American Jewish Committee, the Anti-Defamation League of B'nai B'rith, the American Jewish Congress, the National Jewish Community Relations Advisory Council and the major local area community organizations.

Tragically, for the issue of Jewish survival in America, the capacity of the Jewish establishment for self-delusion is almost limitless. For years this establishment has operated on the principle that the fate of the American Jewish community is inextricably tied to the status of all other minority groups within the society. Thus, during the 1960s the national agencies and their local branches and counterparts increasingly assigned high priority to programs directed at the amelioration of the negative condition of blacks and other non-Jewish minorities. These programs often continued in operation even after the intended beneficiaries expressed anti-Jewish attitudes and/or exhibited overt anti-Jewish tendencies. The liberal-humanist-universalist ethic of the Jewish establishment rendered it incapable of dealing with these manifestations of hostility and resulted in a general attempt to sweep black and other forms of anti-Semitism under the rug. The establishment's philosophic base also inhibited the major communal bodies from coming to grips with significant changes in rank-and-file Jewish attitudes concerning political, religious and social commitment. Thus, the communal organizations could not, and in large measure still do not, comprehend the meaning of the Jewish Defense League, the shift in Jewish voting patterns and the overriding alienation of the masses of American Jews toward their establishment's programs. Most important of all, the establishment fails to perceive the tenuous nature of Jewish existence within the context of a gentile centered society.

This book attempts to describe and analyze the situation of peril currently confronting American Jewry. The book is divided into three sections. The first segment deals with those problems that are international in scope. These include the relationship between Israel and the American Jewish community and the plight of the Soviet Jews. The middle section treats problems that are domestic in nature. These include the relationship of American Jews and the Christian community, black-Jewish relations and the urban crisis, the development and significance of the Jewish Defense League, and the interaction of Jews and the American political system. The final portion of the book examines the growing internal crisis surrounding the issues of intermarriage, education, the alienation of young people, Jewish identity, Judaism and the future of the communal organizations.

I wish to thank Miss Lillian Block of Religious News Service for assistance in the gathering of research materials. I am also indebted to Bernard Braginsky for many helpful suggestions. I simply cannot fully express my gratitude to my wife, Leah, for her patience, love and understanding, and to my children who steadfastly remained calm throughout the length of this project.

I

ISRAEL AND THE AMERICAN JEWS

Of all the problems which will determine Israel's future
and destiny, the No. 1 is the relationship between Israel
and the Diaspora and the responsibility of the Diaspora
for the existence of Israel.

(*Dr. Nahum Goldmann, President, World Jewish
Congress*)

The founding of the State of Israel on May 14, 1948, was
the single most momentous event in the long and troubled
history of the Jewish people. The establishment of Israel
was all the more climactic because it followed so closely,
some would say inexorably, the Nazi Holocaust and the
destruction of the European Jewish community. It is all
but impossible to comprehend contemporary Jewish life
without coming to grips with the tragedy of the near destruction of European Jewry and the triumph marked by
the establishment of a haven for the survivors. These events
have had a most profound impact upon the Diaspora,

particularly upon the American Jewish community, whose sense of remorse for failure to significantly ameliorate the scope of the European disaster has greatly intensified what in any case would have been strong support for the new nation.

Recent historical scholarship has revealed that the American Jewish community was late in perceiving the threat to the European Jews. This failure to understand the seriousness of Nazi intentions was coupled with an inability to successfully marshal the political resources which might have spelled a difference in the eventual outworking of the Holocaust. Arthur Morse and Henry Feingold[1] have in scholarly fashion demonstrated the tardiness of Jewish reaction to events in Europe and the inept manner in which efforts at rescue were undertaken.

Perhaps the key reason for the failure of the American Jewish leadership was their simplistic and almost childlike faith in President Roosevelt. Roosevelt was regarded as the champion of the oppressed who could be trusted to act in accordance with the norms of civilized behavior. Several Jewish leaders had access to the President and were given assurances that the United States would intervene at the proper time. Toward the end of the war when the startling dimensions of the European Jewish martyrdom were revealed it became fashionable to accuse the State Department for the inertia and inaction that marked U.S. policy and to exculpate Roosevelt, who became, in these accounts, the pawn of career officials who were at heart anti-Semitic. Even today there are persons who revere FDR's memory and declare that he was powerless to stop the slaughter. The history of the period suggests a far different interpretation. The fact is that Roosevelt and his fellow defender of democracy Winston Churchill could have given the Nazis a very difficult time as they raced to kill every possible Jew. Nora

Levin[2] and other researchers have demonstrated the allied capability of bombing the rail lines leading to Auschwitz during the 1944 period when one million Hungarian Jews were being transported in sealed freight cars to the waiting gas chambers. The Royal Air Force responded to inquiries as to why such bombing was not conducted by pointing out the "serious technical difficulties" involved in such an operation, this at a time when the Allies had destroyed the Ploesti oil fields in Romania and exercised control of the central European skies. In an even more macabre answer, the same officials declared that the gas chambers themselves could not be targets because "civilians might be killed" during such air strikes. The allied response to the crises facing the European Jews was summarized in the conversation between Lord Moyne, British High Commissioner in Cairo, and Joel Brand, the would-be rescuer of the Hungarian Jews. Brand asked the allies to provide ten thousands trucks to be used as ransom for the lives of one million Jews. Moyne replied that even if the trucks could be obtained and the Germans went through with their part of the arrangement "wherever on earth would I put these Jews."[3] Belated and ineffectual American Jewish interventions to the contrary, Hitler knew from the failure of the Evian Refugee Conference in 1938 through the futile attempt at rescue by Joel Brand that he had carte blanche to destroy the European Jews.

The Burden of Guilt

Thus, the American Jewish community today lives not only with the memory of the Holocaust but also with the heavy burden of guilt for not reacting expeditiously to what in retrospect was history's most monumental attack upon the reality of Jewish existence. This collective memory is perhaps the most determinative force in contemporary American Jewish life. The Holocaust is at once the *sine qua non* for Jewish metaphysical speculation and programmatic articulation. The enormity of the Holocaust's toll in human terms, and the terror of its intention to remove from the earth all traces of Jewish life and culture, presses in on Jewish consciousness, ultimately influencing the manner in which Jews respond to the very real internal and external problems confronting them as individuals and as a community. Thus, it is not surprising that the single most important Jewish commentator of the post World War II period is Elie Wiesel, a survivor of the Holocaust and the period's most definitive chronicler. Wiesel has not only become the interpreter of the Holocaust but also the spiritual guide who provides answers to the thorny questions involved in the survival of the Soviet Jews, the quest for Jewish identity and the recapturing of alienated Jewish youth. It is also understandable that Emil Fackenheim, a theologian who has developed the most systematic philosophic treatment of the Holocaust, is regarded today as the most influential Jewish religious thinker. Fackenheim believes the Holocaust presents Jews with the positive command to survive as a people. God himself speaks out of the slaughter to warn the people against despair of man and his world as well as against despair at the God of Israel. To do otherwise would be to hand Hitler a posthumous victory. Implicit in this construct is the centrality of the State of Israel as the ultimate affirmation of Jewish life and faith.

Jerusalem, while no "answer" to the Holocaust, is a response; and every Israeli lives that response. Israel is collectively what every survivor is individually: a No to the

demons of Auschwitz, a Yes to Jewish survival and security—and thus a testimony to life against death *on behalf
of all mankind*. The juxtaposition of Auschwitz and Jerusalem recalls nothing as vividly as Ezekiel's vision of the
dead bones and the resurrection of the household of Israel.
Every Israeli—man, woman or child—stakes his life on the
truth of that vision.[4]

Fackenheim might have added that the great majority of
American Jews stake at the least their "Jewish" lives on this
proposition. The creation of the State of Israel provided the
new hope and freshness of vision that enabled the Western
Diaspora communities to recover from the shock of the
Holocaust. The American Jewish community, largest in
terms of numbers and resources, has played a crucial role in
the building of the new nation. As Jacob Rubin suggests:

The facts of history confirm, beyond any doubts, the assertion that it was the partnership between Diaspora Jewry
and the pioneers in *Eretz Israel* that made the attainment
of the dream of sixty generations possible. And among
those Jewish communities of the Diaspora that gave their
share in the upbuilding of a Jewish Palestine and the
strengthening of Israel, the American Jewish community
played a most important, sometimes, an almost decisive
role.[5]

American Jews have poured hundreds of millions of dollars into the building and maintenance of Israel and have
been the principal foreign supporters of the nation's right to
exist and flourish. The major role American Jews were to
have in the life of the new State was prefigured before May

1948 in the interventions made by American Zionists with President Truman. The Zionists, who were the brokers in the Jewish community's campaign to establish a Jewish state, found themselves confronted with the same hostile State Department that earlier Jewish leaders had encountered during the Holocaust. Yet on this issue there was a crucial and determinative difference, the White House was occupied by a President who could and would overrule "Foggy Bottom." In addition, the Zionists had one other card up their sleeve, the personal relationship between Truman and an old Kansas City business associate, Eddie Jacobson. Jacobson had been Truman's partner in an ill-fated haberdashery venture in the period following the First World War. Despite this failure the two men remained friends during Truman's rise from county judge to United States Senator to Vice-President and finally to the Presidency. Jacobson, who was a frequent visitor to the White House, placed himself at the Zionists' disposal and arranged several key meetings between Zionist leaders and his Kansas City friend. Perhaps the most important of these Jacobson-inspired sessions involved the greatest Zionist of the twentieth century, Dr. Chaim Weizmann, soon to become the first President of the new nation. There is little doubt that Truman's *de facto* recognition of Israel in the early morning hours of May 14, 1948, was based on his rapport with Weizmann and on the promise of support he had given to Eddie Jacobson. If ever the life of a nation hung on the personal relationship of two men, it was so in the case of Israel and the two Kansas City friends.

In the period between the founding of the State and the June 1967 war, American Jews supported Israel in increasing numbers, so much so that long-established anti-Zionist organizations lost strength and influence. The most important of these groups, the American Council for Judaism, had experienced growing difficulty in raising funds and retaining membership as the reality of a live and dynamic Israel, had its impact upon the Jewish community. American Jews looked with justifiable pride at the growth of the nation and the ability of the new state to conquer adversity and defend herself militarily. Great pride was taken in the accomplishments of the young nation, the reclamation of land, the opening of doors of freedom to the beleaguered Jewish communities in the Arab world as well as to the survivors of the Holocaust, the establishment of a major university, and the founding of hospitals and social-service institutions. This pride was deepened by the knowledge that the American Jewish community had played such a pivotal role in these positive developments. The June 1967 war if anything intensified American Jewish pride in Israel and her accomplishments. The crisis of late May and early June 1967 united American Jewry as never before. The threat to Israeli survival engendered an outpouring of financial and moral support that appeared to lock in forever the destinies of Israel and the Diaspora. As one delegate to the World Zionist Congress declared, "This was the year when every Jew in the world discovered his personal identification with Israel."[6]

The writer can recall spending an evening one week before the war began with fellow students in the home of Dr. Abraham Katsh then director of the Institute of Hebrew Studies at New York University. Everyone present was preoccupied with the threat confronting Israel, and many students had already made inquiries as to the possibility of volunteering for service in the Israeli defense forces. One of the guests, a Sabra who was teaching at the University, would a few days later return home to assume duty as the executive officer of an armored battalion. (Two weeks later the writer telephoned the Israeli's New York home and was astonished to hear the instructor's voice. He had fought in the Sinai and returned to his teaching responsibilities all in a matter of ten days.) The great majority of American Jews could not of course journey to Israel to fight in the war, but they could and in overwhelming numbers did contribute financially to the success of the military campaign and its aftermath.

The enormity of the response of American Jewry floored even the most hard-bitten fund-raising professionals as more money was pledged in one week than in the whole previous history of the United Israel Appeal. The war seemed to mark the internal victory of the American Zionists who had labored so long and hard for the allegiance of American Jewry. The eminent sociologist Marshall Sklare reported that his midwestern survey city of Lakeville,[7] a community that did not have the reputation of being "a hot-bed of Zionist sentiment," was "unambiguously pro-Israel. . . . There was no doubt in their minds as to which side was right. Support for Israel seems to have increased as the Crisis deepened." Sklare also suggested several implications of the response of the Lakeville Jews to the June war.

1. The war attested to the fact that no event during the past decade had an impact upon feelings of Jewish identity comparable to the 1967 crisis.

2. The victory of the Israelis improved the status of American Jewry. Through the results of the war American Jews "had achieved new respect in the eyes of the Gentile."

3. Israel had to be supported as never before because her destruction "would have meant our end as an American Jewry, for we could not survive such a loss of meaning."

An Expression of Jewishness

The Lakeville study is most instructive for what it reveals to us concerning American Jewish support for Israel and involvement in that nation's fate at the crescendo of good feeling and co-operation between the major country of the Diaspora and the Jewish State. Sklare's finding that Jewish identity was significantly affected by the crisis lends support to the theory that for many Jews Israel provides their main outlet for the expression of Jewishness. Those individuals who fall into this category are usually not affiliated with a synagogue or with one of the major communal or service organizations. Prior to 1967 many of these persons had been indifferent or even alienated to recognizable Jewish concerns and had for the most part been only minimal supporters of Israel. The crisis of May and June 1967 caused these individuals to confront their Jewishness and to identify with the Israelis who were putting their lives on the line as Jews. For those Jews who were non-alienated and institutionally affiliated, the crisis intensified their sense of Jewish identification and confirmed the validity of their earlier support for Israel. The Israeli was viewed as the Jew par excellence, whose motivations and actions were worthy of emulation and adulation. The identification of the American Jew with his Israeli brother allowed the American Jew to vicariously share in Israel's astounding triumph. Not only did American Jews desire to enjoy a portion of the Israeli success, they discovered that gentile friends and associates almost automatically assumed that the Israel victory was inextricably connected to American Jewry. As one non-Jew told a Lakeville Jewish business contact, "You Hebes really taught those guys a lesson."[8]

Another important finding of the post June war Lakeville

survey was the feeling of Lakeville's Jews that the crisis presented the possibility of another Holocaust. This Holocaust would, if only because of the geography involved, exempt again the American Jewish community. Jews still living with the two-fold guilt of being shielded from the first Holocaust and of not doing enough to avert the tragedy and aid its victims were presented with the opportunity to cleanse the record of the 1930s and '40s. To allow another Holocaust to occur would, in Fackenheim's terms, grant Hitler a posthumous victory. Such a happening would destroy the new sense of meaning that Israel had brought to Jewish experience. Sklare concludes:

> By upsetting our sense of meaning, a new Holocaust would have plunged American Jewry into total *anomie*. From this perspective, Israel had to be supported as never before. Her destruction would have meant our end as an American Jewry, for we could not survive such a complete loss of meaning.[9]

Yet the most significant finding of the Lakeville study was the lack of long-range impact exerted by the war upon American Jews. Nine months after the war fund raising for Israel had not increased appreciably in Lakeville, and not a single one of the original respondents to the survey had visited Israel. One individual who during the previous May "was practically ready to go over to fight" now had no interest in traveling to Israel. Nor was there any appreciable interest in making *aliyah* to Israel. This last finding was compatible with the overall *aliyah* figures for 1967. In the year that world Jewry contributed $359,000,000 to Israel, 445 fewer Jews came to live there than in the previous year. The Lakeville study's findings concerning the long-range impact of the June war suggest that the conflict, though a one-time phenomenon of great immediate significance, had little capability of fostering a sustained commitment.

Viewed from both the perspectives of the two decades of Israel's life as a nation prior to the war and of the several post-war years, the June 1967 experience can best be described as episodic. Difficult problems, which could not be solved in the emotion-charged atmosphere of military and diplomatic crisis, existed between American Jewry and Israel long before the initiation of hostilities in 1967, and events clearly indicate that tension between the two communities continued in the period between the Six Day and the Yom Kippur wars.

Can Jews Outside Israel Survive as Jews?

From the beginning of the State some Israeli leaders asserted that the new nation was now the major representative of World Jewry and that normative Jewish life was only possible in Israel. These officials, particularly Israel's first Prime Minister, David Ben-Gurion, argued that Jews could survive as Jews only in a Jewish state. The early Israeli leadership believed that it was the duty of Diaspora Jews to emigrate to Israel. Such sentiments were bound to have a deleterious effect outside of Israel particularly in the light of charges made by factions unsympathetic to Israel that Diaspora Jewish support for Israel was an act of dual loyalty. This charge was especially troublesome to American Jews who had struggled to achieve equal status within the context of American pluralism.

In August 1950, Jacob Blaustein, founder of the American Oil Company and president of the American Jewish Committee, journeyed to Jerusalem for a round of private conversations with Ben-Gurion in an attempt to seek a clarification of Israeli aims, vis-à-vis the Diaspora. At the conclusion of the sessions, which were characterized by Blaustein as "long and arduous," Ben-Gurion issued a statement that appeared to delineate Israel's understanding of the role of the Diaspora:

The Jews of the United States, as a community and as individuals, have only one political attachment and that is to the United States of America. They owe no political allegiance to Israel. In the first statement which the representative of Israel made before the United Nations after her admission to that international organization, he clearly stated, without any reservation, that the State of Israel represents and speaks only on behalf of its own citizens and in no way presumes to represent or speak in the name of the Jews who are citizens of any other country. We, the people of Israel, have no desire and no intention to interfere in any way with the internal affairs of Jewish communities abroad. The Government and the people of Israel fully respect the right and integrity of the Jewish communities in other countries to develop their own mode of life and their indigenous social, economic and cultural institutions in accordance with their own needs and aspirations. Any weakening of American Jewry, any disruption of its communal life, any lowering of its status, is a definite loss to Jews everywhere and to Israel in particular.[10]

In his response Blaustein stated his belief that the Prime Minister had taken:

. . . a fundamental and historic position which will redound to the best interest not only of Israel but of the Jews of America and the world. I am confident that this statement and the spirit in which it has been made, by eliminating the misunderstandings and futile discussions between our two communities will strengthen them both and will lay the foundation for even closer cooperation.[11]

The remainder of Blaustein's response bears repeating for it is a very clear articulation of the view held by the non-Zionist segment of the American Jewish establishment.

The American Jewish community sees its fortunes tied to the fate of liberal democracy in the United States, sustained by its heritage, as Americans and as Jews. We seek to strengthen both of these vital links to the past and to all humanity by enhancing the American democratic and political system, American cultural diversity and American well-being.

As to Israel, the vast majority of American Jewry recognizes the necessity and desirability of helping to make it a strong, viable, self-supporting state. This, for the sake of Israel itself, and the good of the world.

The American Jewish Committee has been active, as have other Jewish organizations in the United States, in rendering, within the framework of their American citizenship, every possible support to Israel; and I am sure that this support will continue and that we shall do all we can to increase further our share in the great historic task of helping Israel to solve its problems and develop as a free, independent and flourishing democracy.[12]

Blaustein would later cite the Ben-Gurion statement as contributing to "the growth of a positive attitude toward Israel among American Jews many of whom had had doubts about the State's attitude in relationship to them." Yet the fact that the basic feeling tones of the Israeli leadership remained unchanged was evident in a speech Ben-

Gurion gave to the 1960 meeting of the World Zionist Congress:

> Since the day when the Jewish state was established and
> the gates of Israel were flung open to every Jew who
> wanted to come, every religious Jew has daily violated
> the precepts of Judaism and the Torah by remaining in
> the Diaspora. Whoever dwells outside the land of Israel is
> considered to have no God.[13]

The Prime Minister's address, which was printed in its entirety in *The New York Times,* engendered deep consternation in the United States and caused Blaustein to once again travel to Jerusalem to meet with Ben-Gurion. As a result of this encounter, a statement of reaffirmation was issued concerning the earlier Blaustein-Ben-Gurion agreement. It was also agreed that both the Israelis and the American Jewish leadership should do "everything possible" to prevent future misunderstandings. However, American Jewish uneasiness concerning the true character of Israeli intentions surfaced again in 1969 when a resolution was proposed at Prime Minister Levi Eshkol's Leadership Conference which urged mass imigration to Israel as a priority of American Jewish life. The following year Blaustein met with Eshkol's successor, Golda Meir who assured the American leader that as far as she was concerned the original Blaustein-Ben-Gurion agreement was still in force: Mrs. Meir wrote to Blaustein:

> There is one particular subject on which I would like to
> clear up any possibility of misunderstanding. As you know,
> I was privy to the talks which were conducted on the

occasion of your visit to Israel in 1950 and to the understanding which followed from those talks. This has been a
continuing understanding. On my part, there has been no
deviation from it and it is my intention that there will not
be.[14]

The fact remains, however, that the dearth of American
Jewish immigration to Israel is a constant source of irrita-
tion to the Israel leadership. In a real sense the low incidence of *aliyah* from the United States has signaled the
nadir of the American Zionist movement. As long as there
was a nation to secure, Zionism had, despite significant opposition, a major role in American Jewish life. But as Judah
Shapiro, secretary of the National Foundation for Jewish
Culture, suggests, since 1948 the movement has had little
to say to American Jewry. It is true that there are opponents
of Israel who still talk of Zionist power, and in recent years
the very term "Zionism" has become a code word for anti-
Semites of various shadings. But such expressions are reflex
actions with little base in reality. The American Zionist
movement is fragmented and incapable of fostering a major
change within the Jewish community toward *aliyah*. Part of
this weakness is due to the fantasylike world inhabited by
the American Zionist leadership. Thus, Jacques Torczyner,
president of the Zionist Organization of America told Robert Silverberg:

I honestly believe that you can lead a full Jewish life only
in Israel. I believe that when Bernstein composes music
here, when Irwin Shaw writes a novel, when Norman
Mailer analyzes Chicago, these are American music,
American literature; Jewish art, Jewish literature, you can
only have in Israel. You can be a very good American and

a very good Jew here but . . . you have to maintain your connection with the State of Israel.[15]

More Troubles for the Zionists

The other aspect of Zionist impotency has to do with the character of the American effort to build support for Israel's right to exist as a nation. In the American context, a special-interest group like the ZOA is immediately suspect; thus at almost any given time investigations are being conducted concerning the right of the Zionists to operate in the United States under existing legislation. As a result of the controversy surrounding the movement, the normal functions of the Zionist bodies have been taken over by the non-Zionist major Jewish organizations. Today it is B'nai B'rith, the American Jewish Congress and the American Jewish Committee who are most effective in reaching both Jews and non-Jews with the need for Israel's survival. While these bodies have assumed the major role in the interpretation of Israeli experience, the Zionist groups have been engaged in an internal debate concerning qualifications for membership and major offices. In 1968 the Secretary of the Labor World Zionists suggested that membership in the World Zionist Organization would be limited to Jews who agree to make *aliyah* with their families within five years. This proposal was especially troubling to the American Zionist leadership who had since 1948 been open to he charge of not practicing what they preached.

Mrs. Mortimer Jacobson, the then president of the 325,-000-member Hadassah, rejected the emigration motion and denied that "a Zionist is only one who is committed to living in Israel."[16]

The argument over Zionist *aliyah* was joined with sharper focus at the 1972 meeting of the WZO. There younger

Israeli-born delegates forced through a resolution which held that "a Zionist leader who does not emigrate within two years of holding office must be replaced."[17] This brought about a walkout by the representatives of Hadassah led by their president, Mrs. Faye Schenk, who remarked: "We came to the Congress with high hopes, with stars in our eyes, and found a complete disregard for all we do and all we believe in. The members leave Israel feeling battered and bruised."[18]

The vote was later rescinded, largely through the constructive efforts of the late Aryeh Pincus, then chairman of the Jewish Agency Executive, who explained that many of the Israeli delegates to the Congress were young people who were involved in their first contact with the Diaspora. These young people obviously had little understanding of the problems faced by the American Zionists and may well have been saying that there was little present need for a Zionist structure outside of Israel. Hadassah official, Mrs. Rose Matzkin, summed up the angry reaction of the American delegates to the position of the young sabras:

We found no desire for dialogue, only insults and rudeness and ugliness. Here we were howled down and threatened with assault—this in the land of justice and freedom. Time and time again it was made clear to us in any number of ways that we were not wanted.[19]

The lack of credibility of Diaspora Zionism in the eyes of Israeli activists demonstrates the weakened status of the movement and is suggestive of the difficult future confronting Zionism in America. This difficulty is not ameliorated by the movement's capacity for self-deceit. A recent report based on the future of Zionism summarized the movement's expectations as follows:

> It would be well to consider that the State of Israel will continue to need the support of the Jewish community of America financially, politically, and morally. Whether in times of crisis or in the dramatic normalcy of life in Israel, the Zionist identification is assumed to be more durable for responsiveness to needs and claims of devotion. While Israel will require dedication from the broadest base of American Jewry, that base will be broadest to the extent that Zionism is a continuous influence upon, and an expression of, the Jews of America as individuals and as participants in the array of Jewish organizations which claim their affiliation.[20]

Surely no informed observer would deny the importance of the activities engaged in by Hadassah and other service-oriented Zionist organizations, but it may be time for Zionism as an active political and communal force to pass from the American scene. Though perhaps intemperate in their demeanor, the young Israelis who challenged American Zionists to make *aliyah* or step down from leadership in the movement have logic on their side. If Israel is the fulfillment of the most fundamental tenet of the Zionist dream how can individuals who espouse this dream remain in the Diaspora? Those Zionists who chose to remain outside of Israel compromise the nature of Zionist ideology and communicate a lack of seriousness and dedication which is at once counterproductive and self-defeating.

Events since the June war have also shown that there are areas of disagreement and conflict between American Jewry and Israel. The Zionist goal of total Diaspora subservience to the policies and aspirations of the Jewish State has not been realized, at least in the American context: These differences concern Israel's foreign policy, her internal social problems, her apparent attempts to influence the American electoral process and in a more philosophic frame her role in providing for Jewish survival in a world that still manifests a significant degree of hostility to Jews.

The Vietnam Tensions

In the period immediately following the June war considerable tension developed between the very significant number of American Jews who opposed America's Vietnam involvement and Israeli officials who supported the Johnson and the Nixon administrations' Southeast Asia policy. The Israelis argued that Jewish criticism of U.S. activity would lead to reprisals by the administration, which would cut off the flow of needed military hardware, particularly the much-desired Phantom Jet aircraft.

Many Jewish intellectuals were in the forefront of the peace movement, and the national organizations were under pressure from their memberships to issue statements calling for the end of U.S. participation in Vietnam. That the leaders of these bodies were in a difficult position was apparent in the question asked first by President Johnson then by Nixon to Jewish opponents of U.S. intervention, "How can you oppose me in Vietnam when you favor my getting more deeply involved in the Middle East?" There was of course an answer to this question; the two situations were dissimilar, in the one American troops were actively involved, in the other all that was asked was materiel and the keeping of an earlier moral commitment to secure the nation's survival.

Nonetheless, Arab propagandists operating in the United

States had a field day with the Vietnam issue. The Arab Information Office, a U.S. front for the Arab League, placed an advertisement in *The New York Times* headed, "Will the Middle East Turn Into Another Vietnam?" The ad, which warned that U.S. military involvement in Israel would lead to a Middle East Vietnam, concluded by asking, "Do you want your American boys to perish on the battlefields of the Middle East?"[21]

The Israelis promoted the view that an American retreat from Vietnam would imply a renunciation by the United States of the use of power on behalf of a distant ally and might, in turn, lead to an abandonment of Israel. Whether because of her own foreign policy determinants, or because, as some would claim, Israeli officials had a basically faulty perception of American Jews, the Israelis persisted in their efforts to tone down American Jewish opposition to the Southeast Asia adventure. This effort came under sharp attack in 1970 by Rabbi Arthur Lelyveld, then president of the American Jewish Congress. At a meeting of Americans and Israelis convened to discuss relationships between the two communities, the Cleveland rabbi posed several questions on Vietnam that he suggested the American Jew must consider when assessing his attitude toward Israel:

Does Israel have the right to ask us to be silent on Vietnam because it thinks that in its relationship to the current government of the U.S. it would be tactically helpful for us to do so?

Do American Jews have a responsibility to keep silent when we believe that America's role in Vietnam has been mistaken, iniquitous and immoral?

At what point does such a tactical question become a moral question?[22]

In answer to these questions Rabbi Lelyveld conceded that given the introduction of Soviet military power in the Middle East, no Jew outside Israel "has the privilege of any action or any word that will add one ounce of pressure to the fierce and unremitting threat of destruction that faces her daily."

However he added:

At the same time, American Jewry's integrity and status are important to Israel, tomorrow as well as today. Any expectation that American Jewry will minimize its identity or jeopardize its future for the expediencies of the moment is as short sighted as it is erroneous.[23]

Among the "expediencies" noted by Rabbi Lelyveld as head of the American Jewish Congress was the fact that the Republican Administration continued the war while evincing little interest in domestic issues; what he failed to note, however, was the fact that what is expeditious for American Jewry may be a life and death matter for Israel.

Rabbi Lelyveld, who concluded: "American Jews cannot be expected to be silent on the moral question of United States involvement in Vietnam, despite the fact of Israel's dependence on the Nixon Administration for vitally needed military aid," confronted the larger question involved in the Vietnam debate when he suggested that "An American Jewish leadership that consistently acted only as an instrument of Israeli policy would soon be without a follow-ing."[24]

Israel's Domestic Problems

In recent years Americans have also become increasingly concerned with Israel's domestic problems. Israel has an urban crisis replete with overcrowding, slums, pollution and crime. The Israeli governmental bureaucracy never known for moving with alacrity or efficiency has been un-able to successfully cope with the intensifying problems of Israel's fast-growing cities. These difficulties will only in-crease as thousands, perhaps hundreds of thousands of Soviet Jews emigrate to Israel in the 1970s. American Jews, who have some expertise in urban affairs and who have been among the most influential advocates of massive efforts to solve urban problems, have watched the Israel situation with increasing impatience. The Israelis, who can do little wrong when encapsulated in jet aircraft or tanks, are sharply criticized for their lack of determination and technical skill in solving pressing internal problems. The situation is exacerbated by the elements of discrimina-tion that exist in Israel toward those individuals who have come to the new nation from the non-Western societies. There is a wide chasm that divides the Western and Ori-ental compounds of Israeli society. This gap extends from culture to income, employment, housing, education, mili-tary service, intermarriage and those other concomitants that make for a standard of living. The Israel Government faces a formidable challenge in raising living standards for that segment of the population that is not only a numerical majority but is also largely unlettered and unskilled. Amer-ican Jews who were in the vanguard of the civil rights movement of the early and mid 1960s are especially vexed over the existence of discrimination in Israel. The situation of the Oriental majority is a two-edged sword which on the one hand, will, if not soon ameliorated, add to the rift in Israel-Diaspora relations, while on the other hand contribute to a breakdown in the already unstable Israeli society. The Oriental majority is beginning to feel its potential political muscle. Groups such as the Black Panthers are the first major manifestation of Oriental political power that will surely emerge in this decade to challenge the older Western leadership. Such a fundamental change in the composition of the Israeli Government will have a profound effect upon the American Jewish community, which in the past has been able to smooth over differences with the Israeli leadership on the basis of a common background and culture. Paradoxically, the more American Jews clamor for equality in Israeli society, the more they will find themselves cut off from the mainstream of Israeli life. The failure of most American Jews to recognize the inexorable trend toward Oriental leadership seriously limits their ability to have a lasting impact upon the future course of Israeli life.

Another factor that has produced tension between Israel and American Jewry has been the internal Jewish crisis in America and the growing tendency for American Jewish organizations to allocate funds and programs for domestic rather than Israeli needs. Simply put, the American Jewish leadership has determined that it is impossible to meet the social, educational and religious needs of their constituents and at the same time maintain the extraordinary level of material support for Israel. These leaders, reacting to internal problems that threaten the future of the American Jewish community, have concluded that their main responsibility is to Jewish survival in America. This viewpoint was recently succinctly articulated by Bertram H. Gold, executive vice-president of the prestigious American Jewish Committee. Gold lamented the "excessive" influence Israel holds over aspects of American Jewish life and asked why funds for social and educational programs should be made available to Israel when similar needs are neglected in the United States. The AJC official also told *London Jewish Chronicle* correspondent Raphael Rothstein:

> Who is it that determines it is more important to provide funds for higher education in Israel than funds for Jewish education in the United States? Who is that decides poor Jews in Tel Aviv need improved housing and financial aid more urgently than do the poor Jews in Miami?[25]

The larger issue implicit in Gold's questions concerns the need for a stronger voice by American Jews in consultations between them and Israel. Heretofore the Israelis have generally assumed an attitude of, we talk, you listen. In its practical effect this policy has meant that the Prime Minister or the Foreign Ministry communicated its position on a specific issue to the Conference of Presidents of Major American Jewish Organizations which is then responsible for disseminating the message to its constituent bodies.

If such a device ever had a solid philosophic basis, and this is open to doubt, it surely has no pragmatic validity. The Presidents Conference is an ineffectual body which cloaks its impotence with the appearance of influence and unity. Rothstein correctly concludes that the Conference has created a spirit of disaffection and apathy among American Jews. The time has passed when the American Jewish community should assign credence to an organization that has ears and a mouth but attempts to function without a brain. I do not know many Jewish professionals who take the Presidents Conference seriously or many Jewish leaders who will not countermand that organization's order of the day when it suits their personal or organizational predilections. The tragic fact is that the Israelis once having willed the Conference into being do not realize its bankrupt status. But then the Israelis when scanning the American scene have a remarkable capacity to see what they like and believe will be helpful and to overlook that which is distasteful or potentially harmful. Especially upsetting to the Israelis is criticism of any kind. It is all very well for Albert Arent, chairman of the National Jewish Community Relations Advisory Council, to suggest: "Let us communicate our questions, our doubts, our concerns, our suggestions to the Israelis . . . and let them communicate theirs to us,"[26] or for participants in a recent Presidents Conference junket to desire "a more active role in criticizing defects in Israeli society"[27] but as the *Jerusalem Post* concludes, "Israeli leaders are not willing to listen to criticism."

One of the participants in the seminar, Rabbi David Polish, former president of the Central Conference of American Rabbis, has warned that the Jewish community follows a dangerous course by maintaining "silent and unquestioning support of Israel."[28] The Evanston, Illinois, rabbi, listed two compelling reasons for the necessity of dialogue between American Jews and Israel. First, the process of interchange of views would by its very nature allow each group to better understand each other. Second, regular consultation between the communities would give the American partners an important role disassociated from the single traditional function of fund raising. Rabbi Polish was also concerned with the growing realization among American Jewish leaders that "significant segments of American Jewry are not as unreservedly committed to Israel as we would like to believe."[29] This would certainly be true of a large and articulate number of Jewish young people.

Alienation from Israel in the youth community is due to several factors. Many young people have an overriding concern for social justice, seemingly derived from Jewish principles that cannot accept the social realities of Israel experience. To some the fact of Israel's existence as a Jewish state represents an anachronistic political form that runs counter to their advocacy of political jurisdictions transcending all nationalities and peoples. The very mood of the campuses in the late 1960s and early '70s has been anti-imperialistic and supportive of movements of national liberation. This renders some Jewish students susceptible to the blandishments of anti-Israel propagandists who describe Israel as a Western imperialist imposition upon the Middle East. These same propagandists describe the "plight" of the Palestinians and proclaim the authentic "third world character" of their cause. It is also true that the hostility of some young people toward Israel is an expression of their basic rejection of the Jewish community. As Professor Allen Pollack suggests, "Criticism of Israel has become a way of indicating the depth of their feeling and resentment; and Israel must pay the price for the American Jewish community's inadequacies and failures."[30]

The Radical Youth

Speaking at a recent conference, Paul Jacobs, a radical author and commentator, said that discontent with the "emptiness and sterility of American Jewish life had caused many young Jews to accept the tenets of the new left and in so doing, to reject Israel." Jacobs declared:

Many young American Jews see Israel as a kind of Jewish Disneyland which their parents visit to give vent to their fantasies. They are particularly turned off by what they view as the mindless support of all Israel policies by the Jewish establishment.[31]

Such statements make good copy but fail to recognize that many of the younger critics have never been to Israel and know next to nothing about life in that nation. The often simplistic rejection of Israel coupled with a fervent and adoring support for Fatah and other agents of "liberation" only indicate a lack of judgment and sophistication which hopefully will be remedied by the factors of age and experience. On the other hand, Rabbi Arthur Hertzberg, president of the American Jewish Congress, probably spoke for many of the older generation when he said in response to Jacobs:

Our children come by their passion to improve the world from the tradition we have taught them—or should have taught them—that American Jewry will not become a "colony" of Israel. We insist on the right to criticize Israel when criticism is needed, even if that criticism is likely to be exploited by Israel's enemies.[32]

In the light of increasing criticism, it would seem wise for the Israelis to establish an apparatus to facilitate genuine dialogue with the Diaspora. Recently, the influential

Jewish Post and Opinion suggested the inclusion in the Israeli cabinet of a ministry for the Diaspora that would deal with the complex problems so taxing to the relationship between Israel and Jews of other nations.[33] Bertram Gold of the American Jewish Committee has called for the development of voluntary Israeli organizations that could be associated with voluntarily organized Jewish communities in the Diaspora.[34] Whatever the mechanics of facilitating dialogue, the need for such communication is more urgent than ever.

This point was clearly illustrated in the Israel Government's handling of the film production of the controversial "rock opera" *Jesus Christ Superstar*. Immediately after the Broadway version opened in October 1971, the American Jewish Committee and the Anti-Defamation League objected to what they termed "Superstar's anti-Jewish tendencies." The AJC released a detailed analysis which criticized the depiction of the Jewish priests and Judaism, as well as the show's treatment of the trial and death of Jesus. When the trade media revealed that Universal Pictures planned to shoot the film version of *Superstar* on location in Israel, both American organizations immediately communicated their concern over the potential danger involved in the filming of an anti-Semitic movie in Israel. The AJC pointed out that *Superstar* was at root a passion play, similar in genre to the notorious Oberammergau *Passion Play,* and that as such the production could exacerbate relations between the Jewish and Christian communities. How, the AJC asked, could Jews oppose Oberammergau or the *Great Passion Play* organized in Arkansas by the old-line hate monger Gerald L. K. Smith if an anti-Semitic passion play was made in Israel, presumably with governmental approbation? The Committee also pointed out that its decades-long systematic attack upon the religious sources of anti-Semitism could be seriously set back by the *Superstar* film.

The issue came into public focus in July 1972 when the *Jerusalem Post* published a long article outlining the AJC's criticism of the stage play. The *Post* story engendered a debate in the Knesset which ended with the Minister of Commerce and Industry, Haim Bar Lev, a former general and father of the famous "Bar Lev" line giving assurances that the film would not be anti-Semitic. Bar Lev had talked with the film's producer, Norman Jewison, who advised the general as he had earlier told the AJC and ADL that there would be nothing "objectionable" in the film. Unfortunately, Israel does not take seriously the late Douglas MacArthur's dictum concerning old soldiers fading away. Bar Lev may have been a great warrior but he was a rank amateur when it came to evaluating the mouthings of Hollywood. Months later, when the film was released in the United States and had become the subject of an intensive Jewish furor over its obvious anti-Semitism, it was learned that two other ministries had advised against the project. Michael Pragai, director of ecclesiastical affairs for the Foreign Ministry had read the shooting script and found it to be reprehensible. Pragai's objections were overruled by the Ministry of Commerce and Industry, which apparently viewed the matter as simply a business transaction. This attitude was expressed by Zeev Birger the ministry's director for foreign film production when he told an American motion picture executive that he was "not interested in the content" of the film.

The shortsightedness of the Israel position on *Superstar* is appalling. Anti-Semitism is surely the least problem faced internally by Israel but it is a live and serious phenomenon to the communities of the Diaspora. The incongruity of Israel allowing such a film to be produced within

its borders staggers the imagination and graphically suggests the problems inherent in Israel-Diaspora relations.
One can safely predict that the Spanish and Italian language versions of *Superstar* will have a negative impact
upon the embattled Jewish communities of Argentina,
Chile, Northern Italy, while the German version will surely
reinforce stereotypic images of Jews and Judaism so carefully nurtured over the years by the Oberammergau *Passion Play*. Beyond this it is inconceivable that the Israelis
did not realize that current Arab and Soviet propaganda is
characterized by employment of the deicide charge and
anti-Jewish religious caricature. One hesitates to predict
the impact of the film when it is exhibited in Cairo, Amman
and Damascus. Incidents such as the *Superstar* fiasco have
caused American Jewish leaders to insist upon equal status
for the Diaspora in Jewish decision making and in the future development of Jewish life itself. At the 1973 meeting
of the Rabbinical Assembly, two prominent conservative
leaders called on Israel's leaders to cease from denigrat-
ing the Diaspora. Gerson Cohen, chancellor of the Jewish
Theological Seminary of America warned that:

> the time has come for us to acknowledge that the legiti-
> mate place of the Jewish people, of Jewish culture and
> Jewish religion is not limited to a single geographic loca-
> tion.[35]

Dr. Cohen's colleague, Rabbi Judah Nadich, president of
the Rabbinical Assembly, insisted that the Jewish state
"exists for the sake of the Jewish people, not the Jewish
people for the sake of the Jewish state." Both men argued

that the welfare of Israel depended on the viability of the Diaspora communities. Rabbi Nadich commented:

A strong Diaspora serves to assure the meaningful survival of the Jewish people and thus . . . reinforces the Jewish state in its primary task—the future of the Jewish people.[36]

These views were similar to sentiments expressed earlier by Philip Klutznick, former international president of B'nai B'rith, at a meeting of the organization's board of governors: "There are no assurances for Israel, no matter how strong her military, unless the Diaspora—and particularly the American Jewish community—is also strong."[37]

Hopefully the Israel leadership will give serious consideration to these assertions. Perhaps the beginning of such a process was sounded during the 1973 Israel independence observance by the then President Zalman Shazar:

The sense of Jewish unity must grow deeper everywhere between us and between the dispersion, between Jews in Israel and their brothers everywhere. We have struck root in the land and now we must strike root in the people; educating Jews outside Israel to love the State and Israelis in the State to love the Jewish people.[38]

However, given the context of the current Israeli position vis-à-vis the hostile Arab world, which must in the final analysis be the single most important influence upon Israeli policy, the words of Foreign Minister Abba Eban have much more pragmatic importance than the almost mystical incantation of the late President:

> . . . in the final resort, the decision of our neighbors for peace or war will be determined by the view of their balance of strength. They will ask themselves two questions: do we have a prospect of victory? And, is there an atmosphere of international support and international acquiescence? It is here that the American-Israeli dialogue appears as the determining factor for Middle Eastern peace.[39]

An Indivisible People

The overwhelming empathetic response of the American Jewish community to Israel's plight in the Yom Kippur war confirmed Mr. Eban's analysis of the fundamental nature of the relationship between American Jewry and the Jewish State. The war brought forth a reaction that expressed in graphic terms the indivisibility of the Jewish people. American Jews correctly perceived that contrary to Arab claims the very existence of Israel was at stake as a result of the aggression of Egypt and Syria. "Even handed" persons and pro-Arab apologists could maintain that the war was only limited in intention and designed merely to recapture lost territory, but American Jews knew that Israel's enemies launched the war with the determination to destroy the Jewish State. There is no question but that the Syrian Army hoped to move across the Golan Heights and into the Huleh Valley as a prelude to marching on the populated areas of northern Israel. Likewise, the Egyptians planned to use their bridgehead on the east bank of the Suez Canal as a staging area for attacks across the Sinai which would culminate in an all-out offensive against the Israeli heartland.

In an article syndicated by the *Los Angeles Times*[40] just after the cease-fire, the noted military analyst S. L. A. Marshall described the fierce armored battle launched by the Egyptians in an attempt to seize control of the Mitla Pass, the gateway to Israel proper. This attack was thrown back by the Israelis, who then mounted one of the most daring offensives in modern times by pushing a wedge between two Egyptian armies and crossing to the west bank of the Canal.

American Jews were also made aware in a new and perhaps frightening manner of the continuing hostility of large segments of humanity to Jewish existence. The active involvement in the war of ten Arab nations, the logistical and technical support of the Soviet Union, which cynically utilized the battlefield as a proving ground for new military hardware, the presence of North Korean pilots in the skies and North Vietnamese advisors on the ground coupled with the refusal of Great Britain to sell material to Israel and the pro-Arab stance of France, clearly evidenced the enmity of so many nations to the Jewish State.

The war indicated as never before the existential meaning of the ancient Jewish slogan, *Am Yisroael Chai!* (The People Israel live!) The ambiguous conclusion to the hostilities and the ambivalent role of the United States Government, despite its helpful arms shipments, added to the sense of American Jewish solidarity with Israel. Jews in the United States realized that the situation of Israel vis-à-vis both her Arab enemies and her few allies had significantly changed as a result of the war. October 1973 was, sadly, not June 1967. This time Israel would be forced to eventually make concessions detrimental to her overall security posture. This time the Arabs would not nurse humiliating defeat, but would perhaps nurture encouragement for another go-round where even more sophisticated Soviet equipment could be tested. In any case, most American Jews recognized that life could not be normal again for Israel in quite the same fashion as in the period between the June and Yom Kippur wars. Jews outside of Israel, who had been critical of aspects of Israeli policy and society, would have to take more seriously than ever the caution articulated by Dr. Daniel Elazar of Temple University during the height of the Israel-American Jewish leadership debate:

> The establishment of the State of Israel created a new source of authority for Jews. Certainly after 1968, Israel became the primary authoritative factor, uniting all Jews . . . The authoritative role of Israel functions in two ways. First, Israel is itself authoritative: what Israel wants is what the Jewish community should want, and even those who wish to dissent from any particular Israeli policy or demand must be very circumspect when they do so . . . Secondly, men who can claim to speak in the name of Israel or on behalf of Israel gain a degree of authority that places them in very advantageous positions when it comes to other areas of communal decision making.[41]

In an increasing manner American Jewish organizations who desire to maintain an objective balance in their relationship to the Israelis will be pressed to refrain from criticism of Israel. The factor, while psychologically understandable, will inhibit American Jews from making needed advisory and corrective suggestions to the Israeli leadership. In the sense that genuine two-way communication will be difficult, the war will have achieved a result that, in terms of its relationship to the Diaspora, is inimical to Israel's best interests. The rightward turn in Israel's political composition and her renewed determination to go it alone understandably bolstered by world hostility and indifference, will act to further complicate the relationship between Israel and American Jewry.

In the period immediately ahead, both Israel and the American Jewish community will be severely tested by internal pressures and outside events and forces. There will be needed as never before an effective and two-way channel of communication. Each partner will have to make a new and concerted effort to understand each other's strengths, weaknesses and peculiar problems. Without such a relationship, Israel and American Jewry will be susceptible to ideological attacks which will surely be forthcoming from their many and formidable enemies.

II

THE SOVIET JEWS

In the past year an increasing number of American Jews have taken to wearing necklaces and pendants inscribed with the names Platnick, Kusnetsov, Zalmanson. These items of costume jewelry symbolize solidarity with the struggle of the three-million-member Soviet Jewish community to achieve basic human and religious rights. The necklaces and pendants represent real persons incarcerated in Russian prisons and testify to the very severe dangers confronting the Jews of Russia. Indeed, it may be correctly said that outside of the Arab nations the policy of the Soviet Government vis-à-vis its Jewish minority is the only example of official anti-Semitism in the world today.

To understand the rationale behind both the repressive anti-Jewish policy of the Soviet Government and the militant response of Jewish activists in the period since the June 1967 war, one must first examine the history and character of Jewish experience in Russia.

Jews have lived in Russia for less than two hundred

years. For most of its history as a nation-state, Russia was *"Judenrein."* The absence of Jews prior to the late eighteenth century was not a chance occurrence but resulted from a well-defined and clearly articulated government policy. The basic cause for this closed-door treatment was theological. The Orthodox church held as a basic tenet the ancient Christian teaching that the "Jews" as an entity killed Christ and thus were to be regarded as rootless and homeless persons, doomed to spend their earthly days wandering the earth. The Russians, who as late-comers to Christianity felt a special imperative to evidence piousness and allegiance to church doctrine, manifested, in the case of the Jews, a zealousness that went beyond the normally wide boundaries of Orthodox excess.

By the last quarter of the eighteenth century, however, Russian expansionism created the problem of absorbing the vast Jewish population of the Polish Empire. At first the traditional policy held firm, and those Jews who lived in the lands ceded to Russia were simply expelled. But in 1795 Russia received a greater portion of former Polish territory and with it approximately one million Jews. As a result of this development Russia became the home of the single largest concentration of Jews in the world. The fact that a huge number of Jews were now included in the Russian state did not signal a basic change in government policy. To deal with the situation a plan was put into effect that, by restricting Jewish residence to areas formerly under Polish jurisdiction, kept Jews from Russia itself. These areas—comprising Poland, Lithuania, White Russia and the Ukraine—were known collectively as the Pale of Settlement. Jewish life in the Pale was at best difficult. The Jewish community was heavily taxed and lost many of its young men to a twenty-year period of military conscription.

Jews who had been employed in the Polish governmental bureaucracy were forced to surrender their positions to officials assigned by Moscow. Jewish artisans and traders were hard-pressed to compete in the economic sphere on the more sophisticated levels of Russian commerce and industry. The coming of the industrial revolution to Russia in the middle of the nineteenth century placed the Jews in especially dire economic straits. Professor Allen Pollack concludes, "the development of Russian industry meant the further dislocation and pauperization of Russian Jewry."

More ominous for the Jews was the appearance in the 1860s and 1870s of a revolutionary movement. The movement, which undoubtedly attracted a number of young Jews who had recently gained admission to the universities, was responsible for the assassination of Tsar Alexander II. The reaction of the government to this act was centered in a program of repression which, in the fall of 1881, resulted in the introduction of pogroms or organized physical onslaughts directed at the Jewish community. These pogroms, which marked the first modern manifestation of anti-Semitism, were built on the foundation of a deep-rooted Russian antagonism to Jewish life. The pogroms were intended to be diversionary tactics to deflect attention from the real issues that confronted Russian society. The outbreaks of anti-Semitic behavior were followed in 1882 by a series of legal actions that further crippled and isolated the Jewish community. The May Laws, as these acts were called, set up a *numerus clausus* or quota system for Jews in the universities and prohibited Jews from residing in rural areas. This provision, aimed at segregating Jews from the peasantry, effectively closed 97 per cent of the Pale of Settlement to the Jewish community. The Jews of Russia, forced to move to the larger cities and towns and cut off from their basic sources of income, were faced with economic strangulation. By 1900 almost one third of the Russian Jewish population was totally dependent upon charitable aid from abroad.

Jews reacted in several ways to these new and awesome difficulties. Many simply left the country, so that by 1910 over three million Russian Jews had emigrated to other world areas, with a major share settling in the United States. However, the high birth rate among those Jews who remained indicated that emigration was not the solution to the problems of Russian Jewry. In 1914 despite the millions who had fled, the Jewish population of Russia was 40 per cent higher than in 1881. Those Jews who did remain attached themselves to various ideological movements whose programs were directed at amelioration of the trying Jewish situation in Russia. Some individuals joined in the thrust toward an intensified religious life while others found the preachments of the new Zionist movement to provide answers to their existential dilemma. Still others suggested that the Jewish problem in Russia could only be solved as part of an all-encompassing and radical change in Russian society. Allen Pollack succinctly summarizes the rationale underlying Jewish interest and involvement in the revolutionary wave of early twentieth-century Russia:

No people needed a revolution more than the Jews; no people worked for the revolution more than the Jews; no people greeted the revolution with more glee than did the Jews; no people devoted themselves to the new revolutionary regime as did the Jews; and no people were as betrayed by the revolution as were the Jewish people of Russia.[1]

Jews and the Revolution

Jews played an important role in the development and ultimate outcome of the revolutionary activity. The revolution of 1917 brought a significant change to the difficult pattern of Russian Jewish existence. Anti-Jewish legislation was abolished and Jews were granted full civic equality. Anti-Semitism was declared a punishable crime, and orders were issued to all Soviets to destroy the anti-Jewish movement at its roots. These measures, though official and seemingly far-reaching, could not significantly suppress the endemic anti-Semitism that permeated all layers of Russian society. The 1920s witnessed outbreaks of overt anti-Semitism which frequently occurred even within Communist Party ranks. By the early 1930s a program of political education began to make a dent in the surface level of anti-Jewish behavior, but the ephemeral nature of this change was clearly evident with the introduction in the middle 1930s of another period of official discrimination. Individual Jews, some of them highly placed in the government and Communist Party were murdered, imprisoned or exiled during the great Stalinist purges of 1936–37. Even more troubling was the liquidation of institutions that had been created to service the educational, social and cultural needs of the Jewish population. World War II placed the Jews of Russia in an ambivalent position.[2] At the beginning of the conflict the position of Soviet Jews was improved in an attempt to convince Jews in other nations to rally behind the Russian cause. For the first time since the October revolution, an official Jewish delegation was sent to the West to inform Jewish communities of the benefits achieved by Jews under Soviet rule and to request assistance in the struggle against Fascism. At the same time the Nazis were able

to exploit to the fullest the underlying anti-Jewish character of Russian society. Approximately one half of the Jewish
population was killed during the war. These murders were
in many instances facilitated by the co-operative efforts of
Russians, Ukranians and Lithuanians.

Some Jews who joined with the anti-Nazi partisan forces
suffered persecution, and many of the half million Jews
who served in the Russian Army were subjected to discrimination and harassment. The period immediately following the war did not ease the plight of Soviet Jewry. In
many instances Jews who returned to their homes, particularly in the Ukraine, found their former places of residence
occupied by gentiles who had no desire to relinquish them
to their rightful owners. The government adopted a hands-
off policy, and dispossessed Jews who wished to regain their
property were left without legal recourse.

The official Soviet accounts of hardships caused by the
struggle against National Socialism omitted mention of the
extreme suffering of the Jews.

By 1948 the Jewish Anti-Fascist Committee was abolished as were those cultural institutions that had been allowed to function during the war years. This was an especially difficult period for individuals involved in Jewish
cultural life. Jewish writers and artists were arrested and
sent to prisons or labor camps in the Siberian wasteland.
The campaign directed against Jewish intellectuals was
climaxed in August 1952 with the execution of twenty-four
of the most prominent Jewish literary figures. These murders devolved from a concerted government effort to de-
prive Soviet Jewry of its spiritual leadership and to prepare
the Jewish community for absorption into the general population. There are also indications that Stalin, who considered the Jews foremost among "enemies" of the regime, regarded the August 1952 executions as the first step in a

program that would lead to the physical destruction of the Jewish community. Such a theory finds striking confirmation in the events of early 1953, particularly in the arrest of six prominent Jewish physicians (along with three non-Jews) who had allegedly plotted to murder Soviet leaders under the guise of performing medical duties. The news of the so-called "Doctor's Plot" spread quickly throughout Russia and resulted in a wave of anti-Jewish activity. Many Jews were dismissed from their jobs, Jewish children were assaulted in the streets and all Jews were regarded with hostility and suspicion by their gentile neighbors. Just at the moment when it appeared that Russia was headed for a government-sponsored serious anti-Semitic outbreak, Stalin died. The dictator's death led to the release of the physicians and to the announcement in April that the "Doctor's Plot" was a fabrication of the secret police. Yet the fact that large numbers of Russians were ready to believe the worst about their Jewish fellow citizens did not auger well for the future.

The period immediately following Stalin's demise did little to reassure the Jews that their situation would materially change. Stalin's successors were not concerned with redressing wrongs brought about during his reign. A general liberalization of policy did occur after Premier Khrushchev's famous 1956 report to the Twentieth Congress of the Russian Communist Party, but this new mood did not markedly affect Jewish life. Indeed, the process of anti-Jewish discrimination and the dissemination of anti-Jewish propaganda continued and in some cases was intensified during the Khrushchev era. The Jewish religion was treated in an inferior manner to other religions. Jewish cultural institutions that had been closed during the Stalin period were not reopened. Jewish history and the contributions of Jews to the October revolution were falsified or ignored in textbooks and in educational curriculum. Jewish identity was treated in a wholly negative manner. Professor Shmuel Ettinger of the Hebrew University suggests that Jewishness

had no meaning other than to subject them to discriminatory and humiliating treatment, to bar them from many jobs (particularly in Party administration and the diplomatic corps), to restrict access to higher education, to demean their social status and to limit their public and government representation.[3]

The Jews of Silence

Indeed, Jewish nationality implied an untrustworthiness and expressions of solidarity with other Jewish communities or with Israel's cause were regarded as a breach of faith in the Soviet system. The June 1967 war had important repercussions for Soviet Jewry. The government, which unconditionally supported the Arab states, unleashed an anti-Israel propaganda campaign whose flavor quickly became overtly anti-Semitic. Soviet publications raised the specter of an international Zionist conspiracy to which the Russian Jews owed allegiance. Most disturbing was the pronounced and vicious attack upon Judaism that formed a major part of the propaganda effort. Trofim Kichko, a notorious anti-Semite who earlier had written *Judaism Without Embellishment*, a crazy-quilt tract replete with the most absurd charges concerning Jews, published in late 1967 a new and even more offensive book, *Judaism and Zionism*.[4] This work linked the religious practices of Judaism to an anti-Russian political ideology and suggested that Judaism held to the belief that "the entire world belongs to the Jews."

That such views were not uncommon in the period following the June war is evidenced by the spate of anti-Semitic books, monographs and articles that appeared with government sanction. In 1970, for example, a book entitled *Love and Hate* contended that Jews are characterized by "an overwhelming love of money, a repugnance of physical labor and an absolute refusal to integrate into Soviet life."[5] The Six Day war marked a watershed in the life of Russian Jewry. Soviet Jews despite, or perhaps because of, the stepped-up campaign of government-fostered anti-Semitism, experienced the same feelings of identification and solidarity with Israel's struggle for existence felt by all other communities of the Diaspora. To some degree the process of an intensified Jewish consciousness had already begun to develop in the early 1960s. Elie Wiesel in his remarkable *The Jews of Silence* described the joyous experience of witnessing thousands of young Jews gather in the Moscow synagogue to celebrate the festival of Simchat Torah in 1965.

> I spent hours among them, dazed and excited, agitated by an ancient dream. I forgot the depression that had been building over the past few weeks. I forgot everything except the present and the future. I have seldom felt so proud, so happy, so optimistic. The purest light is born in darkness. Here there is darkness; here there will be light. There must be—it has already begun to burn.[6]

By early 1968 Wiesel's Jews of Silence were becoming quite vocal. Petition campaigns, demonstrations at Soviet Government offices, (particularly at the OVIR, Office for Visa Registration) and sit-ins at the Kremlin itself characterized the first phase of Soviet Jewish direct action. At the same time an underground press featuring a newsletter, translations of novels and poetry and tapes of Yiddish and Hebrew songs came into existence. The most striking aspect of the first wave of activism were the scores of petitions written either individually or by groups asking for the right to emigrate to Israel. The petitioners ranging in age from twenty to forty-five boldly listed their names, addresses and occupations. The petitions were sent to several audiences. Some were addressed to high Israel Government officials such as the Prime Minister and President. Others were forwarded to the United Nations. Still others were directed to non-Soviet personalities ranging from President Nixon to the head of the British Communist Party, while a final segment were sent to Soviet officials including the Premier, Party Secretary and President. The petitions forwarded to Soviet officials comprised only a small portion of the whole and reflected the lack of faith Russian Jews had in obtaining redress from their government. Many of these internal documents, which, incidentally, were also released to the free world, detailed the fruitless efforts of Jews to secure the right of emigration over a period of several years. It is obvious from the number of petitions (over two hundred between February 1968 and October 1970) and their ultimate destination that the Jewish activists had decided upon a strategy of internationalizing their protest. A major plank in this program was an appeal to the world community to encourage the Soviet Government to adhere to the Universal Declaration of Human Rights. This document, which was formally ratified by the Soviet Union on January 22, 1969, obligates governments to recognize that "Everyone has the right to leave any country, including his own." It should be noted that the Soviet Union, which is also a signator to other international agreements concerned with freedom of emigration, includes in its own constitution, provision for citizens to leave for other nations. The petition tactic must also be understood in the light of Premier Kosygin's December 1966 promise that "the door is open" for all Soviet Jews who wish to be re-united with their families in Israel. The rising Russian Jewish consciousness manifested in petitions, the introduction of a Jewish press, and a renewal of interest in Jewish religious practice brought forth a repressive response from the government. By late 1970 a number of Jewish activists were arrested and then tried for engaging in "anti-Soviet activities." Several of these individuals were sentenced to prison terms while others were detained in mental institutions, the latter a favorite device of the Soviet authorities when they wish to remove dissidents from the society.

The Trials

The rising number of Jews applying for exit visas and the world-wide publicity garnered by these efforts apparently caused the Soviet Government to assume a hardened attitude. On December 15, 1970, a group of Jews charged with aerial hijacking were placed on trial in Leningrad. The trial was preceded by an almost hysterical press campaign directed at the defendants. An attack upon Zionism was at the heart of the government propaganda effort. According to the Soviet press, Zionists were racists who sought world domination through co-operation with the imperialist states. The Ukranian *Komsomolskoye Znamia* asserted that the aim of Zionism was to

impede all progressive changes; its characteristic method of action is a mixture of police violence and programs. It is

to carry out these aims of Zionism that cold-blooded
murderers are being raised.[7]

In the light of Russian history it would have been difficult
for the Soviet authorities to have come up with a more
hypocritical statement. Nonetheless, as all previous Russian
enemies of Jewish existence had discovered, such false and
potentially destructive rhetoric found wide acceptance
within the greater Russian community. Although the government was most anxious to disseminate information concerning the defendants and their "crime" prior to the
beginning of the trial, the proceedings themselves were
closed to public scrutiny. Most foreign correspondents were
not allowed in the courtroom, and those who questioned the
black-out policy were informed that "this is a special case."

The authorities, however, had not counted upon the impact of the petition drive to energize world public opinion.
From the June day when the arrests were first announced
many individuals and institutions, particularly in the West,
were both concerned over the ultimate fate of those ap-
prehended and suspicious of the charges brought against
them. When the trial began, a major protest erupted and
was directed not only at the plight of the defendants but
also at the situation confronting the entire Soviet Jewish
community. The Leningrad trial and subsequent similar
proceedings over the next several months served the purpose of further detailing the perilous situation of Soviet
Jewry in a manner far more comprehensive than had been
possible before.

From a judicial perspective the Leningrad trial was a
sham. The background of the case, the nature of the arrests and the propaganda efforts waged by the authorities
all suggested that the entire affair was part of a plot to dis-

credit the Jewish activist movement. The court, which had to rely on highly questionable confessions and on evidence based largely on letters and cards sent to the defendants by friends in Israel, found the accused "plotters" guilty and sentenced two to death and assigned harsh prison sentences ranging up to fifteen years to the others. The verdicts engendered a world-wide outcry, particularly from church groups who pleaded with the Soviet leaders to modify the sentences by executive action. The Kremlin could probably have taken the criticisms of the churches and other Western institutions in its stride, but they had genuine difficulty in fielding the objections of almost all of the Western Communist parties as well as the appeals articulated by working-class groups normally sympathetic to Soviet objectives. The weight of protest apparently caused the Soviet Supreme Court to commute the death sentences to fifteen years at hard labor. This action, while of course not totally satisfying to those individuals and groups engaged in aiding the defendants, did indicate the growing susceptibility of the Russian Government to outside pressure. World Jewish leaders, heartened by the assistance lent by governments, churchmen and workers and encouraged by the reaction of the Soviet leadership to outside pressure, decided to press their case for further amelioration.

In February 1971 a World Conference of Jewish Communities on Soviet Jewry attended by 760 delegates from thirty-eight countries convened in Brussels. The Brussels Conference accomplished two major objectives: first, the conferees were able to increase knowledge and awareness of the situation of the Soviet Jews; and second, the Conference clearly evidenced a global Jewish solidarity with the three million Russian Jews. The Brussels Declaration issued on the final day of the historic conference stridently enunciated this sense of unanimity:

We the delegates of this Conference, coming from Jewish communities throughout the world, solemnly declare our solidarity with our Jewish brothers in the Soviet Union. We want them to know—and they will take encouragement from this knowledge—that we are at one with them, totally identified with their heroic struggle for the safeguarding of their national identity and for their natural and inalienable right to return to their historic homeland, the land of Israel.[8]

The Visa Tax

Events in the Soviet Union indicated that the Conference had an important impact upon the Jewish community. In the days following the Brussels meeting, Russian Jews intensified their demands for the right of emigration and initiated a wave of protests, demonstrations and sit-ins which resulted in an easing of the restrictive emigration policy. On March 10–11, 1971, for example, over 150 Jews from Moscow and Riga converged upon the offices of the Presidium with a petition demanding both authorization to emigrate to Israel and an end to the policy of intimidation directed at petition signers. The protestors refused to heed warnings that they disperse and instead began a hunger strike. On March 11 the Minister of the Interior met with the group and promised that representatives of his agency would carefully examine the pending visa applications submitted by group members. Three months later almost all of the demonstrators involved in the unprecedented March 10–11 incident had safely reached Israel. During the spring of 1971 reports emanated from Western press sources in Russia suggesting that the Soviet Government was about to adopt a more liberalized emigration policy. The pertinent statistics for the spring months seemed to confirm that a significant shift had occurred. Jewish emigration figures continued to rise throughout 1971 and 1972. During 1972 over thirty thousand Jews were able to leave the Soviet Union with the great majority of emigrees settling in Israel. The emigration policy of these years, while affording more Jews than ever before the opportunity to leave, was both arbitrary and capricious. Some petitionists were detained by the police or jailed for fixed periods of time while others received exit visas on a stepped-up basis. Most distressing was the policy of granting a visa to one or more members of a family but not to the entire family.

During the summer of 1972 the Soviet position on Jewish emigration took a new and more difficult turn. In August the government began to impose an exorbitant exit visa tax. This fee in some cases ran as high as thirty thousand dollars in U.S. currency. The exit surcharge was prorated on an ascending scale according to the numbers of years of formal education experienced by the applicant. The Soviets claimed that the high visa tolls were aimed at inhibiting those individuals who had received advanced degrees from leaving the country. The officials argued that since the government had underwritten the cost of the individual's education, it had a right to demand repayment if the person wished to remove his skills to another country. The question of the exit fees caused deep consternation among the Russian Jews and served to draw more worldwide attention to their freedom struggle. The period between the fall of 1972 and the late spring of 1973 was marked by an intensified Jewish effort both within and without the Soviet Union to force the government to withdraw this new and retrogressive policy as well as to finally grant unrestricted emigration to the Jewish community. Then in May 1973, just before Communist Party Chief Leonid Brezhnev visited the United States, the Soviet Government quietly dropped the exit visa tax. This concession seemed to signal the possibility of a new and more favorable policy, and expectations were high that the Brezhnev-Nixon conversations would result in a major Soviet shift vis-à-vis emigration and the status of Soviet Jewry in general.

The Summit Talks

Just prior to the summit talks a small group of Jewish leaders met with President Nixon and Dr. Henry Kissinger and submitted to the latter a list of one thousand persons who had encountered extraordinary difficulty in obtaining visas. In addition, the Jewish spokesmen asked the President and his top foreign policy advisor to raise the question of the Jewish prisoners of conscience both in terms of their current physical status and the possibility of their accelerated release. It should be noted that a similar meeting had taken place shortly before Mr. Nixon's 1972 visit to the Soviet Union. Immediately after the Moscow summit, Dr. Kissinger told newsmen gathered in Vienna that the subject of Soviet Jewry had been raised by the President in his conversations with the Russian leadership. Dr. Kissinger would not indicate, however, the substance or results of that conversation. Nonetheless, the fact that the Nixon Administration had listened with apparent seriousness to the concerns voiced by Jewish authorities on the earlier occasion gave hope that the June summit would result in a significant amelioration of the problems confronting both the prisoners and the rank and file of Russian Jews.

The openness of the White House to Jewish articulations of concern was not entirely due to humanitarian stirrings within the Nixon inner circle. By the spring of 1973 the status of Soviet Jewry had become a major American political concern. This was due in large measure to amendments submitted in both the House of Representatives and Senate to an administration trade bill that proposed to grant most-favored-nation status to the Soviet Union. The amendments that threatened the success of Mr. Nixon's new economic policy toward the Communist bloc were submitted by Senator Henry M. Jackson and Congressmen Wilbur Mills and Charles Vanik. The Jackson amendment and the Mills-Vanik bill would bar most-favored-nation standing as well as United States Government credit and investment guarantees to countries that deny their citizens the opportunity to emigrate or prevent their citizens from emigrating by imposing exorbitant taxes as the price for departure. What was especially disconcerting to Mr. Nixon was the remarkable expression of support elicited by the trade amendments just days after they were first proposed. By early June seventy-six Senators were recorded as cosponsors of the Jackson amendment while two hundred seventy-eight Representatives joined in cosponsoring the Mills-Vanik bill. Credit for this remarkable achievement should be assigned not only to the Congressional initiators but also to the indefatigable efforts of staff personnel such as Richard Perl of Senator Jackson's office and Mark Talisman, legislative assistant to Congressman Vanik. The Jackson/Mills-Vanik amendment was also important in the sense that it provided an alternative to private diplomacy. Thus, what Mr. Nixon could not or perhaps would not win in personal encounter with the Soviet leadership might be accomplished through the action of the Congress. As matters turned out it was well that the fate of the Soviet Jews did not rest on the secret interventions of Messrs. Nixon and Kissinger. To put it in the vernacular, Nixon and Kissinger did a number on the Jewish leadership. The great expectations built up as a result of the leadership briefing sessions and sharing of lists produced no tangible result.

The days following the Brezhnev visit were not marked by dramatic changes and breakthroughs. The prisoners remained incarcerated and there was even evidence to suggest that a new hardening of policy was about to occur. Just two months after the summit several key activists were arrested and detained and Yevgeny Levich, the son of one of the most important Jewish activists, was sent to a labor camp within the Arctic Circle. Overt acts of anti-Jewish behavior began to take place with some frequency as, for example, in Moscow where the authorities stood by while vandals destroyed eleven of twelve Torah scrolls.

The American Jewish community, whose strong minority support for Mr. Nixon in the 1972 election was predicated in part on the Chief Executive's apparent solidarity with the cause of Soviet Jewry, was genuinely disappointed with the results of U.S.-based summit conversations.

The failure of the American-Soviet discussions to make an impact upon the condition of the Russian Jews was outlined in a meeting conducted on July 19 between Dr. Kissinger and three key Jewish figures involved in the Soviet Jewish issue: Richard Maass, chairman of the National Conference on Soviet Jewry; Jacob Stein, chairman of the Conference of Presidents of Major American Jewish Organizations; and Max M. Fisher, White House advisor and chairman of the Council of Jewish Federations and Welfare Funds. Dr. Kissinger informed the Jewish leaders that while he still expected the release of many of the individuals whose names appeared on the list submitted by the Jewish officials to the administration in the earlier White House meeting, he could not guarantee that such action would occur. Kissinger also indicated a lack of progress regarding the forty Jewish Prisoners of Conscience. In addition, he could not report a positive change in the pattern of harassment experienced by those who applied for visas. Mr.

Maass, in a memorandum to the membership of the National Conference on Soviet Jewry, described his reaction to Kissinger's remarks, "We expressed disappointment in the lack of visible results to date, especially in regard to our demands on emigration and emigration procedures."[9] The Kissinger report was especially disturbing to the Jewish leaders since their organizations had urged the American Jewish community to act circumspectly during the Brezhnev visit. The Jewish establishment believed that militant demonstrations similar in character to those staged in Canada in 1971 on the occasion of talks between Prime Minister Trudeau and Premier Kosygin would weaken Mr. Nixon's hand in discussions concerning the Soviet Jews. The major Jewish agencies' advocacy of a "cool it" strategy clearly echoed the desire of the administration to have the summit discussions conducted in an atmosphere conducive to *détente*. At the same time, American Jews of a more activist bent chafed at the restrictions set down by the major organizations. Members of the Student Struggle for Soviet Jewry and the Union of Councils for Soviet Jews grudgingly submitted to the discipline of the establishment-oriented National Conference on Soviet Jewry which sponsored the only mass meeting related to the visit of the Soviet Party chairman. On June 17 while Brezhnev relaxed at Camp David, about ten thousand persons, mostly from the middle Atlantic and northeastern states gathered at the Capitol to express solidarity with the Soviet Jewish community.[10]

The size of the crowd was insignificant and left the impression that American Jews were not all that concerned with the fate of their coreligionists in Russia. In retrospect it would have been better if the rally had not taken place. The "low key" ground rules made for confusion of direction and eventual failure. The only benefit accrued to the Jewish Defense League, whose attempts at disruption were prominently featured in media accounts of the rally. The establishment's handling of the summit meeting was not enhanced by the appearance of Jacob Stein, chairman of the Conference of Presidents of Major American Jewish Organizations, at the black-tie dinner given in honor of Brezhnev by President Nixon. Stein's reprehensible acceptance of the White House invitation caused many grass-root individuals who were actively supportive of the Soviet Jewish struggle to question the depth of commitment of the establishment to the cause. To be sure, Stein may have acted as an individual but his presence at the state dinner dramatized the susceptibility of Jewish leadership to seduction by the Presidency.

The Jewish failure to influence the Nixon-Brezhnev summit, called into question many of the presuppositions underlying the establishment's program relative to Soviet Jewry. That the National Conference on Soviet Jewry was open to the strongest criticism should not obscure the fact that the Conference is the creation of the major national organizations and remains dependent upon these agencies for its financial life line. The National Conference is an umbrella body which must adhere to the policy directions formulated by its constituent organizations. These directions are normally predicated on a philosophy built around the concepts of public pressure and quiet diplomacy. In recent months the National Conference has been unable to resolve the tension inherent in these two positions. It should be pointed out that the inability to balance pressure and diplomacy is in no way the fault of the National Conference staff or of its able chairman, Stanley H. Lowell. The problem is rather centered in the infrastructure of the American Jewish community and particularly in the ideological and pragmatic divisions that separate one organization from another. If, for example, the American Jewish Committee and the Anti-Defamation League cannot agree on the co-operative treatment of a specific program area, how can they be expected to work effectively in concert with thirty-odd other organizations in the National Conference? This situation is complicated by the fact that many of the National Conference's constituent agencies have specialists working in the area of Soviet Jewry. These organizations are not likely to emasculate their own programs (which have important fund-raising potential) in favor of the programmatic thrust of the National Conference.

Christian Support

Interestingly, the program of the National Conference is perhaps best complimented by the activities of a coalition whose base of support is interreligious in nature.

The Jewish community which has experienced significant difficulty in winning support for Israel among American Christians has fared better in its effort to enlist interreligious support for the cause of the Soviet Jews. In late 1971 plans were developed for a National Interreligious Consultation to be held in Chicago in March of the following year. This Consultation would be the first meeting of its kind and would, hopefully, lead to the establishment of a permanent interreligious secretariat to systematically treat the question. It is noteworthy that the several Christians and Jews who met at the Chicago Theological Seminary for the initial Consultation planning session resisted the temptation to make of the March meeting an exploration of the many human rights issues currently affecting large segments of the world population. The planners who were determined to focus in on the problems confronting Soviet Jewry feared that an opening of the Consultation to other and genuinely important concerns would act to wash out the Jewish factor. In addition, it was rightly suggested that there were already several organizations working on an interreligious basis for the amelioration of human rights problems in other world areas. The Chicago Consultation included an impressive honorary sponsorship, chaired by R. Sargent Shriver and running the gamut from William F. Buckley to Dorothy Day and from Ralph David Abernathy to William Randolph Hearst, Jr. The actual chairmen who represented the Protestant, Roman Catholic, Greek Orthodox and Jewish communities were ably directed by Sister Margaret Ellen Traxler, then serving as executive director of the National Catholic Conference on Interracial Justice and President of the National Coalition of American Nuns. The Consultation which brought together two hundred religious leaders from all parts of the nation heard addresses by Fayette, Mississippi, Mayor Charles Evers, Ambassador Rita Hauser, United States Representative to the United Nations Commission of Human Rights and Representative Robert Drinan, the first Roman Catholic priest to be elected to the Congress.

The delegates also heard a dramatic message delivered by Archbishop Fulton J. Sheen. The aging but still forceful prelate electrified the audience when he referred to the upcoming visit of President Nixon to Moscow:

Every man has two or three critical moments in his life when he can save his soul. President Nixon had one such moment in China and will have another like moment when he visits Russia. May the God of love inspire our President to plead for all the persecuted people in Russia even as we raise our voices against the persecution of the Russian Jews and other religious groups.[11]

The Consultation concluded with the adoption of a Statement of Conscience, which became the basis of the formation of a permanent Interreligious Task Force on Soviet
Jewry. The Statement, which received wide circulation in
the Christian community, said in part:

> The National Interreligious Consultation on Soviet Jewry,
> meeting in unprecedented deliberation on March 19 and
> 20 in Chicago, Illinois, calls upon the conscience of man-
> kind to make known its profound concern about the
> continued denial of the free exercise of religion, the
> violation of the right to emigrate, and other human rights
> of the 3 million Jewish people of the Soviet Union and of
> other deprived groups and nationalities.[12]

The Interreligious Task Force was instrumental in developing Christian support for the 1972 Solidarity Day program and lobbied strenuously on behalf of the Jackson/
Mills-Vanik legislation. In May 1973, during the height of
discussion concerning the trade bills, the Executive Committee of the Task Force met with Senator Jackson and
Congressman Vanik to declare total support to the measures
introduced by the two legislators.

In a genuine sense it may be easier for Christians than
for Jews to support measures that appear to be at odds with
American foreign policy. The Jewish community must walk
a tightrope in its criticism of the trade legislation or in
efforts to place items of internal Jewish concern on the
agenda of a summit meeting. There is the real danger that
Jews will be viewed by the larger society as being interested
only in self-serving issues. Many in the general community
ask why the move toward *détente* with the Soviet Union
should be impeded because of the grievances of three mil-

lion Russian Jews. The questioners insist that the stakes involved in *détente* are too high for outside considerations to upset. A relaxation of tension between the two superpowers would signal an end to the cold war. A new relationship between the two nations would result in a decrease in military spending thus freeing monies for much needed domestic reform. *Détente* would also bring increased trade, and a major boost to the American economy. The question has also been raised as to why United States policy vis-à-vis the Soviet Union must be developed in accordance with that Government's handling of a domestic situation. Tom Wicker, an associate editor of *The New York Times,* criticized the Jackson amendment as an undue attempt to influence the internal affairs of Russia.[13] It is interesting to note that Wicker, whose argument is regarded as persuasive by an increasing number of liberals, completely fails to mention the humanitarian implications of the issue. This unbenign neglect is strange coming from one who has persistently defended the rights of felons, convicted through due legal process, currently incarcerated in American prisons. Wicker's argument against the Jackson amendment is also suspect in the sense that he has been an outspoken critic of the policies of the governments of South Africa and Rhodesia.

Beyond this, Wicker's argument cannot stand up against the over-one-hundred-year record of U.S. initiatives on behalf of oppressed minorities in Russia. In the past century at least ten American Presidents have intervened either directly or indirectly on behalf of Jews in Russia. In the historical precedent most like the pending Jackson/Mills-Vanik legislation, the U. S. Congress in 1911 voted to abrogate an eighty-year-old commercial treaty with the Russian Government on the basis of that Government's persecution of Jews.[14]

Wicker would also do well to ponder Senator Jackson's assertion that the United States, as a nation of immigrants, should support the right of individuals to emigrate freely.

Little Basis for Optimism

Those organizations and individuals in the American Jewish community who are vitally concerned with the status of the Russian Jews have little basis for optimism. All indications point to a hardening of the Soviet position. Emigration will likely be fixed at about 25,000 to 30,000 per year. The program of harassment directed against activists and persons seeking exit visas will continue. Jews who wish to remain in the Soviet Union will continue to encounter grave difficulties in practicing Judaism and manifesting Jewishness in any overt manner. Worst of all, there are no immediate grounds to expect that the Prisoners of Conscience will be freed or even that their sentences will be materially reduced. Likewise, it is unrealistic to expect that the harsh regime that characterizes their incarceration will be eased. On the contrary, one might safely predict that more Jewish activists will be jailed in the coming months. The Soviet leadership is quite obviously relying on a diminution of interest in the situation of Soviet Jewry on the part of the American public. Brezhnev and his cohorts believe that support in America for the Soviet Jews will eventually be vitiated thus allowing for at least a compromise in the trade legislation. There are also indications that intra-Jewish squabbles involving community priorities and the programmatic right to the Soviet Jewish issue will seriously weaken the effort to save Soviet Jewry.

The effort to ameliorate the situation of the Soviet Jews has also been hampered by inadequate funding. It is shameful that the American Jewish community has not provided sufficient financial backing to those organizations programmatically involved in the Soviet Jewish issue. The National Conference on Soviet Jewry has operated on a shoestring for the last few years. In the fiscal year 1971–72 one third of the Conference's constituent national organizations either did not make their dues payment or allocated funds significantly below the assigned rate. A similar situation pertained in 1972–73.[15] Another complication arises from the role assumed by the Israeli Government in the Soviet Jewish problem. The American Jewish groups rely on the Israelis for intelligence concerning the day-to-day experience of Soviet Jewry and for more analytical projections of trends regarding emigration and Soviet policy directions. Israeli officials often meet with representatives of the major American Jewish agencies to discuss the Russian situation. In general, the Israelis have urged American Jews to continue and even accelerate efforts aimed at keeping pressure on the Soviet Government. Yet in the weeks immediately prior to the Yom Kippur war there were vibrations that suggested that the Soviet Union and Israel were close to at least a partial diplomatic rapprochement. Such a thaw in Soviet-Israeli relations would not necessarily mean a turn for the better in the life of the Russian Jewish community. The Stalin regime supported the creation of a Jewish state in Palestine during the period immediately following World War II while at the same time internally reintroducing anti-Jewish measures. A case could be made that diplomatic rapport between Russia and Israel can only come at the expense of the long-range interests of the Soviet Jews.

It would appear that time and momentum are on the Soviet Government's side. The American Jewish community has been slow to respond to the crisis confronting its brethren in Russia, and there are no signals suggesting that change in the form of a major programmatic effort will soon occur. There is also very little reason to expect that the present U. S. Administration will be of any meaningful assistance. Henry Kissinger, who had been described by a Jewish official as a "committed Jew," will likely make every effort to separate his Jewishness from foreign-policy planning and objectives. Those in the Jewish community who expect Dr. Kissinger to serve as a catalyst for major change in the condition of Soviet Jewry are sadly mistaken. Kissinger may, as in the past, be helpful in individual cases, but he cannot and surely will not place the interests of Russian Jews above the aims of American foreign policy if he believes they conflict. Likewise, there is simply no reason to believe that President Nixon, who never again requires the political support of Jewish voters, will suddenly champion the cause of Soviet Jewry at the expense of his predilection for *détente* at any price.

It may be that, given the realities of Soviet hostility and intransigence, American governmental policy and American Jewish inertia, the overwhelming majority of Soviet Jews have little chance of ever gaining their two-fold objective of freedom of emigration or of being able to live as Jews with dignity within the Soviet system. However, I would hope that the Jewish establishment, which certainly has the financial and professional resources to systematically deal with the question, will yet rise from its lethargy and indifference and adopt a crash program to save Soviet Jewry. Perhaps the odds are too great, perhaps such an effort is doomed to failure, but at the very least, the attempt itself will put muscle into the posturing concerning the need for Jewish solidarity so prevalent within the contemporary American Jewish community.

Finally, such an effort might inhibit the next generation of Jews from asking their elders, "Where were you when the life of Soviet Jewry hung in the balance?"

III

AMERICAN JEWS AND THE CHRISTIAN COMMUNITY

The pluralistic character of American Christianity provides special problems for the Jewish community. Jews must relate in sometimes passive, sometimes active fashion to several branches of Protestantism, ranging from ultra fundamentalist to unitarian liberalism, to Roman Catholics (who themselves are split into conflicting camps), to the Orthodox churches many of whom are tied to Middle East churches and to the black churches, long a seminal force in the life of the black community.

As is the case with so many other areas of community concern, no single voice speaks for Jews in relationship to Christians. National secular agencies such as the American Jewish Committee and the Anti-Defamation League and to a lesser degree the American Jewish Congress have program departments or individual staff dealing with interreligious affairs. These programs operate independently of each other and manifest surprisingly little duplication.

Theoretically, the National Jewish Community Relations Advisory Council should act as a co-ordinating body, but except for issuing annual program projections, which are promptly ignored by its constituent national organizations, the NJCRAC plays a relatively minor role in the sphere of interreligious relations. (The NJCRAC's ninety-three local community relations councils do perform a more active function in the interreligious area, particularly in those communities where the national defense agencies do not have local professional representation.) Likewise, the Synagogue Council of America, the co-ordinating body for the three major religious bodies has little active involvement in interreligious activities save its largely ceremonial function of sitting in a summit-type troika with the National Council of Churches and the secretariat of the National Conference of Catholic Bishops.

The basic mission of the interreligious affairs sections of the national defense agencies is twofold: a) to combat the religious sources and manifestations of anti-Semitism, and b) to educate Christians concerning the nature and experience of Jewish faith.

The Dangerous Tradition

In recent years, particularly since the June 1967 war, these agencies have also expended a good deal of time and resources in interpreting Israel to the Christian community. The problems faced by the Jewish organizations in their relations with Christians are enormously complex. This complexity is not difficult to understand when one recognizes that the relationship began with a traumatic event that set the stage for centuries of animosity and mutual distrust. At its best, this relationship has been tenuous and problematic; at its worst, it has been marked by persecution and violence.

One can trace several stages in the development of the Jewish-Christian relationship. In the early centuries church and synagogue struggled against a pagan Roman jurisdiction and mystery cults and religions pressing in from the Eastern world as well as against each other. It was in these formative years that a Christian tradition of teaching was born which placed primary responsibility for the crucifixion upon the Jewish people. According to this tradition the "Jews" by killing Jesus had forfeited all human and divine rights. Jewish religion was denigrated and the life experiences of the individual Jew were caricatured and dehumanized. The Jew was destined to spend his earthly days awaiting and experiencing the divine wrath. Moreover, for a Christian to attempt to alleviate Jewish suffering was to thwart the will of God. After the fourth century and the political triumph of Christianity Jews suffered under social, economic and civic restrictions imposed by Church law.

During the medieval period the image grew of the Jews as enemy of God, agent of Satan and obdurate foe of Christendom. It was during this period that mythologies developed depicting Jews as poisoners of wells, as killers of children, and as participants in a world-wide heinous conspiracy to destroy Christianity and Western culture. The early modern period and Enlightenment did bring some respite from the pattern of denigration and degradation, but from time to time pogroms would arise from the smoldering ashes of Christian opposition to Jewish life, to bring widespread death and destruction. Our own generation has witnessed the Holocaust, the systematic destruction of over five million men, women and children, simply because they were Jewish.

One can surely argue as to whether the great pioneer of

modern Jewish-Christian relations, James Parkes, is correct when he draws a straight line from the ancient negative Christian tradition of teaching concerning Jews to the death camps, yet it must be said that there was active in European civilization a definite anti-Jewish conditioning that helped create a climate in which Jews were regarded as subhuman and worthy of destruction. Hitler and his cohorts surely did not invent legislation dealing with economic restrictions and social limitations. Precedents for these sections of the Nuremberg Laws came from canonical legislation dating from the formative period of church history. Neither did the Nazi ideologues initiate a new philosophic understanding of Jewish experience. While it is true their ideology concerning Jews was an amalgam containing nationalistic, racial and religious strains, there was clearly present the notion of Jewish guilt and the concomitant need, yea divine fiat, for corporeal punishment. The fact that the German churches largely parroted the National Socialist line was due not only to existential realities but also to a long and largely unbroken strand of theological anti-Semitism dating from the Protestant reformation—particularly the teaching of Martin Luther. It is striking to note that even the "confessing" church which opposed Hitler said little and did less to ameliorate the lot of the Jews. Indeed, some of the great heroes of the resistance, who today are transmogrified into twentieth-century prophets by many "with it" churchmen, were at heart decidedly anti-Semitic. Martin Niemoller wrote in 1939 of having to marshal all his inner resources to accept converted Jews "into the bosom of the church,"[1] and one looks in vain in the writings of the martyred Dietrich Bonhoffer for words of empathy concerning the plight of the Jews.

The definitive explanation of National Socialist policy vis-à-vis the European Jews came after the war from Higher

SS General von dem Bach-Zelewski who testified at Nuremburg of the National Socialist goal of "exterminating Judaism."[2] In essence, what the Nazis attempted, was the destruction of Jewish civilization itself. Thus, in a few blood-drenched years, Hitler and his associates tried to accomplish what nineteen hundred years of tension and turmoil could not achieve; the final victory of Christianity over the mother faith.

Sadly, the record of the American churches during the Nazi years is marked by ambivalence and indifference. The World War II period witnessed no significant outpouring of Christian concern over the fate of the European Jews. Those churchmen who did comment on events across the ocean often cited Hitler as the anti-Christ or dealt with the unfolding tragedy as another sign of the fast-approaching end time. In that sense, what was done to the Jews was a part of the larger fabric and could not be actively opposed lest the return of Christ and the setting up of the millennial kingdom be inhibited. Christians who held to such views found it convenient to cite the Holocaust as one more divine act of retribution for the failure of the Jewish people to accept Jesus as the Christ. Incredible as it may seem, such ideology still commands significant allegiance within some fundamentalist circles. As recently as the 1960s the Assemblies of God, a major pentecostal denomination, published a Bible study that, after rehearsing Jewish history since the crucifixion, described the Holocaust and the execution of millions of Jews. The publication flatly states that all Jewish suffering occurred as a result of the "rejection" of Jesus. "What a price to pay," the study concludes, "His blood be upon us and on our children."[3] Recent textbook research indicates that such teaching, though in a somewhat modified form, characterizes much of Protestant educational comment on Jews and Judaism.

A Tedious Enterprise

This onerous theological and experiential background makes the mission of improvement of relations between Jews and Christians a difficult and tedious enterprise. So uneasy is the past and so arduous is the labor involved to achieve peaceful coexistence and eventual mutual respect that many in the Jewish world refrain from entering into dialogue with Christians. Indeed, some influential leaders, particularly in the orthodox community, actively oppose efforts to improve interfaith relations. Rabbis Eliezer Berkovits of Chicago and the much revered Joseph Soloveitchik of Boston have long held that such dialogue cannot help Jews and in the long run only act to undermine Jewish religious and communal commitment. This viewpoint, while understandable in the light of past events, is, in the American pluralistic context, shortsighted and self-defeating. The very fact of Jewish minority status in America, currently less than 3 per cent of the population with a steadily declining birth rate, makes communication with the majority an incumbent responsibility. Dialogue allows Jews to state their religious and communal concerns and often provides an effective channel for the articulation of current Jewish agendas. Too often the impetus for dialogue comes solely from the Jewish side, but Christians in an increasing manner have responded positively to such overtures and have in some notable instances themselves initiated discussion with Jewish counterparts.

These discussions invariably deal with the major theological questions separating the two faith communities. Topics such as the meaning of Messiah, conversion, law and grace, salvation, and the future of monotheistic religion are expounded in scholarly papers and in lively, informed discussion. Often the deliberations are published and circulated among clergy and interested laymen thus widening the circle of dialogue participation. It must also be said that these encounters, while spiritually and intellectually stimulating to those involved, seldom have noticeable effect upon the average Christian or upon the total life experience of the churches as they relate to Jews and Judaism.

The National Council of Churches

The most important interaction between the two religions comes in more indirect and politicized settings. Thus, in the last few years Jewish representatives have been able to most effectively articulate their positions by participation as active observers at national meetings of individual denominations and at the general board sessions of the National Council of Churches. It is in such arenas, where Christians set policy, that a Jewish presence acts to inform and often modify or change the direction of statements or programs that are viewed in the Jewish community as antithetical to Jewish interests. In a real sense such efforts are a justifiable attempt to keep the Christian bodies from making concessions to other groups and interests at the expense of the Jewish community. These activities are all the more justifiable when one realizes that other groups have instant entree to the deliberations of the major church organizations, and that there exist in local areas important segments of Christian opinion that are disturbed by the one-sided treatment of the Arab-Israel conflict by the liberal Protestant establishment. The liberal Protestant attitude toward Israel has been explored by Hertzel Fishman in a recent study entitled, *American Protestantism and the State of Israel.* Fishman, an official of the Israel Ministry of Education suggests:

> An anti-Israel theological bias is still very much evident within American Protestantism. More latent than overt, it has been manifest in negative attitudes toward cultural pluralism—as applied to Jews—in the United States, the admission of Jewish refugees from the European Holocaust to America; Jewish nationalism in contrast to the nationalism of other peoples, especially the Arabs; the establishment of a sovereign Jewish state in Palestine; the security of Israel.[4]

The theological bias Fishman describes can be traced to that tradition of Christian teaching which viewed Jews as weak and without spiritual resources as a result of the rejection of Jesus. The modern articulation of this thesis which has had the most significant impact upon mainline and liberal Protestantism is Karl Barth's formulation of the Jews as being a sign of God's judgment in the world. Barth in commenting on the traditional Christian view of the two basic natures of God, the one of mercy, the other of judgment, saw the continued existence of Jewish life as a sign-warning of God's side of judgment which will come down upon those Christians who live disobediently. Barth, who in his personal life was well-disposed toward individual Jews even to the extent of helping facilitate the rescue of colleagues from the Nazi terror, repeated in his teaching the distortions of the past by making of the Jewish people abstractions to be neatly fit in a theological system. Thus, he contributed to the continuation of theological anti-Semitism. His disciples in the American churches mirror his views to a remarkable degree. Many of them would fight valiantly for the individual Jew in distress but could not come to grips with the reality of a vibrant and dynamic Jewish state which is the living antithesis to weakness and judgment. For these persons the June 1967 war was a trauma of immense proportions, and in the intervening years many mainline Christians have attempted to turn aside the victory of Israel through resolutions, statements and at times active involvement in the affairs of the Middle East nations. What these Christians fail to comprehend is that the situation of the Jews insofar as Israel is concerned has radically changed. As Robert Alter suggests:

> Millions of Jews from the First Crusade to the Final Solution were passive victims because their location as a minority, as resident-aliens on sufferance, made it politically, tactically, psychologically impossible for most of them to be anything but passive victims. By establishing a sovereign state, Jews have resuscitated the possibility of initiating action rather than merely responding to the action of others, of controlling in some significant degree the conditions that are literally matters of life and death to them.[5]

Dr. Franklin H. Littell, director of graduate studies in religion at Temple University, accurately summarizes the liberal Protestant failure to comprehend this new situation:

> The thing, the 19th century Liberal Protestant, the Christian humanitarian, cannot grasp is the Jew who is a winner, a citizen soldier of liberty and dignity, who does not have to beg protection of a patron or toleration of a

so-called Christian nation, who can take the Golan Heights in six hours if necessary. This is precisely the reason why Israel is a stone of stumbling, and why also the generally covert anti-Semitism of liberal Protestantism can be just as dangerous as the overt anti-Semitism of the radical right.[6]

Other factors aiding in the development of this bias vis-à-vis the Middle East are the long history of mainline Protestant missions in the Arab world, the continuing investment in terms of personnel and material in Middle East church work, and the long "on site" experience of key staff responsible for administering Middle East affairs for the American denominations.

The October war further exacerbated tension between the Protestant establishment and the Jewish community. A few days after the hostilities began, the governing board of the National Council of Churches convened in New York at their regular semi-annual session. This meeting was marked by the most outspoken and viciously anti-Israel debate and private discussion the writer has yet witnessed.[7] On October 15, the governing board passed a resolution on the war that was regarded by the Council's leadership as "even handed and balanced." The American Jewish Committee, however, in a statement issued immediately after the resolution was adopted assailed the statement for its "total inability" to morally condemn Egypt and Syria for their violation of the cease-fire.[8] The NCC resolution also appeared to lack balance in its appeal to the U. S. Government to "effect an immediate-mutual cessation of arms shipments" without making a similar request of the U.S.S.R. In the light of the fact that the resolution was passed while a massive Soviet shipment of arms to Egypt and Syria was going on, the NCC sentiment could only be interpreted as supporting the cause of Egyptian and Syrian aggression while advocating the crippling of Israel's capacity for self-defense. The AJC also pointed out that the resolution placed the National Council in a position anomalous to the many Christians who had already "publicly expressed strong support for Israel at this hour of crisis." It should be noted that the NCC statement originated in the Council's overseas ministry staff and was then approved by several denominational leaders who are headquartered in the Interchurch Center in close proximity to the NCC. The mainline leadership led on this issue by William Thompson, stated clerk of the United Presbyterian Church, was fully committed to the resolution and fought tenaciously to retain its original "even handed" language. The anti-Israel thrust of this leadership was articulated on the floor by Mr. Thompson who clearly expressed his pro-Arab feelings. In private conversation some mainline leaders were even more outspoken in their distaste for Israel. On Sunday evening, October 14, a top executive of the United Church of Christ, the Reverend David Stowe, told me that Israel "might have to die" to prevent World War III.[9] Three days later Stowe, who serves as executive vice-president of the United Church Board of World Ministries, sent a telegram to Secretary Kissinger in which he suggested that the United States should at once "seize the opportunity" offered by Egyptian President Sadat and work for a truce based on the pre-1967 boundaries.[10] In his message to Dr. Kissinger, Stowe also expressed support for the NCC Middle East resolution.

In the light of the NCC reaction to the Yom Kippur war and that organization's past record on Israel and on specific issues of concern to the Jewish community, I would urge Jewish bodies to carefully reassess their relationship with the National Council. I refer in particular to the Synagogue Council of America, which maintains a formal relationship with the NCC at the chief-executive level. I would urge the Synagogue Council to pull out of this alliance with the NCC if there is no immediate evidence of a change in NCC policy on the Middle East situation. The Synagogue Council has not made any significant contribution to the Jewish community's attempt to interpret Israel to the NCC, its governing board and its constituent members. Most distressing is the fact that the Synagogue Council has not sent observers to Council sessions on any consistent basis and failed to provide any representation at the October 1973 NCC governing board meeting in New York. The Synagogue Council's executive vice-president, Rabbi Henry Siegman, compounded the failure of his organization to closely follow NCC actions by apologizing for the NCC's failure to condemn the Egyptian and Syrian Yom Kippur war aggression. Questioned by *The New York Times* just after the NCC statement on the war was adopted, Rabbi Siegman expressed regret at the resolution but noted "that unlike individuals, the NCC was obliged to issue carefully worded statements because many of its 30 member denominations had Middle East connections."[11]

The Middle East issue will also cause the Jewish community increasing problems in relating to the United Church of Christ and the United Presbyterian Church, the two most prestigious mainline denominations. In the coming months Jews will likely seek active coalition with more moderate bodies such as Methodists, Disciples and Baptists. Mainline Christian support for the Arab position is especially disturbing because this activity flies in the face of the experience of the past three decades in which Jews and liberal Protestants worked together to bring about needed social reform. One can almost suggest that the Jewish community was being used by Protestant counterparts who in their collective gut had little interest in the underlying Jewish agenda. I would hope that in the future Jews will think carefully before entering into alliances of any sort with the liberal Protestant community.

The Protestant establishment's record on Israel clearly reveals at best a lack of sensitivity on Jewish concerns and at worst a latent hostility that is inimical to Jewish continuity and survival.

The Roman Catholics

Viewed from the perspective of the last decade, the work of Vatican Council II marked a watershed in relations between Jews and Roman Catholics. The Declaration on the Relation of the Church to Non-Christian Religions promulgated by Pope Paul VI on October 28, 1965, set the stage for a new beginning in Jewish-Catholic affairs.

To be sure, the section of the Declaration dealing with Judaism and the Jewish people did not go as far as some in the Jewish community had hoped, but there is little doubt that the document's rejection of the historic deicide charge, its condemnation of anti-Semitism and suggestion of the validity of Jewish religious faith has had a profound impact upon Roman Catholic thought and experience. This impact can be measured on the bureaucratic level by the establishment of a Vatican office of Jewish-Catholic relations and by the setting up of similar secretariats in individual nations.

In the United States, the secretariat for Catholic-Jewish relations, ably directed by Father Edward Flannery, is an integral part of the National Conference of Catholic Bishops. The secretariat furnishes information and documentation to local dioceses and provides program co-ordination for diocesan committees involved in Catholic-Jewish affairs. The very fact that such a secretariat exists indicates the seriousness with which the American Bishops view the Jewish community. In contrast there is no counterpart office in the American Protestant denominational establishment. The National Council of Churches received a foundation grant in 1973 to establish a staff position to co-ordinate relationships with the Jewish community. However, in the light of the negative history of NCC activity dealing with Israel, I would not expect the NCC to make a significant contribution to Jewish-Christian amity.

The impact of Vatican II can also be measured in terms of Catholic education. In a 1970 survey conducted by Sister Rose Thering of Seton Hall University, Catholic colleges and seminaries reported a significant growth in courses in Judaism, lectures by Jewish scholars, and interaction with local Jewish communities.[12] The impetus given by Vatican II has also affected lay people in the two faith communities. Dialogue groups and seminars at the parish and synagogue level have sprouted up in many parts of the country.

Yet once all of these welcome and positive developments have been reported one must recognize the growing gulf that exists between the Catholic and Jewish communities. This separation, interestingly, is not due to theological or liturgical distinctions but to wide divergence on the philosophic and practical aspects of several major contemporary issues. Simply put, most Jews and Catholics differ on questions such as public aid to parochial schools, abortion, birth control. In recent months there has been a growing tendency for bishops and other church authorities to ask for a *quid pro quo* with the Jewish community. Thus, if Jewish leaders seek Catholic support for Israel or for the release of Soviet Jews, Catholics will counter by asking for

Jewish backing for anti-abortion legislation or for assistance in the struggle to fund Catholic education through
public sources. Several key bishops have manifested an increasing impatience with Jewish issues and there now exists
the potential for a renaissance of ill feeling between Catholics and Jews. During the last few years the Catholic press
has given inordinate attention to the views of two outspoken opponents of Israel, Archbishop Timothy Ryan of
Alaska and Father Joseph Ryan, a Cambridge, Massachusetts, Jesuit who most recently served in Iraq.

Father Joseph Ryan is an interesting study in that he re-
flects a kind of Christian masochism in which one's support
for the Arab position increases proportionally with the
amount of emotional and religious abuse inflicted by the
objects of mission. Thus, Ryan became an even more ardent
proponent of Arab aims after he was summarily bounced
from Iraq.

The fact that the subject of Israel complicates the Catholic-Jewish relationship can be traced in large part to the
Vatican's failure to recognize the Jewish state. There is of
course no great mystery surrounding the position of non-
recognition. Arab pressure on the Church has been enormous from the period prior to the establishment of Israel
and the presence of representatives to the Holy See from
each of the Arab nations allows for constant pressure to be
exerted. In addition, certain Vatican officials are basically
anti-Israel in their approach to Middle East questions. Outstanding in this category is Frederico Allesandrini, a key
press officer and writer for *L'Osservatore Romano*. It was
Allesandrini who out maneuvered the Israeli press officials
immediately after Prime Minister Golda Meir's 1972 visit
with the Pope in the Vatican. While diplomatic officials
were working out the last details of what was basically a
positive and mutually respectful communique, Allesandrini

was informing the world press that the session between the Pope and Mrs. Meir was cold, formal and non-productive. Jewish reaction in the United States to the media accounts based on the Allesandrini briefing reflected a general suspicion of all things emanating from Rome. The Allesandrini-inspired news reports confirmed for many Jews the futility of working seriously with Catholics, and even the yeoman efforts of American Jewish officials to communicate a more realistic account of what had transpired in the Vatican session could not dispel the uneasiness alive in the community.

American Jews also look with apprehension at the increasing trend in the Catholic sphere toward individual piety and emotional religious experience. Thus, the growth of Catholic pentecostalism and the support given the Key 73 evangelistic campaign by several major archdioceses (not to mention the endorsement of the National Conference of Catholic Bishops) has engendered Jewish concern over a rightward turn in American Catholicism. The challenge confronting Jews and Catholics in the remainder of the 1970s is whether the initial momentum provided by Vatican Council II can be enlarged and channeled into fostering depth discussion over the very real differences which divide the communities. Given the political and social climate of America and the ambivalence of Rome concerning the right of Israel to survive as a nation, the prognosis for the future of Catholic-Jewish relations is not promising.

The Evangelicals

As late as ten years ago the suggestion that there could be a meaningful relationship between American Jews and evangelical Protestants would have been rejected out of hand. Traditionally, the two communities were at odds not only in an overwhelming theological sense but also from a sociological and historical perspective. Indeed, there had been in America a tendency for anti-Semitism to find root in evangelical soil. Studies undertaken as late as the middle 1960s showed a high correlation between conservative theological commitment and anti-Semitic attitudes. On the experiential level there was almost no formal contact between the Jewish community and the evangelical establishment. When Jews sought to relate to Protestants they seemed to naturally look to the mainline churches. The June 1967 Arab-Israel war radically changed this pattern as Jews who felt abandoned by old allies in the Christian world found that the evangelical community was by and large quite friendly to Israeli aspirations and exercised little inhibition in articulating this position.

Evangelical support for Israel is largely based upon theological grounds. For many years prior to the establishment of the State of Israel in 1948 evangelicals had taught that Jews would return in numbers to their ancient homeland. This restoration of the Jewish people to their land would be a precursor of the return of Jesus to the earth and the setting up of his millennial kingdom.

This expectation of a mass Jewish return to the Middle East was highly speculative and the source of much derisive criticism of evangelicals in the liberal Protestant seminaries. It is thus understandable that when the State of Israel came into being, evangelicals viewed the event as a signal confirmation of their theological beliefs. The miracle that the prophets had promised and that evangelicals had propounded through many a dark and unlikely night had come to pass. To be sure there was and is much about Israel that troubles evangelicals, but it is unthinkable that once the divine will has been exercised in the restoration of Israel that the believer can do other than support the nation's right to exist. In any case, many evangelicals believe that at the end of time there will be a massive Jewish conversion to Christianity which will be centered in Israel, so that patience with the unseemly aspects of contemporary Israeli life will eventually be rewarded. One might expect that, given the ultimate evangelical expectation of Jewish conversion, the Jewish community would not have much interest in relating to evangelicals. However, pragmatic considerations must be taken into account. If one concedes that American support is a major determinant as to whether Israel continues to exist as a nation, and if one further recognizes that Christian attitudes help mold American public opinion on the Middle East question, then the subject of evangelical backing for Israel is of more than academic interest to Jews. In the light of the hostility of some Protestants and the indifference of others, the keen and active interest of evangelicals cannot be taken lightly.

In 1971, for example, when support was growing in both the mainline Protestant and Roman Catholic communities for internationalization of the city of Jerusalem, it was a group of evangelical leaders who made the strongest comment favoring retention of a unified Jerusalem under Israeli jurisdiction.[13] The framer of the statement, issued immediately after the close of the June International Jerusalem Conference on Biblical Prophecy was Dr. Arnold T. Olson of Minneapolis, president of the Evangelical Free Church of America and immediate past president of the National Association of Evangelicals. Dr. Olson, an elder statesman and a widely respected and beloved figure within the evangelical movement, undertook an even more important mission in 1973 at the time when evangelicals' tempers were frayed over the alleged mistreatment of Christian missionaries in Israel. Olson visited Israel in

April and met with missionaries, Israeli Government officials and representatives of the more liberal churches. Statements such as that issued by Chief Rabbi Goren, "I say we must uproot this affliction called mission," reports that the government was planning to expel one hundred missionaries, and a recent fire of suspicious origin at the Mount of Olives International Center for Holy Scriptures alarmed even those American evangelicals who had been outspoken advocates of the Israeli cause. On May 2 Olson addressed the influential National Association of Evangelicals gathered in annual session at Portland, Oregon.[14] He reported the anti-missionary activity was mainly the work of extremist groups, and that the government had given assurances that it would respect Christian freedom of conscience and the right of missionaries to air their views provided they did not exercise coercion or engage in willfully misleading practices. The Olson report quelled an incipient outbreak of anti-Israel feeling at the NAE meeting and made an important impact upon evangelicals throughout the nation.

It is little wonder then that the Jewish establishment has given increasing priority to relating to persons such as Olson and to the evangelical churches in general. Both the American Jewish Committee and the Anti-Defamation League have sponsored theological dialogues with the twelve-million-member Southern Baptist Convention, and in 1969 the AJC marked an interreligious first by bringing Jewish scholars to the annual meeting of the Evangelical Theological Society. On June 7, 1972, the Southern Baptist Convention, meeting in Philadelphia, became the first major evangelical group to adopt a statement condemning anti-Semitism. The resolution, introduced by Dr. B. Elmo Scoggin, professor of Old Testament at the Southeastern Baptist Theological Seminary declared anti-Semitism to be unchristian, and pledged Southern Baptists to "work positively to replace all anti-Semitic bias with the Christian attitude and practice of love for Jews, who along with all other men, are equally beloved of God."[15]

The AJC has also conducted extensive programming around the World Wide Pictures (a Billy Graham subsidiary) production, *His Land*. This film is perhaps the most positive Christian media statement on Israel ever developed, and at last count had been viewed by over twenty million Christians in the United States and Canada.

Billy Graham's attitude with respect to Israel is instructive because it indicates that evangelicals can go beyond their initial theological commitment, to an appreciation of the human dimensions of Israeli life. Many evangelicals can understand Israel only in abstract terms. Israel is the great stage upon which the last great drama of history will be played out, but there is little comprehension of the reality of contemporary Israel. A Sunday school lesson prepared by an evangelical publisher just after the June 1967 war vividly illustrates this failure to come to terms with the human quotient involved in certain evangelical theological formulations. The lesson after stating that Israel had just won a smashing military victory pointed out that another war could start at any time and that Israel might be destroyed in such a conflict. The lesson then concluded that if such a result ensued, "we shall simply know that God's time has not yet come for the Jews."[16] This appalling lack of sensitivity is not unlike some Christian reactions to the Nazi Holocaust. Graham has transcended this shallow position. True, his starting point in relating to the reality of Israel was based on the theological necessity for a restored Jewish state, but then through active experience with Israelis in many walks of life, Graham gained an enormous appreciation for the human, living fact of Israel. Today

Graham is perhaps the world's single most important Christian friend of Israel. The *His Land* film, which movingly describes Israel as it is while presenting with integrity the evangelical theological viewpoint, was made at significant risk to Graham's relations with Christians in the Arab world. Indignant letters and threats to cut off aid came from Arab Christians in the Middle East and the United States when the picture was released. Graham characteristically took the criticism in stride and gave instructions to World Wide Pictures that the film be given the widest possible exposure. Beyond the film and sermons and talks in which he speaks positively of Israel, Graham is a staunch and treasured friend of many Israeli leaders, and it is not unreasonable to assume that he has had some positive impact upon the conclusions reached in the past by Presidents Johnson and Nixon concerning Israel.

The "Jewish Missions"

While Israel has been the foundation upon which improved relations between evangelicals and Jews have been built, conversion-oriented evangelistic overtures to the Jewish community may well erode the newly developed Jewish-Evangelical understanding. For years there have been organizations operating on the fringes of evangelicalism whose sole *raison d'être* has been the conversion of Jews to Christianity. These groups, until very recent years, have met with meager success. Indeed, if one were to do a budget analysis of what it costs these groups to convert one Jew, donations would likely fall off sharply.

The American Board of Missions to the Jews, the largest of the more than one hundred organizations working full-time in "Jewish evangelism," had a total budget in 1971 of 1.9 million dollars. Most of this money comes from the gifts of local churches and individuals. The question is often asked why these institutions and persons support an activity that has traditionally met with such singular failure. The answer to this lies, as might be expected, on theological grounds. New Testament evidence suggests that the Apostle Paul, himself a convert from Judaism to Christianity, urged that the gospel be preached first to the Jewish community and then to the gentiles. Paul's own practice upon visiting a new city was to go to the synagogue and make a witness to Jesus as Messiah or Christ. Quite generally he met with a negative reception and thus went off to preach to the non-Jews of the community. There is then deep in the recesses of the evangelical mentality an imperative to tell Jews about Christianity. Also, to adherents of a missionizing faith like Christianity who are always seeking new confirmations of their beliefs, there is no catch quite like a Jew. Churchmen reason that if a Jew is willing to forsake Judaism with all the trauma and perhaps personal loss this entails, then the Christian religion must be true; ergo the experience of the individual gentile believer must necessarily be real. Nevertheless, most gentile Christians find it extremely difficult to "witness" to Jews. First, they know almost nothing about Judaism; second, they know even less about Jewish culture and everyday life; and finally, they realize that it takes a large slice of internal fortitude to speak to a Jew about accepting a religion that has helped to provide so much pain to his people over the centuries. In the light of this, it is not surprising that gentile Christians have been more than willing to turn over the function of "Jewish missions" to specialized organizations. These organizations presumably provide the expertise required to properly confront a Jew with the claims of Christ.

Manny Brotman, founder of The Messianic Jewish Movement International, explains why the act of witness to Jews is such a unique enterprise:

I knew of many extremely dedicated Gentile believers who were trying to reach the Jewish people, but the more I observed, the more I realized their approach "turned off" the Jewish people. By overemphasizing the cross and the name of Jesus, they were unknowingly aggravating sensitive areas to the Jewish nonbeliever.[17]

The mission groups are invariably run by converted Jews like Brotman who because of their background are thought to be especially equipped to expedite Jewish witness. Normally, the account of their conversion is portrayed in dramatic terms. One can for example, write in for the publication, *But You Don't Look Very Jewish,* the "amazing story of Manny Brotman." Interestingly, many of these individuals, who like Brotman are prone to a kind of megalomania ("one day I prayed 'God give me the world's Jewish population for Messiah Yeshua'"),[18] do not know much at all about Judaism although they usually stress the orthodoxy of their childhood.

In studying the publications of scores of these groups over the years I can recall only a few instances in which a mission leader described a reform or non-aligned Jewish background. The Judaism they oppose and preach against is quite generally a caricature composed of a combination of past personal unhappiness, dim memory of childhood and Christian and other extant forms of anti-Jewish attitudes and ideas. In the light of this it is not surprising that some of the most virulent expressions of theological and at times sociological anti-Semitism emanate from the mission organizations. Indeed, one could safely conclude that the stock in trade of these bodies is an anti-Judaism that denigrates Jewish religious leadership and the spiritual experience of the individual Jew. A brochure distributed by the American Board of Missions to the Jews states:

> Never before in Israel's history has the Jew been in sorer need of the Gospel. The Jew is adrift from the moorings of his Old Testament. . . . Bewildered and misled by the emptiness of Judaism and the false aims of Zionism, he is on the hunt for something to replace what he has lost.[19]

In similar fashion an article in *The Chosen People,* a publication of the American Board of Missions summarizes Jewish religious experience

> Finally the hardening of Israel has manifest itself in their absolute ignorance of the nature and purpose of the law . . . The rabbis have conceived of the law as an excellent system whereby man can find favor and merit with God. The regulations imposed by them upon the nation with this view in mind are sometimes downright absurd.[20]

Prior to 1971 this literature and the larger ministry it represents had never surfaced in any significant way so as to represent a major problem to the Jewish community. But in that year, possibly as a result of the attention being given the Jesus movement but more probably because of the developing national strength of evangelicalism, the Ameri-

can Board of Missions to the Jews and similar organizations
took on a more militant stance.

The Board produced a half-hour television program
called *The Passover* which articulated a christological interpretation of the character and implements of the Jewish
Seder and ended with an overt pitch for conversion. The
program was scheduled for broadcast in major Jewish population centers with the kick-off to be, naturally enough, in
New York. Executives at WPIX-TV, the station scheduled
to air the program in New York, invited Jewish representatives to a screening just days before *The Passover* was to be
shown. Suffice to say, the screening caused great consternation on the part of the Jewish viewers who readily recognized the program for the patent deception it was. As a result of the objections voiced by Jewish organizations, particularly the Board of Rabbis, the program was canceled.
This brought charges of censorship from the American
Board and gave the group for the first time in its ninety-
year history a front-page story in *The New York Times*.[21]

Some observers, including this writer, thought the Board
of Rabbis made a tactical mistake in demanding that the
program be withheld. This view was based on the assump-
tion that groups such as the American Board need occa-
sional martyrdoms to feed their psychological as well as
financial needs. In any case, the controversy apparently
proved to be a windfall for the American Board and several
months later the organization took a full page advertisement
in *The New York Times* at a cost of eight thousand dollars.[22] The ad which pictured about twenty-five smiling
persons standing in a circle was entitled, "So Many Jews
Are Wearing 'That Smile' Nowadays!" Insult was added to
injury by the fact that the ad appeared on a Friday. Predictably the reaction of Jews throughout the metropolitan area
was one of shock and outrage. The advertisement which

eventually appeared in seven daily newspapers and was later used as a fund-raising device in the evangelical press was characterized by the American Jewish Committee's Rabbi Marc H. Tanenbaum as "trying to sell Christianity the way you sell toothpaste."[23]

Dr. Franklin Littell raised an objection from a Christian perspective by stating that the ad showed a "shocking degree of insensitivity." Littell added that Christianity "had better spend its time and money proving its credibility through actions of goodwill toward Jewish people and Israel."[24]

"Jews for Jesus"

One of the most significant by-products of this increased activity by the American Board and other adult-oriented groups has been the formation of independent or off-shoot organizations whose program is specifically directed at evangelizing Jewish young people. The most important of these groups is the "Jews for Jesus" founded by the Reverend Martin Meyer Rosen, an ordained Baptist minister and long-time staff member of the American Board of Missions to the Jews. Rosen, who has served as a missionary and director of training for the Board, left the American Board's staff in the fall of 1973 to form a new organization known as Hineni Ministries. The Board, which for a time took great pride in Rosen's work, apparently had a falling out with Rosen over his activist methodology.[25]

The fortyish Rosen, who is generally garbed in dungarees and jacket, works out of Corte Madera, California, but keeps an extensive lecture schedule throughout the country. His following, which was originally based on the apparent success of the Jesus movement to attract Jewish students to

Christianity, is quite aggressive and can be seen at the San Francisco airport or in the downtown areas of the city busily passing out "broadsides" and "witnessing." In an interview with the *Village Voice* Rosen described these street corner activities:

> Maybe we're a little over enthusiastic . . . Maybe we go out on street corners and push literature, maybe we brag too much, maybe we become obnoxious because of our zeal. But if you've really got Jesus, you've got that kind of enthusiasm. You want to run out screaming "Jesus is the way! Jesus is the way!"[26]

Rosen's *Voice* interview also revealed his megalomanic tendencies:

> If Jesus is the Messiah, your life isn't your own anymore. It's His. He's got a right to order me around. He can say, "Moishe, go to New York; Moishe, go to Honolulu" . . . I'm not going to get into how He talks to me; it's too spooky. You wouldn't believe it anyway; most of the time I don't believe it, but he does . . .[27]

Just how many devotees the Jews for Jesus, the Young Hebrew-Christian Alliance which operates a coffee house in Philadelphia called "the Hidden Matzoh," the Student Involvement Program of the American Messianic Fellowship and other similar groups have is difficult to ascertain. A cardinal rule in evaluating the activities of these organizations is to never believe their statistics. One can generally reduce by at least 50 per cent the figures released by these groups. On the other hand there evidently has been an increase in the number of young Jews who in the last three years have turned to Christianity. In 1972 Rabbi Samuel Fishman, assistant national director of the B'nai B'rith Hillel Foundations, conducted two surveys of over eighty college and university campuses in order to determine the Jewish student response to Christian evangelism. Fishman indicated that fifty of the schools experienced conversionary activities by one or more groups, with fifteen of the fifty schools reporting actual conversions. Fishman did flatly reject the claim published in the June 12, 1970, issue of *Time* "that young Jews are converting to Christianity at the rate of six to seven thousand a year." The Fishman survey made the following observations concerning the motivations for Jewish conversion:

1. For a number of individuals the attraction seems to be the current step in a series of experiments, and follows involvement with drugs, transcendental meditation, Eastern religion, astrology.

2. Conversion to Christianity is the latest manifestation of the student's fundamental rejection of family, synagogue and community.

3. In some cases psychological factors play a significant role in accounting for the student's behavior.

4. For some Christianity provided a spiritual experience of heretofore unknown dimensions.[28]

Moishe Rosen attributes Jewish student conversion to Christianity to the failure of Judaism and Jewish religious institutions. Writing in *Christianity Today,* Rosen states:

Another factor increasing Jewish interest in Jesus is rabbinical Judaism's *lack of solution to the difficult situations* confronting people today. Rabbis have decried the problems of dope, of degraded sex, and of the dehumanization of society and have shown great concern for finding answers. But they have generally failed to recognize these problems as symptoms of a spiritual hunger and emptiness in man . . .

Another important factor is the role of the synagogue . . . the idea that God cares for man and acts to intercede on behalf of individuals is rare in Jewish teaching. For the most part, sermons in the temple deal with the role of a Jew in a Gentile society and seem to be more properly suited for college lecture material than religious instruction.[29]

One could legitimately ask what qualifies Rosen, who by his own admission has had no contact with organized Judaism since the early 1950s to make such sweeping generalizations. The denigration of Judaism implicit in Rosen's writings and speeches acts to feed already deeply imbedded anti-Jewish mythologies and keep stereotypes alive in the Christian community. It is reasonable to assume that despite the desire of Rosen and others engaged in Jewish missions to target their tracts to Jews, most of their material falls into non-Jewish hands. Coupled with this is the fact that the *Chosen People* and similar magazines are read almost exclusively by evangelical Christians. Likewise, the missionaries spend a good deal of time in fundraising efforts through appearances in church services and before women's, youth and other special-interest groups. In these settings the missionary invariably takes Judaism and Jewish leaders to task, often in emotionally charged terminology. Fortunately for the Jewish community most missionaries are like the fighter who leaves his fight in the dressing room. They are great when dealing with the already saved but experience enormous difficulties when confronted with a Jewish person. Moishe Rosen, however, may represent a new breed. He is something of a charismatic figure who has convinced some rabbis and Jewish professionals in the Bay area of his sincerity. Like his elders in the area of Jewish missions he sides with Israel and the Soviet Jews but with a more persuasive articulation. More importantly, he really seems to understand the Holocaust and the primary importance of Israel and would likely not suggest as an American Board colleague did at UCLA that, "had the six million who died in the Holocaust become Christians, Jesus would have saved them from the gas chambers."[30] Rosen also is able to communicate far more effectively than other missionaries the traditional "Hebrew-Christian" claim that you can believe in Jesus and remain "Jewish." In a tract entitled "Christmas Is a Jewish Holiday," he writes:

All we need for Christmas or a celebration is Jesus. He is the world's oldest living Jew (since He is still alive!) . . . All of Jesus's apostles spoke with a Jewish accent! . . . If you knew what we know that Jesus really is the Messiah— then you would agree that Christmas should be a Jewish holiday.[31]

In his ministry, Rosen attempts to present a Christianity which is about 80 per cent Jewish. The tag line at the bottom, however, includes Christian baptism and identification with a local church. It is difficult to conclude whether Rosen is purposefully deceptive or if he just has not thought through the implications of his teaching. He should know, however, that in the real world one cannot be a Christian and a Jew at the same time. Rosen's keen understanding of the media and his reasonably solid financial base should keep him active over the next several years. He will likely continue to meet with some success in converting young Jews but as Rabbi Stephen Shaw of the City University of New York suggests perhaps the greater danger to Jewish youth comes from the Eastern religions. In any case, the Jews for Jesus and Hineni Ministries will likely provide a measure of bizarre excitement as they latch on to many issues of communal interest to Jews. Thus, the Jews for Jesus picketed the theater in San Francisco which played the film version of *Jesus Christ Superstar*. The bravado of the group was reported by Herb Caen in the *San Francisco Examiner* when he described the new definition of *chutzpah* developed by Rosen and his cohorts in asking the theater cashier to validate their parking tickets once the picketing was completed.

The Campus Crusaders

The recent activities of the older Jewish mission organizations and the appearance of bodies such as the Jews for Jesus are of course disturbing to the Jewish community. However, what has been even more troubling has been the greatly accelerated efforts at Jewish conversion undertaken by organizations whose activities are normally focused at the general student population.

Groups such as Young Life, Youth for Christ, Hi-Teen, Intervarsity Christian Fellowship and, pre-eminently, The Campus Crusade for Christ have assumed an active stance on high school, college and university campuses vis-à-vis the Jewish student population. To some degree they have usurped the functions of the specific Jewish mission organizations and a bitter intraevangelical struggle is taking place over who will be broker for the conversion of Jewish youth.

The most militant student-oriented group is the Campus Crusade for Christ founded in 1951 by Bill Bright a California businessman and millionaire several times over who felt led to leave the world of commerce in order to evangelize students. Campus Crusade currently has mission bases in thirty-seven countries and employs four thousand people on a full-time basis. Approximately twenty-five hundred of these staff members operate on campuses in the United States.

Bright zoomed to the top of the campus organizational heap when he staged a spectacular week-long youth rally in Dallas (where else?) in June 1972. The meeting known as Explo '72 was attended by over eighty thousand very straight young people from the United States and Canada and was budgeted at eight million dollars. The Explo '72 program featured daily seminars and nightly mammoth sessions in the Cotton Bowl and ended with a Saturday music extravaganza set on a blocked off freeway. Over one quarter million people gathered to hear almost every major musical group currently on the make for the Christian youth market. Explo was to be a training experience that would enable students to return to their respective schools geared up to fulfill the Campus Crusade goal of bringing the world to Christ by 1980.

Shortly before Explo '72 opened, the writer and his colleague Rabbi A. James Rudin, Associate Interreligious Affairs Director of the American Jewish Committee, met privately with Bright in his cramped Dallas hotel room to express concern over the report that the subject of Jewish missions was to receive a high priority at Explo. It is difficult to gauge what impact the session had on Bright, who obviously had never been in dialogue before with representatives of the Jewish establishment. In any case, during Explo, I discovered that the Jewish mission groups were highly agitated over the cavalier treatment they had received from Campus Crusade officials. In contrast to other seminars held in locations easily accessible to the great bulk of delegates, the one Jewish missions seminar was conducted at a church on the outer periphery of Dallas. A young representative of the American Board of Missions to the Jews told me that the one hundred or so "Hebrew-Christians" present were boycotting the Cotton Bowl rallies, in protest against Explo's "unfair policy" on Jewish missions.[32]

In retrospect it is difficult to assess whether the slighting of the specific mission organizations was due to a basic change of heart by Bright or because he saw an attractive opportunity for his own organization to move into the Jewish mission field in a major way. What is clear is that over the next year Campus Crusade operatives made a concerted effort to bring their message of the "four spiritual laws" of salvation to as many Jewish students as they could possibly reach. Many of these endeavors were coercive in nature. The door of a Jewish student's room would be flung open late at night and a clutch of young evangelists would enter singing hymns and offering testimony. At Arizona State the situation became so agitated that officials forbade all solicitation in the dormitories. This action caused problems to more legitimate parties than the evangelistic groups. Rabbi Barton Lee, the ASU Hillel director, whimsically told me that he could no longer go into the dorms to solicit UJA pledges. In a number of instances half-times of athletic events were turned into Jesus rallies by the Campus Crusade affiliate, Athletes in Action. The group also used deceptive practices to lure

Jewish young people to so-called "coke parties" and "hamburger bashes" where Crusade representatives would witness and not always in a subtle or ethical manner. The justification offered by the Crusade was that the organization worked for a higher power not obliged to recognize the laws of mere mortals. This reasoning sounded strange coming from a segment of the population which has normally been strongly supportive of the concept of "law and order." These divisive Crusade practices continued through the 1972–73 school year.

Key 73

If the work of traditional Jewish missions groups, the development of Jews for Jesus and the new Jewish ground plowed by the campus evangelicals was troubling the Jews, the most disturbing aspect of recent evangelical programs was the launching of a nationwide evangelistic campaign known as Key 73. This campaign owed its origin to a series of meetings held in 1967 at a motel near the Key Bridge linking Arlington, Virginia, and Washington, D.C. The sessions were called by Carl F. H. Henry, then editor of *Christianity Today* and long-time resident intellectual guru of evangelicalism. Henry was disturbed at the helter-skelter approach of the churches to evangelism and wanted to develop a co-operative effort that would cover the entire North American continent for a specified period of time. Henry was also perceptive enough to realize that the religious tide was moving back to the evangelicals.

Henry correctly saw that mainline Christianity had gotten itself so over-involved in the civil rights movement that it had lost the allegiance of many lay people. What Henry could not know in 1967, but may have wisely guessed was that disillusionment with the liberal denominations, would grow to a crescendo by 1972. In a real sense George McGovern, social gospel Methodist and former delegate to the World Council of Churches, was the candidate of the mainline bodies. His electoral disaster also marked the tolling of the bells for liberal Protestantism. Thus, whether through design or happenstance the prospects for the Key 73 movement were most promising.

Jewish leaders were not only concerned over the coming together of almost all the legitimate evangelical bodies in a year-long evangelistic program but also by the ecumenical nature of participation in Key 73. As early as April 1972 the National Conference of Catholic Bishops endorsed Key 73; later major archdioceses such as Los Angeles, Chicago and St. Louis would actively participate in the event. This meant that Roman Catholic priests and lay people would be working hand in hand with some of the very people in the evangelical world who had heretofore regarded every Catholic as a target for conversion. The Chicago situation was most interesting. In 1958 a tragic fire in a West Side Roman Catholic parochial school killed over one hundred pupils and teachers. All flags in the city of Chicago flew at half staff on the day of the mass funeral, except one. The lone holdout was the Moody Bible Institute, a bastion of evangelical education and the self-advertised "West Point of Christian Service." When asked why the Moody flag was not at half staff in honor of the dead, an Institute official replied that the flag would not be lowered for Catholics. Now in 1973 much had changed. The writer was startled to hear a Roman Catholic nun in uniform from Chicago cry out at the Key 73 panorama, "Halleuia, Praise the Lord," and to note the enthusiasm her appearance generated.

One does not have to be too jaded or cynical to suggest that at least one reason for Catholic participation in Key

73 was the attempt to relate to the more traditionalist and right-wing segments of the Catholic community who were troubled by what they construed as a leftward drift among the hierarchy and some younger activist priests and nuns. Key 73 was an occasion for the bishops to say to this audience that the church was still interested in individual spiritual experience. The ecumenical character of Key 73 extended also into a more unlikely area, the inclusion of several mainline Protestant bodies. Thus, the United Methodist Church, the nation's second largest denomination and the American Baptist Churches, formerly known as the American Baptist Convention, joined with evangelicals in the Key 73 movement. Here again one could clearly trace the realistic view of top leadership within these denominations that participation in Key 73 was a way to cut losses. For several years individuals on the right wing of the two groups were opting out and joining conservative churches. Key 73 provided an opportunity to convince the doubters that the denominations were still interested in personal salvation and the old time religion. For the Methodists, participation in Key 73 provided particular problems vis-à-vis their relationship with the Jewish community. In 1972 the denomination's General Conference passed a far-reaching statement on interreligious dialogue with Jews which seemed to place attempts to convert Jews outside the pale of Methodist life. Several leading Methodists were acutely troubled by the seeming contraction involved in the Methodist stance on Key 73, and at the October 1972 Panorama these individuals quietly lobbied for a Key 73 statement that would clarify the intentions of the movement toward the Jewish community. Unfortunately these Key 73 central committee members were unable to prevail and the movement never issued a definitive comment on its

aims vis-à-vis Jews. Many American Jews were deeply concerned over the following implications of Key 73:

1. How much of the projected evangelistic activity would be specifically directed to the conversion of Jews or the Jewish community?

2. What effect would these programs have on intergroup and community relations programs?

3. What impact would such programming have on the emerging Christian "theologies of Judaism" that view the Jewish religion as a living, valid, permanent faith?

4. What were the implications of this evangelism for the pluralistic character of American society?

1. There was general Jewish unease over the question of whether the Key 73 program which took as its aim, to "confront every person on the North American continent with the chains of Christ," would target Jews since the Jewish mission groups would obviously jump on the Key 73 bandwagon. These fears were not alleviated when the Key 73 resource book was released. The book contained a section on "Witnessing Messiah to the Jew" and the fact that Bill Bright was the author of the section exacerbated Jewish concern. Indeed, Bright was one of the luminaries of the Key 73 movement. He was a member of the executive committee and at the October 1972 Panorama was treated to a rousing welcome by the assembled delegates. The Jewish organizations justifiably believed that any direct attempt of the campaign to missionize Jews would play into the hands of the specific mission groups by giving

them encouragement and credibility. The looseness of Key 73 operation and its almost inept central administration meant that any organization could claim affiliation with Key 73 and be virtually unchallenged in its assertion.

2. The plans for various community-wide activities such as Bible and New Testament distribution, prayer rallies and religious census raised the possibility that intergroup relations could be adversely affected by the Key 73 program. In several instances confrontations occurred, particularly over the issue of religious canvass. The canvass would usually involve one or more people who would come to a home and ask about the person's religious affiliation. If the individual replied that he or she was a Jew, the canvasser would usually break into a fervent period of witness and leave "appropriate" literature. Similar experiences, though on a less-frequent basis, were reported with reference to city-wide Bible distributions.

3. Those individuals in the Jewish community who were professionally or avocationally involved with Christians in dialogue and discussion were especially troubled over the potential impact of the campaign upon the developing Christian theologies of Judaism which regarded the latter as valid and eternal in nature. Scholars such as W. D. Davies at Duke, Coert Rylaarsdam at Marquette and John Pawlikowski at the Catholic Theological Union were working to impress Christians with the authenticity and viability of Jewish religious faith. The writings and lectures of these and other like-minded theologians had begun to make an impact within the churches, and particularly within seminaries, and denominational curriculum publishing houses. Key 73 posed the question: if Jews were legitimate targets of Christian conversion, how could Judaism be valid and meaningful?

4. Implicit in the Jewish consideration of Key 73 was

the question as to whether the evangelical renaissance posed a threat to pluralism in America. Some observers feared that the evangelical revival could result in a regression to that earlier stage of American history marked by the concept of evangelical empire. This philosophic construct supported a Christian theocratic perception of American institutions and had serious consequences for religious minorities. Key 73 appeared to imply that the terms "American" and "Christian" were synonymous, and that one had to be a Christian to be a *good* American, an implication that, at least in this writer's opinion, may have been the greatest problem the ideology of Key 73 held for the Jewish community.

In the coming months and years Jews will be increasingly faced with the problem of how to assure freedom of religion while at the same time preserving the pluralistic character of American society. The potential erosion of the liberal Christian understanding that Jews are full partners in the American experience is the most significant threat posed by the resurgence of evangelism. It is exactly this point that several Jewish leaders missed when they easily dismissed Key 73 as of little concern to the Jewish community.

Key 73 itself was not an overwhelming success, but there is every indication that the militant efforts of Key 73 oriented evangelicals will continue through the decade, that evangelism is here to stay and that the underlying problems for the Jewish community simply cannot be wished away. There are also growing indications as the United Methodist participation in Key 73 suggests that the mainline churches are hedging on earlier pledges to refrain from evangelizing Jews. Even the National Council of Churches, the coordinating body for liberal Protestantism in the United States, was involved through its evangelism division in the activities of Key 73. That many NCC governing board members agreed with this activity was apparent when a resolution introduced at its February 1973 Pittsburgh meeting which would have declared the NCC as opposed to efforts to convert Jews failed to obtain the necessary votes.[33] The most outspoken opponent of the proposed resolution was Mr. William Thompson, chief executive officer of the prestigious United Presbyterian Church. Thompson and his church, who in recent years have argued for the integrity of many minority groups and have actively supported the right of freedom of expression of Angela Davis and other radical dissidents, could not support the integrity of Judaism and the right of this faith to exist independent of Christianity.

A Meeting with Billy Graham

In striking contrast to the NCC action, Dr. Billy Graham issued a statement the following day disavowing coercive evangelistic efforts and clearly indicating his belief that God has a special relationship with the Jewish people.[34] A few days before the statement was released the writer and Rabbi Marc H. Tanenbaum spent four hours with Graham at the evangelist's home in Montreat, North Carolina. In this conversation, Graham described his study of Judaism and outlined his views on the unique place he believes Jews have in the divine economy.

I was most impressed by Graham's understanding of Jewish concerns related to evangelism.[35] Although his statement fell short of citing the evangelization of Jews as totally out of bounds, it seemed clear that Graham was moving in this direction. If Graham clarifies his position and recognizes the validity of Judaism for the individual Jewish believer, he will spark a revolution in evangelical thought and greatly contribute to understanding between evangelicals and Jews. His March 1, 1973, statement did send shock waves through the ranks of the specific Jewish mission organizations since a great many of their contributors take their marching orders from Graham. It is not unreasonable to suggest that a clear articulation of the hands-off policy toward Jews, which the evangelist seems to have privately arrived at, could put some of the mission organizations out of business. This would be a most welcome and wholesome development. These organizations are anachronistic, divisive and non-contributive. Indeed, the basic Christian need to convert Jews should have long ago been excised from the life of the churches.

If Christians spent all of the next thousand years propping up their own house and bringing backsliders to the fold, they would be more than occupied on a full-time basis. The Christian mission to the Jew is a specialized form of Christian evangelism which has no proper place in a pluralistic setting. Given the dismal record of Christian failure of missions in almost every world area, one would expect that American evangelical Christians would be most circumspect in their dealings with other communities. However, we cannot expect such a radical reorientation of values to come easily or quickly. The Jewish community over the next several years will likely face continued onslaughts from conversion-minded evangelists. This coupled with the impasse Israel has produced in mainline Protestant-Jewish relations and the wide divergence between Catholics and Jews on major contemporary issues will continue to cause tension in Jewish-Christian affairs.

There is however one area of Jewish concern that has brought forth a positive across-the-board Christian reaction. The issue of the Soviet Union's denial of basic human and religious rights to her three-million-member Jewish minority has elicited genuine concern by every segment of American Christianity. Several major Protestant bodies, including the United Presbyterian Church and the United Methodist Church, have passed resolutions condemning Soviet treatment of Jews. In 1971 the United Presbyterian Church gave a platform to Mrs. Rivka Aleksandrovich who was in the United States to plead for the release of her daughter from a Russian prison. Mrs. Aleksandrovich was the first Jew in the 183-year history of the Presbyterian General Assembly to address that group. In 1972 the cause of Soviet Jewry brought together for the first time in American history three of the nation's major Baptist bodies. The presidents of the Southern Baptist Convention, the American Baptist Convention and the black Progressive National Baptist Convention jointly released a strong statement of moral and spiritual support for the Jews of Russia.[36]

On the Roman Catholic side, several bishops issued pastoral letters in observance of the 1972 Solidarity Day program for Soviet Jewry. In the same year Roman Catholics joined with Greek Orthodox and Protestant brethren to form the National Interreligious Task Force on Soviet Jewry. The task force held a major two-day consultation in Chicago in March 1972 and issued a statement of conscience stressing Christian support of the Russian Jews. During the summer of 1972 Representative Robert F. Drinan of Massachusetts, a Jesuit priest and participant in the work of the task force, spent days on an around-the-clock basis to work for the release of Gavriel Shapiro from a Moscow jail. The response of the churches to the plight of Soviet Jewry was singularly instructive since Christians are usually programmed into viewing humanitarian issues through a universal prism. One might have expected Christian leaders to ask how they could separate out the problems of the Russian Jews from consideration of the plight of the Basques, the situation in Northern Ireland, the racism of South and South West Africa. Often in the past when Christians agreed to work on Jewish problems their preoccupation with other issues tended to wash out the Jewish component. This has not occurred in the case of the Soviet Jews. What is more remarkable is the fact that Christian sympathy for this beleaguered minority flies in the face of a long-standing mainline Protestant and liberal Catholic softness on the Soviet Union. Christian support for the Russian Jews should give pause to those in the Jewish community who decry all efforts at dialogue and communication between the two communities. At the April 1973 executive committee meeting of the National Interreligious Task Force one of the participants after listening patiently to an explanation of the need for trade legislation with Russia given by the Assistant Secretary of State for European Affairs, told the official, "Christians will no longer be silent when the rights of Jews are threatened. We will not allow another Holocaust to take place." While such sentiments should not be construed as being representative of the majority of Christians, there is hope that the Soviet Jewish issue could serve as a model for future relationships between Christians and Jews.

A leading rabbi recently published an article in a Methodist publication entitled, "Do You Know What Hurts Me?"[37] When Christians are able to respond in the affirmative to this plaintive query, the way will be prepared for contact and communication characterized by mutual respect and an absence of the mentality of aggrandizement. The unfortunate reality, however, is that aside from the issue of Soviet Jewry many changes in the basic Christian conception of Jews and Judaism will have to occur before such communication is achieved. In the light of the serious internal problems confronting the various Christian bodies it is not likely that meaningful change is on the near horizon. Rather, in the forseeable future theologically based antagonism to Jewish experience will continue to provide a foundation upon which more overt forms of anti-Jewish behavior can be constructed.

IV

THE BLACKS, THE JEWS AND THE URBAN CRISIS

Perhaps the most troubled of the several relationships American Jews have with other segments of the population involves interaction with the black community. The crisis in black-Jewish affairs is of rather recent vintage and can be traced to the period immediately following the June 1967 Arab-Israel war. For the roughly hundred-year period between the conclusion of the Civil War and the June 1967 war Jews and blacks though, of course, in contact on an individual basis either in the small towns of the South or in the changing neighborhoods of the urban North were basically preoccupied with internal concerns and the struggle to achieve a degree of security and status in the larger American society. Those contacts that did occur were generally friendly, and in the period before the initiation of a civil rights movement or even the thought of one many Jews sought to aid the black community, quite probably out of compassion for the problems of another minority group. Men such as Julius Rosenwald who donated millions of dollars to improve the education of blacks in the South and Joel Springarn who provided the resources necessary for the organization and growth of the National Association for the Advancement of Colored People, epitomized the genuine concern Jews had over the apparent plight of their black fellow citizens.

During the Roosevelt years of the 1930s and early '40s Jews in the administration's inner circle advocated federal programs to help the black community. When the civil rights movement emerged in the late 1950s individual Jews and the organized Jewish community were consistent in their support for black aims and gave generously both in terms of financial support and staff time to the movement. Many young Jews journeyed to the centers of action in the South to lend their bodies to the black cause. Two of these young people, Michael Schwerner and Andrew Goodman joined the ranks of martyrs in the struggle for black equality.

During this period many rabbinical and communal leaders shared the experience, in a score of southern and increasingly northern locations, of A. James Rudin, a young rabbi who worked for voter registration in Hattiesburg, Mississippi, and later risked his life in a march through Chicago's Gage Park with Dr. Martin Luther King, Jr. A growing camaraderie developed between the established black leadership and Jewish religious and secular officials, and the flow of Jewish material and emotional support intensified as the great legislative goals of the mid 1960s were set and eventually realized. By early 1967, with a solid string of victories under their belt, the civil rights leaders turned their attention to the northern cities and the problems of school integration, housing and employment opportunities. As the movement focused in on the urban centers, the Jewish community, only marginally represented by population in the prior areas of civil rights activity, would be confronted with black demands that threatened to erode the hard-won achievements of its individual members. At the same time the civil rights movement was undergoing significant change. The Southern Christian Leadership Conference, which set up offices in Chicago, was not the same organization that had engaged the southern establishment in St. Augustine, Florida, Albany, Georgia, and Selma, Alabama.

For one thing, the Conference's president, Dr. King, was becoming more and more preoccupied with wider national and international issues such as the problems of poverty and, especially, the Vietnam war. For another, it soon became obvious that Chicago was not Selma and that Mayor Daley was not Joe Smitherton. There were some white civil rights advocates who suggested that Dr. King had lost his operational touch and that he was out of his element in the complex urban North. Other supporters were concerned over King's increasingly hostile position vis-à-vis the Johnson Administration because of its policy on the war. King seemed to be devoting too much energy in criticizing the nation's Southeast Asia position and not enough time attacking the very real problems still confronting the black community one hundred years after emancipation and months after passage of the omnibus civil rights and voting rights acts.

The civil rights movement itself had undergone important change, the Student Non-Violent Coordinating Committee was fast becoming known as the Non-Student Violent Coordinating Committee, and its leaders would not be silenced in 1967 as John Lewis was at the Lincoln Memorial and in the White House on August 28, 1963. New aggressive and tough-talking individuals, such as Stokely Carmichael and H. Rap Brown of SNCC and Roy Innis of the Congress of Racial Equality, had replaced the more moderate leadership of a few years before. These militant young men appeared to speak for the masses of blacks, particularly those residing in urban areas. Their increasingly incendiary rhetoric fanned the flames not quite extinguished from the traumatic (for white liberals) Watts riot and appeared to prefigure a larger and more disastrous wave of unrest and violence which would force America to make the fundamental societal changes required to bring justice to her twenty-two million blacks. The Newark and Detroit "Civil Disturbances," which in the spring of 1967 suggested that the nation was on the brink of a major internal crisis, sent the public and private establishments scurrying to create programs that would placate the black masses and their largely self-appointed prophets.

The Jewish community, historically uneasy and vulnerable in times of social upheaval, was especially troubled by the pattern of wanton destruction of Jewish-owned businesses which emerged from the two great riots. Jewish fears were not at all eased when it became clear that one of the leaders of the Newark black community was the anti-white racist and anti-Semitic poet Leroi Jones. Apparently the days when it was fashionable for Jewish audiences to extend to Jones standing ovations after listening to his desire "to stick a knife in a Jewbelly," were at an end. Nor was Jewish concern lessened when notions of Jewish conspiracy and of Jewish power began to creep into the blandishments of black militant leaders.

The Breakdown of a Coalition

The hostile and hysterical black militant reaction to the Israeli victory in June 1967 was perhaps the single most important factor breaking down the black-Jewish civil rights coalition. American Jews were identified with the Israeli "killers of Middle East black people," and placards were sighted in Harlem stating "Jews get out of Palestine, its not your home anyway, Moses was the first traitor, and Hitler was the Messiah!!!" Stokely Carmichael, who had emerged as the chief ideological spokesman of black extremism and whose SNCC newsletter had featured a viciously anti-Semitic article,[1] confessed to a national convention of black students that he had once been "for the Jews" but had now reformed.[2] In September 1967 black delegates at the National Conference of the New Politics in Chicago voted with the majority to condemn "Zionist aggression" against the Arabs,[3] while black author Harold Cruse in a book praised by media such as *The New York Review of Books* condemned Israel as part of a world conspiracy against the black, and claimed that "the emergence of Israel as a world power in miniscule meant that the Jewish question in America was no longer purely a domestic minority problem. A great proportion of American Jews began to function as an organic part of a distant nation state."[4]

For many Jews who had accepted the half-century-old dictum of Louis Marshall, a founder of the American Jewish Committee, that "we do not recognize the existence of a Jewish Question in the United States," Cruse's words should have been chilling. The truth was that with the breakdown in relations between Jews and blacks, some blacks, surely out of non-altruistic motivation, were raising the specter of a Jewish question in America. The growing anti-Semitism of the black movement presented a challenge to Jewish security, but many in the Jewish community were reluctant to countenance this possibility and there began a series of Jewish apologies for the overtly anti-Semitic remarks and attitudes articulated by black leaders and their followers.

Thus, editor I. F. Stone would state, "It will not hurt us Jews to swallow a few insults from overwrought blacks,"[5] and writer Nat Hentoff would suggest that the CORE official who lamented Hitler's failure to make more Jews into lampshades be invited to a panel discussion.[6] Even establishment leaders were not immune from glossing over expressions of black anti-Semitism.

Dore Schary, chairman of the Anti-Defamation League, warned against exaggerating fears of Negro anti-Semitism and proclaimed that there existed "no organized anti-Semitic group among Negroes,[7] while the chairman of the National Jewish Community Relations Advisory Council insisted that Jews have a massive stake in the urban crisis and should not be diverted "because some Negroes are violent or ungrateful or anti-Semitic."[8] Events over the next eighteen months were to severely try the patience and credibility of those Jewish leaders and organizations who heretofore could not take seriously black anti-Semitism. These events would have nationwide ramifications because they occurred in the city that housed more Jews and more blacks than any other urban center.

The Crisis in New York's Schools

In the fall of 1967 John T. Hatchett, a teacher in the New York City public school system, openly attacked Jewish colleagues in an issue of *The African-American Teachers Forum*. Hatchett charged:

We are witnessing today in New York City a phenomenon that spells death for the minds and souls of our black children. It is the systematic coming of age of the Jews who dominate and control the educational bureaucracy of the New York Public School system and their power starved imitators, the Black Anglo-Saxons.[9]

Hatchett's article brought a storm of protest from Jewish organizations and signaled the beginning of a crisis in the New York public schools. Hatchett, who defended his position by stating that the article was not anti-Semitic but anti-establishment, "that is, it was against those in a position to change the system,"[10] was shortly thereafter hired by New York University as director of the Dr. Martin Luther King Afro-American Student Center. This action of a major educational institution whose enrollment was largely Jewish was provocative to say the least. Jewish leaders who protested to the University's President, Dr. James Hester, also pointed out the incongruity of appointing an anti-Semite to direct a center named for a black leader who had consistently attacked anti-Semitism. The Hatchett affair, which included the considerable mediatory expertise of Arthur Goldberg, president of the American Jewish Committee, marked a coming of age for the Jewish organizational leadership and served as a training aid for the upcoming school crisis.

Goldberg's decision that Hatchett should retain his NYU position (later countermanded by President Hester) brought the established Jewish organizations into open conflict with the majority of New York's huge Jewish population and put these agencies on notice that acquiescence to black anti-Semitism would not be tolerated by the rank and file of Jews.

The school crisis which came on the heels of the Hatchett episode took place in the Ocean Hill-Brownsville area of Brooklyn, once mainly Jewish but by 1968 almost all black in population. As in many other black areas of the city, there still remained some Jewish businessmen, mostly entrepreneurs of so-called "momma and poppa" grocery and clothing stores. In addition, blacks encountered Jews in positions of authority in the welfare centers and in the neighborhood's schools. As Bayard Rustin remarked: "If you happen to be an uneducated, poorly trained Negro living in the ghetto, you see only four kinds of white people —the policeman, the businessman, the teacher and the welfare worker. In many of the cities three of those four are Jewish."[11]

The Ocean Hill-Brownsville school district was the center of an experimental "decentralization" project which allowed the local community-elected school board a degree of control over policies in the district's eight schools, thereby circumventing the authority of the central Board of Education. The project was financed by the Ford Foundation whose chief executive, former Kennedy and Johnson aide McGeorge Bundy seemed to personify the WASP establishment. Not surprisingly the project was vehemently opposed by the United Federation of Teachers, which feared that its power as bargaining representative for the great bulk of the city's teachers would be undermined if the decentralization were to be applied to the entire school system.

The Union's argument with the Bundy Plan, as it became known, dovetailed with the opposition of the nine-hundred-member New York Board of Rabbis, who on January 31 expressed concern that the Bundy Plan would "institutionalize separatism and segregation and establish in the selection of personnel on all levels, the primacy of ethnic origin over such values as merit and individual ability."[12] It is noteworthy that the Board of Rabbis who contended that the Bundy Plan would increase racial tension issued on the same day a statement that called on "responsible leaders" of the black community to exercise their influence and restraint on the "extremist among their own people to refrain from taking the law into their own hands."[13] Rabbi Gilbert Klapperman, the Board president added:

> The proliferation of militants and extremists among the Negroes and their tendency to turn their extremism into anti-Jewish and anti-Israel propaganda is not only dangerous for intergroup relations but it can destroy America in the process. It is ironic that the Jewish people who have been leaders in the civil rights movement should now be singled out by these extremists in their blind hatred of the white community.[14]

The crisis over decentralization reached an active stage when the school board summarily attempted to transfer ten white teachers, nine of whom were Jewish, for allegedly attempting to sabotage the decentralization project. The Union retaliated by staging three separate city-wide walkouts, which virtually immobilized the system for a thirty-six-day period. Black parents denounced the striking teachers as "Jew pigs" and literature was disseminated in the Ocean Hill district that contained virulently anti-Semitic sentiments: One anonymous tract distributed during October said in part:

> It is impossible for the Middle East murderers of colored people to possibly bring to this important task the insight, the concern, the exposing of the truth that is a must if the years of brainwashing and self-hatred that has been taught to our black children by those bloodsucking exploiters and murderers is to be overcome.[15]

The Anti-Defamation League which the year before had almost triumphantly issued the preliminary findings of a five-year study to "sharply refute widespread sensational Negro attitudes toward Jews,"[16] released a study that indicated that there was no evidence of an organized effort behind the materials. The ADL research notwithstanding, the persons most directly concerned with the situation, the Jewish teachers, correctly understood the larger stakes involved in the dispute. As one teacher remarked:

We don't deny their equality, but they shouldn't get it by pulling down others who have just come up. It's wrong and reactionary for them to pit their strength against a group that struggled for years to make teaching a profession.[17]

Certainly there was nothing in the Brahmin background of McGeorge Bundy to enable him to understand what it meant for the children of immigrants to struggle against overwhelming odds to achieve a measure of status and security for themselves and their children. A similar disability characterized the life experiences of Francis Keppel, former U. S. Commissioner of Education and author of the Bundy Plan, who later admitted to "a lack of acuity in understanding anti-Semitism."[18]

Some Jewish leaders reacted to the Ocean Hill situation in typical fashion. Rabbi Jacob Rudin, president of the moribund Synagogue Council of America, deplored black anti-Semitism but stressed that the phenomenon was unrepresentative of the majority of blacks.[19] Arthur Goldberg, president of the American Jewish Committee, stressed in a letter to the organization's membership that "Negro anti-Semitism was still confined to an unrepresentative minority" and that Jews "must continue an unrelenting support for the civil rights movement."[20] However, Bertram H. Gold, the Committee's executive vice-president, later urged black leaders to face forthrightly the issue of anti-Semitism within the black community.

Gold's position was in line with the conclusions of a report prepared by a retired New York judge, Bernard Botein, who after studying hate literature distributed in the schools, stated "continued silence" by most white Christian and most Negro leaders was adding to the rising tide of anti-Semitism in the city.[21] This view was also articulated by Will Maslow, then executive director of the American Jewish Congress, who told *The New York Times,* "what appalled most of the leaders of the Jewish community was the utter silence of the Christian community and the Negro leadership in the face of flagrantly anti-Semitic utterances and articles."[22] Mayor Lindsay, who had requested the Botein report, had already experienced the growing fury of the Jewish middle class. During the school strike he had been shouted down at the East Midwood (Brooklyn) Jewish Center when he tried to discuss the school issue. Even the intervention of Rabbi Harry Halpern had not been able to calm the audience and allow the Mayor to speak.[23] The criticism directed at the Christian community was well taken. During the Ocean Hill affair arrangements had been made to bus in Christian bureaucrats from the New York-based denominational staffs for a firsthand examination of the situation. Many of these individuals, who lived for the most part in the New Jersey suburbs adjacent to the George Washington Bridge, bought the school board argument in toto. In accepting the school board version of the situation,

these officials were acting out a larger mainline Protestant
blind advocacy of the black cause which had little use for
nuance or distinction between legitimate legal means and
militant or even violent efforts to achieve social change.
James Forman in his "reparations" gambit would find these
same liberal Christians ready to accede to the most fantasy-
ridden and potentially destructive elements of his program.

I can vividly recall a meeting held between Jewish professionals and top National Council of Churches staff some-
time after the school strike. One of the NCC participants
had just returned from a six-month overseas sabbatical and
was unfamiliar with the details of the situation. During the
discussion, he was pressed by the blacks present to take a
stand on the black contention that Jewish teachers and
other civil servants should be replaced by blacks. The
official emphatically responded that if dislocations of Jews
had to occur to satisfy black demands, so be it. Such thinking was the rule and not the exception in the mainline
Protestant world during the late 1960s and early '70s, and
I have seen little evidence to suggest that there has been
any significant change in the Protestant predilection to sacrifice Jewish interests on the altar of black progress.

The Poem and the Exhibition

The school strike had barely ended when a new incident
occured involving Leslie Campbell, a black schoolteacher
who read a poem over radio station WBAI-FM which was
dedicated to teacher union president Albert Shanker. The
poem began, "Hey, Jew boy, with the yarmulke on your
head/You pale faced Jew boy—I wish you were dead."[24]
The Campbell affair was exacerbated by Albert Vann, president of the Afro-American Teachers Association who reacted to Mayor Lindsay's criticism of Campbell for reading

"an obviously anti-Semitic poem" by charging that the Mayor had attempted to "appease the powerful Jewish financiers of the city."[25]

A few weeks later another incident caused tempers to flare to a new pitch. In mid January 1969 a photo exhibition called "Harlem on My Mind" opened at the Metropolitan Museum of Art. The exhibit's catalogue contained an introduction written by a sixteen-year-old black schoolgirl which said in part:

Behind every hurdle that the Afro-American has yet to jump stands the Jew who has already cleared it. Jewish shopkeepers are the only remaining "survivors" in the expanding black ghettos. The lack of competition allows the already exploited black to be further exploited by Jews.[26]

With the release of the catalogue Jewish complaints were immediately directed to another super WASP, Thomas T. P. Hoving, chief executive of the museum and a former key aide to Mayor Lindsay. The Jewish protest was accompanied by a strong denunciation of the introduction issued from the Mayor's office. Hoving, who with the catalogue's publisher, Random House, agreed to insert a disclaimer written by the same schoolgirl, declared that the issue was "totally out of perspective."[27]

Hoving, who earlier had been criticized for the showmanship that appeared to mark his tenure as museum director, had always taken pains to emphasize the continuing high standards of the famous institution. Yet it did not seem incongruous to him that a sixteen-year-old high school student with no background in sociology or race relations would be commissioned to write a serious piece for a museum publication. Hoving's attitude in approving the original assignment and in allowing the disclaimer to be prepared by the same schoolgirl reflected the atmosphere of condescension that characterized much of the WASP approach to the race problem. On January 26 David Rockefeller, president of the Chase Manhattan Bank, and a member of the Executive Committee of the National Urban Coalition, expressed surprise over the controversy set off by decentralization and the Campbell and Ellison episodes. The banking executive, whose huge institution employed few Jews at the executive level and few blacks at any level, remarked:

> The whole school strike has become based on a struggle between two groups that have been most subject to discrimination. That they should now be attacking one another is both ironic and tragic.[28]

Another establishment view was articulated by an individual described by *The New York Times* as a prominent lawyer with a distinguished record in the foreign service. This person deplored recent denunciations of anti-Semitism as "exacerbating" the situation and declared:

> I think the Jewish community is making a mistake. I may not be an over-all judge of anti-Semitism but several of my most valued partners are Jewish. Anti-Semitism has been on the wane ever since World War II, but this great furor has just been overemphasized by the Jewish community.[29]

The controversy over the museum catalogue brought forth predictable comments from the major Jewish organizations who still believed that black anti-Semitism could somehow be brushed off into a corner. Dore Schary of the ADL, while acknowledging his organization's objections to "portions of the introduction," stressed that the League did not seek withdrawal of the publication.[30] The American Jewish Congress in an advertisement in *The New York Times* deplored the catalogue but insisted that all would be well if black extremists would desist from attacking the "natural" alliance between Negroes and Jews.[31] Rabbi Henry Siegman, executive vice-president of the Synagogue Council of America, announced a $54,500 grant from the Ford Foundation to develop a program designed to lessen tension between Negro and Jewish groups. Siegman in a classic incantation of the liberal Jewish expectation that reasonableness would cure all manifestations of tension remarked:

That such differences exist is no cause for alarm, as long as we retain the ability to discuss them rationally with one another and to work toward compromises which do not deny the fundamental hopes and aspirations of each group.[32]

The National Jewish Community Relations Advisory Council claimed that overt anti-Semitism was at a low ebb despite some "acute" manifestations among some Negroes and intellectuals and urged the Jewish community not to be deflected from its support of equality for Negroes.[33] Leonard Fein, of the Harvard-MIT Joint Center for Urban Studies warned against Jewish "hysterical overreaction" to black anti-Semitism,[34] while Rabbi Arnold Jacob Wolf, a devotee of the new left, asserted that Jews were overreacting to "black Zionism."[35] In the light of these statements it was not surprising to learn that the editor of the museum catalogue, Alan Schoener, was himself a Jew. Schoener had assured Hoving before publication that the Ellison introduction was not anti-Semitic, although he did ask the young lady to "soften" the piece somewhat. Hoving accepted Schoener's evaluation because the editor had previously been assistant director of the Jewish Museum. One of the more ironic aspects of the catalogue incident devolves from Miss Ellison's reliance on the book *Beyond the Melting Pot*, a famous study of minority adjustment in America. Nathan Glazer, the book's coauthor with Daniel Patrick Moynihan, commented that the catalogue controversy indicated a change in atmosphere in the United States with Jews worried about anti-Semitism for the first time in many years.[36]

The question remained, however, what Jews? The major organizations still desired a piece of the shrinking civil rights pie while middle-class Jews were increasingly disenchanted with the positions held by the establishment groups. More ominous for the future was the emergence of the Jewish Defense League as a force in the Jewish community. The New York-based national organizational leadership who had been repudiated as early as 1966 when the majority of the city's Jews voted against the establishment of a civilian review board for the police department were out of touch with what was happening in the Jewish neighborhoods. In addition, they failed to gauge the impact events in New York would have on local Jewish communities in other sections of the country. The fact was that the masses of American Jews were beginning to take black anti-Semitism very seriously. At least one leader of a national organization did recognize the growing Jewish concern over participation in the civil rights movement. Bertram Gold, chief operating officer of the American Jewish Committee cautioned delegates to an AJC session:

> Jews are beginning to feel that their national leadership is more concerned with bettering intergroup relations than protecting the interests of the Jewish community. Though we must reject demands for withdrawal from the civil rights struggle, the committee's leadership would not be fulfilling its functions if we were to ignore the legitimate demands for greater power by the Negro community at the expense of hard-won gains made by individual Jews.[37]

The Factors Behind Black Anti-Semitism

When the controversy over the school strike and the museum catalogue died down, some commentators attempted to analyze the root causes of the flare-up of hostility and the longer range implications of these tensions. A number of factors were advanced as forming the background to the crisis.

1. The movement of blacks into neighborhoods that had previously been largely Jewish and the ensuing competition between those Jews who remained and the blacks.

2. Reports of crimes against persons and property in these areas and differing views over law and order held by Jewish shopkeepers and black residents.

3. The move by black militants to take over the direction of the civil rights movement and to exclude Jews from participation.

4. The growing employment of anti-Semitic and anti-Israel rhetoric by these militants.

5. The developing professional and economic conflict caused by blacks moving into vocational fields such as teaching and social work that had previously attracted large numbers of Jews.

One of the questions frequently posed by analysts was whether the incidence of black anti-Semitism should be viewed as mere rhetoric or as an expression of hostility toward white men in general. After all, these experts reasoned, blacks often described the world of white men in Jewish terms. Thus, a black would refer to his "Jew landlord" even if the man's name were Kowalski or O'Brien, or to a Cadillac, even if black-owned, as a "Jew canoe." In black areas of cities, such as Detroit, white storekeepers were often called "Goldberg" though the actual owner might represent any one of several non-Jewish ethnic groups. Jews according to this theory, symbolized the white world and its power hold on the black community. Other observers suggested that blacks were evidencing an expected psychological reaction in their rejection of those who had been their staunchest allies in previous days. Daniel Watts, the outspoken editor of the radical monthly *Liberator* said that in the light of this past brotherhood blacks were outraged by what they perceived as a betrayal by Jews.

We expect more of him and when its not forthcoming that love turns to rage. The Jew has been a hypocrite. The liberal Jew has been in the forefront telling the South to integrate, while he lived in lily-white communities in the North. That hurts more than a Wallace, who is at least honest.[38]

A black educator, Dr. Nathan Wright, Jr., suggested that Jewish fears of black anti-Semitism stemmed from the difficulty Jews faced in the changing of their relationship to blacks from that of patrons or parents to that of peers.[39] Perhaps blacks were tired of being told to emulate Jews who, as the older black leadership constantly reminded their constituents, "know how to handle money, know how to make it, invest it and multiply it; have a deep reverence for learning are passionately devoted to education and achieve academic distinction; and above all stick together and help one another."[40]

There were of course other and deeper seated factors involved in black anti-Semitism. These had to do with the character of American society. Blacks who have suffered from a sense of inferiority due to the exploitation and oppression of the dominant white majority could, by manifesting anti-Semitic attitudes, identify with that majority. There is little reason to doubt that some militant leaders seized upon this psychological mechanism already active in their communities. Such leaders knew full well the history of anti-Semitism in America and were cognizant of the anti-Jewish attitudes widely prevalent in the white society. As the sociologist Earl Raab has commented:

Whether it is a matter of Jewish aggressiveness, Jewish clanishness, Jewish shrewdness, or whatever, the great majority of Americans still hold to *some* pattern of differentiating, and negative, stereotypes about Jews. And there is scarcely an American who does not know what these stereotypes are, even if he does not profess to hold them. *The instrument is there, readily available in our culture* (italics added).[41]

Concomitant to this is the fact that American Jews constitute a highly visible minority close to the top of the economic ladder but without real power. As Richard Rubenstein suggests in a provocative *Reconstructionist* article,[42] Jews arouse envy, they are disliked, they can be displaced. "This has happened elsewhere it can happen here." Rubenstein adds that blacks, unlike Jews, have the potential to seriously disrupt the normal functioning of urban society. If blacks employ an intelligent use of this capacity, they can wring important concessions from the white establishment. To some degree violence may be used to force the establishment to submit.

Blacks also know that "violence perpetrated against Jews, especially within the ghetto, will not be regarded as seriously by white Christians as violence done to Gentiles outside the ghetto." Such a theory would appear to suggest the possibility of a white power structure-black alliance to win advances for the black community at Jewish expense. Earl Raab, in defiance of predictable charges of paranoia and hysteria, was the Jewish authority who first most cogently outlined the evolving black power political strategy, one aimed at forcing the WASP establishment into making concessions at the expense of Jewish interests. Writing in the January 1969 issue of *Commentary,* the executive director of the San Francisco Jewish Community Relations Council said:

There is the possibility of a classic marriage, a manipulative symbiosis, between the privileged class and the disprivileged mass—in this case a WASP class and a black mass in these cities: the kind of symbiosis that existed in the 1920's between respectable Republican leaders and the KKK, and which permitted temper of repression and bigotry to flourish.[43]

After examining the record of the last several years, can the teacher, store owner, welfare investigator or other middle-class Jew doubt that the Bundys, Keppels, Hovings and Rockefellers would sell them out in an instant if their own power and interests were threatened? Racial quotas, preferential treatment, open enrollment all presage the coming of a revolution which, unless checked, will contain the seeds of destruction for a way of life built on study, perseverance and other verities heretofore considered sacred in America. Yet the bulk of American Jewish leadership still talks of rebuilding coalitions and co-operating on programs despite—as the National Women's Division of the American Jewish Congress noted—"reports of tension and conflicts between blacks and Jews." William Wexler, former president of B'nai B'rith, calls for the rebuilding of the "shattered relationship" between the Jewish and black communities while his organization deplores the collapse of the "once sturdy working relationship" between Jewish and black groups, citing each group as a "loser."[44] Carl Gershman, described as a young Jewish writer and activist, is quoted in the February 1971 issue of *Keeping Posted,* a publication of the Union of American Hebrew Congregations, as saying, that much of the anti-Semitism expressed by some blacks results from the "difficult and frustrating" situations blacks face as they strive for identity. "They simply strike out against that which is nearest at hand, and Jews are the group that has been most closely associated with Negroes.[45]

Writing in *Reform Judaism,*[46] Joseph Robison, director of the Commission on Law and Social Action of the American Jewish Congress, suggests that Jews must assume a self-sacrificial stance in relation to black demands for a greater share of the economic pie. He argues that the total society is in danger of serious disruption if inequities suffered by blacks are not ameliorated through the utilization of quotas. Jews, according to Robison, "stand to lose more by destruction of society's tranquility than by borderline economic handicaps."

Thus, Jews "cannot oppose—we must even support measures that require us to pay part of the price to be paid by whites generally."

This call to martyrdom is accompanied by the assertion that "some of us got the jobs from which the blacks were excluded." This might be true for some Jews but can hardly pertain in Robison's situation since there is not the remotest possibility that Robison's position at the American Jewish Congress could be filled by a black. Aside from the personal hypocrisy inherent in Robison's exhortation, he fails to note that quotas and preferential treatment penalize unjustly individuals who bear no personal responsibility for historic, economic and vocational wrongdoing to blacks.

One can easily dismiss Robison's argument as well as the pronunciamentos of an organization like B'nai B'rith whose satellite body, the Anti-Defamation League, bombards the community with "scientific" studies proving blacks are less anti-Semitic than whites while releasing other research surveys that indicate the growing danger of black anti-Semitism. Yet what of other more credible organizations and individuals who sincerely believe that a black-Jewish coalition did once exist, that this coalition helped to improve the condition of blacks (thus helping to improve the status of other minorities, such as Jews) and that the renaissance of this coalition will have profound positive impact upon the nation as well as upon each partner community. Apparently the need or feeling of intelligent and well-placed Jews for such a coalition will not easily die. Nor will the belief that if only a few extremists could be silenced, then blacks will revert to their natural state of loving Jews and joining with them in the struggle to overcome evil. How else, for example, can one explain the continued devotion of Jewish organizations to voter registration drives and legislation that would widen the franchise when the emerging pattern of the last few elections has indicated that blacks will vote their own self-interest (which often is diametrically opposed to Jewish interests) while being strongly influenced by militant appeals. What is especially difficult to understand has been the disposition of some Jewish organizations to fund black projects and programs. Or, as in the case of the American Jewish Committee, to solicit and accept funds from the Ford Foundation for a program of "depolarization" which would bring ethnics and blacks together. Together for what, one might ask?

The existence of anti-Semitism in the white ethnic communities is very real. I can recall Sister Margaret Traxler, former president of the National Coalition of American Nuns, describing her astonishment at the degree of anti-Semitic attitudes expressed by white ethnic Catholics in the Chicago area during the summer of 1973. Has anyone asked if what serves the interests of the Ford Foundation, serves the best interests of the Jewish community? Does the Committee believe that the anti-Semitism of white ethnics and the anti-Semitism active in the black community will cancel each other out? Or will these new allies, if the program succeeds, come to the joint understanding that anti-Semitic attitudes and behavior can be of pragmatic value in the American context?

Rabbi Bernard Weinberger, former president of the Rabbinical Alliance of America raised several important questions concerning the urban affairs program of Jewish social agencies. In the fall 1969 issue of the *Journal of Jewish Communial Service*[47] Rabbi Weinberger suggests that the funds available to Jewish organizations "are nowhere near what is needed to make the slightest impact" upon the problems faced by blacks. There is also the question of what justification Jewish agencies have for disbursing monies raised for Jewish purposes for non-Jewish efforts. Such Jewish-supported programs continue the benefactor-beneficiary relationship that blacks apparently resent "even more deeply than the lack of the services these programs can provide." Finally, Jewish-sponsored programs convey the impression that Jews are guilty for not having done enough for blacks and are now desperately attempting to catch up. Rabbi Weinberger then asks an obvious question but one that many Jewish professionals have not bothered to consider: "Should we not ask for some documentation that Jews . . . have had any role in causing the suffering of blacks?"

One might ask, have Jews created the ghettos? Do they, in fact, own the great bulk of property in the inner cities? Do they control the banks and lending institutions that fix mortgage rates and determine who will obtain funds for restoration, rehabilitation and initiation of housing stock? Do Jews control the commercial and industrial organizations that have systematically discriminated against blacks in employment practices? Are Jews in control of the political structure that provides inferior services to ghetto residents and legislates in prejudice and bigotry? The answer, of course, to all of these questions is a resolute "no." This writer agrees completely with Rabbi Weinberger's assertion: "I totally repudiate any attempt to ascribe to the Jewish community any blame for the sad condition of black Americans."[48]

"If I'm Not for Myself, Who Am I?"

There are of course issues around which Jews and blacks may gather, but I would maintain that the Jewish communal leadership must end its policy of alignment with the black movement on grounds that Jews are guilty, or that blacks are also a minority or because the Jewish ethic demands participation in the black struggle. Jewish decision making at the national organizational level should reflect enlightened Jewish self-interest. Many Jewish leaders point to the first portion of the famous dictum of Hillel's, "If I am only for myself, what am I?" but too quickly, and perhaps too self-consciously, pass over Hillel's conclusion, "If I am not for myself, who am I?" Certainly recent events including American black militant support for the Arab and particularly Palestinian positions, the increasing anti-Jewish rhetoric of the Black Muslim movement, the approbation extended by some black spokesman to Uganda's General Amin, combined with the growing struggle over quotas and affirmative action do not foster hope that relations between blacks and Jews are on the threshold of improvement and conciliation.

An especially disturbing expression of black hostility to Jews was contained in a recent attack on the Jewish community by Dr. Carlton B. Goodlett, president of the black-oriented, National Newspapers Publishers Association.

Goodlett made his charges at a "summit conference" involving black publishers and Jewish leaders.[49] The session was convoked naturally enough by the Anti-Defamation League of B'nai B'rith which continues to believe that a mutual airing of grievances will resolve differences between the black and Jewish communities. Goodlett who referred to Jews as the "chosen people" asserted that blacks were disturbed over Jewish opposition to quota systems. He also mentioned the feelings of young blacks, concerning "the role of international Zionism and its drive through Israel to implement an expansionist policy in the Middle East." The publisher then described black opposition to the appointment of Dr. Henry Kissinger as Secretary of State:

In terms of academic training, breadth of experience in the university setting as well as high governmental decision making levels, Dr. Kissinger possesses many of the important qualifications to be an outstanding Secretary of State.

However, his appointment brings to the surface, a number of potential areas of friction which must be discussed. Because of economic power and because of the exaggerated amount of political power which Jewish finance permits the Jewish community to exert upon the foreign policy of the United States vis-à-vis the State of Israel, we feel that for 6,000,000 people to literally have veto power over U.S. foreign policy, i.e., via the Presidency, the Congress, and the influence of public media, is potentially a serious threat to the well-being of the nation.[50]

These words, which could have been uttered by Gerald L. K. Smith, come not from an extremist but from a presumably responsible black spokesman. It should be noted that the ADL-black "summit" came less than a month before the beginning of the Yom Kippur war. Goodlett's comments provide a background to the genuine difficulty the Jewish agencies had in eliciting black support for Israel during the first two weeks of the conflict. There were, of course, a few exceptions, men such as Dr. E. V. Hill, president of the California State Baptist Convention and Pastor of Mt. Zion Baptist Church, Los Angeles, Percy Sutton, Borough President of Manhattan and Roy Wilkens and a number of black trade unionists did publicly express concern for Israel's plight but there were many other black leaders who refused to join in the outcry against the Egyptian and Syrian aggression. Perhaps the ADL can discuss this situation when it next decides to provide a platform for Dr. Goodlett and his colleagues.

Almost seven years ago, Richard Rubenstein wrote on "Jews, Negroes and the New Politics" and concluded:

It is very difficult for any community suddenly and radically to reexamine its fundamental political strategy. The Jewish community faces precisely that necessity. The presuppositions of American-Jewish liberalism worked well in the America of the thirties, forties and fifties. Even then, Jews were as powerless to secure effective allies in their struggle for the survival of Europe's Jews in the forties as we were to secure allies during the recent Six Day war. The challenges of the sixties are infinitely more complex than those of the earlier periods. The Jewish community can no longer remain true to its own fundamental aspirations in America or its deep commitment to the safety and prosperity of Israel and, at the same time support the Negro revolution. That revolution will have to play out its own drama with its own cast, its own inner compulsions, and, I believe, its own tragic end.[51]

These words, though written before much of the turmoil between blacks and Jews which marked the late 1960s, retain much pertinence. It is now time for every major national Jewish organization and each local community relations council to re-evaluate programs related to the urban crisis. The intransigence of militant blacks and the failure of moderate black leadership to either stifle or criticize the excessive rhetoric and in some cases actions of militants would in and of itself seem to suggest the need for such re-evaluation. When one adds to this the sorry record of non-accomplishment of establishment programs to improve racial relations the importance of taking stock would appear all the more evident. Finally, in the light of the serious internal crises confronting American Jewry it is incumbent upon the communal bodies to direct the major share of resources and programs toward specifically Jewish needs.

V

THE JEWISH DEFENSE LEAGUE

In the spring of 1968 Meir Kahane, an obscure Rabbi troubled by the climate of tension extant in several Jewish neighborhoods of New York City, invited interested persons to meet with him in a Manhattan synagogue to discuss ways of combatting the rising tide of violence and anti-Semitic outbursts that were making life uncomfortable for a significant number of Jews. The Rabbi, who by virtue of his dual roles as spiritual leader of the Traditional Synagogue of Rochdale Village in Queens and as an editor of the *Jewish Press,* a weekly Brooklyn newspaper with a predominately Orthodox Jewish readership, was daily and directly in touch with the huge New York Jewish middle and lower middle class. As a result of this contact Kahane had become increasingly concerned that the problems experienced by these Jews were not priority items on the agendas of the establishment organizations whose leaders worked in Manhattan and lived either in that borough or in the prosperous suburbs of the metropolitan area. Kahane, gratified by the attendance at his hastily called meeting and by the enthusiastic response to his suggestions for counteracting the increasing neighborhood turmoil, joined with two long-time friends to establish yet another Jewish organization, the Jewish Defense League.

Martin David Kahane

Martin David Kahane (he changed his name to Meir after ordination as a rabbi) was born in Brooklyn in 1932. His paternal grandfather was a rabbi in Safed, Palestine, and his father, Charles, also a rabbi, had emigrated from Safed, long a dynamic center of Jewish religious life, to the United States at age eighteen. The father, who graduated from Yeshiva University and became the rabbi of a congregation in the middle-class Jewish section of Bensonhurst, was an ardent Zionist who followed the philosophy of the militant revisionist Vladimir Jabotinsky. On one occasion, Jabotinsky, who was in the United States on a lecture tour, spoke to a small group at the Kahane home, and Charles Kahane would remember the deep impression the fiery leader made on the young Martin. The youngster who was sensitive and sentimental, was also precocious—at the age of five, after a mastoid operation, he asked his nurse for a copy of *The New York Times*. Martin experienced a happy childhood, he was an ardent Yankee fan in the midst of fanatical Dodger rooters, and played basketball and ran track in school. He completed elementary and high school work at the Yeshiva of Flatbush, an Orthodox day school, and went on to take rabbinical training at Mirer Yeshiva in Brooklyn. Yet the normalcy of Martin's formative years was clouded by a growing realization there were forces in society that were hostile to Jewish life.

The Nazi Holocaust made a profound impression upon Martin, and in 1947 he joined with a group of young men who threw tomatoes at the visiting British Foreign Minister Ernest Bevin. Kahane, who was clubbed by a mounted policeman during the demonstration, reflected the general opinion of the Jewish community that Bevin was the man behind the noxious British policy of inhibiting the Holocaust survivors from emigrating to Israel. A year earlier Martin had joined Betar, the militant youth branch of the Jabotinsky movement. He received ideological and military training at a Betar camp in the Catskill Mountains and often journeyed to the New Jersey docks where he and other Betar members would pack and load illegal gun shipments for the underground Irgun organization in Palestine. After graduation from the Rabbinical academy (he had concurrently attended Brooklyn College and earned a B.A. degree) Meir, as he now called himself, took an LL.B. from New York Law School and a Master's degree in international law from New York University. This period of Kahane's life, during which he also married, was marked by a pattern of high expectation followed by failure. He took a law degree but failed the New York State bar examination; he served a congregation for two years but left because his approach was too orthodox for his conservative-minded congregants; he traveled to Israel but did not realize his prediction of soon becoming a member of the Israeli cabinet. From Israel he informed his family of an offer to become director of the department of international affairs of Bar-Ilan University, but when this fell through he accepted a post as rabbi in a *kibbutz*. During his service on the agricultural settlement he apparently met with major rabbinical personages, at least he wrote to his mother of meeting with the chief rabbis of Jerusalem, the "first American rabbi, and so young, to be admitted among them."[1] But after three months on the *kibbutz,* Kahane returned to New York, "very upset at all the fighting among Jewish factions in Israel."[2]

The Jewish Press

In 1963 Kahane began writing a column in *The Jewish Press,* a weekly with a circulation of 130,000. He used the pen name "Michael King," and in 1965, still under the name Michael King, started work at Consultants Research Associates, an organization founded by a close Brooklyn friend, Joseph Churba. Kahane and Churba soon organized a venture called the "July Fourth Movement" which was aimed at mobilizing campus support for American involvement in the Vietnam war.

The two organizers apparently had different motivations for setting up the movement. Churba felt "there was a need to strengthen our presence in Southeast Asia." Kahane, who believed that widespread opposition to the war threatened continued U.S. aid to Israel, also feared that an American defeat in Southeast Asia could become the cause of an upsurge of anti-Semitism in the United States. As he later remarked during an appearance at the University of Pennsylvania, "After the war in Vietnam is over they will forget the Kennedys and the McCarthys . . . but they'll remember the names of Goldberg and Javits."[3] On June 29, 1965, a quarter-page advertisement, announcing the formation of the July Fourth Movement, appeared in the *New York Herald Tribune.* A few days later, the *New York Journal American*[4] printed a story describing the aims and activities of the Movement. The story, which included a photograph identifying Kahane as Michael King, claimed that chapters of the Movement set up on six campuses, including Fordham and the

University of Wisconsin, were counteracting the anti-war activities of student groups. The reality, however, was far different. As Kahane would later admit to *The New York Times,* "The *Journal American* account was just nonsense and exaggeration. There was never anything more to it than Churba and myself." Once again Kahane had been engaged in a futile exercise for—as he later said—the anti-war movement had "crested by the time the July Fourth Movement was organized."

Between the summers of 1965 and 1967 Kahane and Churba continued their association as consultants, researchers and writers for various government agencies and congressional committees. During this period close relatives of the Kahane family heard that Meir was doing very well and was in close touch with important people in Washington. There are also indications that Kahane and Churba attempted to convey the impression that they were involved in some way with the government's intelligence apparatus. On August 2, 1967, the two men set up as a partnership the Crossroads Publishing Company, for the sole purpose of publishing a book they had been researching. The book, entitled, *The Jewish Stake in Vietnam* was underwritten by private individuals and was never copyrighted. *The Jewish Stake,* whose basic thesis suggested that Jewish life could not exist under communism, sold under three thousand copies and was another segment in the string of reverses that seemed to define Kahane's life in the 1960s.

Soon after this Kahane and Churba joined in another venture. They contracted with Information, Inc., a mail-order publishing house, to prepare a book on the social and political life of North Vietnam. This book, which occupied most of Kahane's time for the next year and a half, was not published, because Kahane and Churba could not produce the promised endorsement which would have attested to the validity of their data.

It was after this additional disappointment that Kahane broke off his relationship with Churba and accepted a position as rabbi of the Traditional Synagogue of Rochdale. At the same time, his relationship with the *Jewish Press* deepened and he was offered and accepted a position as an editor at a salary of $17,000 a year. Kahane, who had dropped the name Michael King after coming to Rochdale, began to learn from his congregants and from letter writers to the *Jewish Press* of their growing apprehensions concerning the quality of life in Jewish sections of the city. Perhaps the most common thread that seemed to run through these articulations of fear and uneasiness was the lack of identification these Jews sensed with the established Jewish organizations. Jews living in neighborhoods significantly removed from Manhattan in life style and psychological climate looked for an organized voice to give representation to their feelings and needs. Kahane who was impressed by the frequency and poignancy of these expressions of Jewish concern and by the fact that similar communications were coming to the *Jewish Press* from other urban centers placed an advertisement in his newspaper announcing a session to discuss Jewish grievances. The results of that meeting and the subsequent formation of the JDL clearly indicated that whether by chance or calculation, Kahane, for the first time in his adult life, was on the threshold of success. Garbed in "official" JDL blue berets, emblems and buttons, and chanting the organization's watchword, "Never Again," Kahane and his minions were ready to do battle with the anti-Semites and with the Jewish establishment which they believed had failed to correctly gauge the threat such extremists presented to American Jewish life. The motivating ideology of the movement was an amalgam based on Kahane's preoccupation with Jewishness and with his reaction to the problems confronting urban Jews in the late 1960s. To Kahane Jewish defense did not only imply physical action but also included those measures needed to safeguard the continuity of the Jewish people. As Kahane stated in a long and wide-ranging interview with Walter Goodman:

> The Jewish Defense League came into being to physically defend Jews. It also came into being to go out among Jews and instill within them a feeling of Jewish pride, to defend the Jews from simply fading out. Our major goal is to come to Jews—and say, Jewish is beautiful. Be proud that you're a Jew, identify with it . . . Study and see what made your ancestors such stubborn people who refused to give up.[5]

Much of Kahane's rhetoric, however, suggested the need for violent confrontation. To Kahane, America in the late 1960s bore a striking resemblance to Germany in the 1920s. Economic problems, the rising demands of blacks, the intransigence of white ethnics who viewed Jews as supporters of the civil rights movement, disillusionment over the American role in Vietnam all would combine to produce a great upsurge in anti-Semitic attitude and activity. To counteract the expected tide of anti-Jewish behavior, Jews needed to both arm themselves for self-defense and to change their image as liberals while opting out of alliances with the black community. The eclectic nature of Kahane's system is certainly of more than passing interest. His insistence that "Jewish is Beautiful" was obviously borrowed from the black militants, while his American "Weimar" vision fits hand in glove with the "Amerika" theories of the new left.

Soon after the League was organized Kahane resigned his position as Rabbi of the Traditional Synagogue in Rochdale to devote more time to the nascent organization. Later, in 1968, he would be fired by the *Jewish Press* for allegedly using the JDL as a "personal political club." The initial organized activities of the League were centered around patrols on the periphery of Jewish neighborhoods bordering on the Brooklyn and Bronx black ghettos. JDL cars, equipped with radios would cruise the streets while foot patrols prowled for muggers and rapists. The appearance in the streets of an independent Jewish protection apparatus would presumably ward off crime and reduce tension. The JDL operatives who roamed the troubled sections of the city were ever mindful of Kahane's injunction:

If someone calls you a Jew bastard, hit him so hard he'll never do it again. You know what you'll get, Respect![6]

To those who felt that such violent activity was a negation of Jewish religious and philosophic principles Kahane had a ready answer:

Violence is not un-Jewish. The Bible tells us that Moses came across an Egyptian beating a Jew. What did he do? What he did not do was form a committee to study the root causes of Egyptian anti-Semitism. The Bible tells us, "And he smote the Egyptian."[7]

Camp Jedel

To train young people for service in the street patrols Kahane established Camp Jedel in Woodburne, New York. Here during the course of a nine-week period youngsters would rise at 5 A.M. to receive instruction in karate, weapons training and close-order marching. Instruction was also given in Jewish history and in the history of anti-Semitism. Camp Jedel was modeled after the Betar camp Kahane had attended as a young man. Despite the initial neighborhood interest garnered by the new organization, Kahane realized that funding for its expansion and development would not come unless he could make a wider impact through the media. As a result, Kahane devised a series of "outrageous acts" to attract public attention. He would later describe this phase of the League's existence by saying:

"We have no great funds, no great influence, so the answer is simple: to do outrageous things."[8]

In May 1969 a squad of about thirty JDL members, armed with clubs and chains appeared in front of Manhattan's Temple Emanuel-El in anticipation of a visit by James Forman, the black militant who was then making the rounds of religious institutions in quest of reparations for real or imagined wrongs inflicted by white society upon blacks. Forman did not appear, but as Kahane must have expected, the incident elicited wide press coverage. Some weeks later Kahane seized on the notoriety of the Emanuel affair by running an advertisement in *The New*

York Times which featured a photograph of JDL members in battle dress. The caption to the photo read, "Is This Any Way for Nice Jewish Boys to Behave?" The advertisement, which of course answered this question in the affirmative, stated:

> Maybe there are times when there is no other way to get across to the extremist that the Jew is not quite the patsy some think he is.[9]

Kahane and the JDL had, of course, been previously involved in activities related to expressions of black anti-Semitism. In January of 1969 the League had both picketed the Metropolitan Museum of Art to protest the introduction to the Museum's catalogue of the "Harlem on My Mind" exhibition and had publically demanded that WBAI-FM dismiss from its staff Julius Lester, a commentator who had read on the air an anti-Semitic poem written by a fifteen-year-old black girl. In February JDL members interrupted a meeting of the New York City Board of Education to protest the Board's retention of two teachers who the League cited as having engaged in anti-Semitic activities. In May the League went to court to obtain an injunction to force Dr. Buell Gallagher, then president of the City College of New York, to reopen the institution after a shutdown precipitated by the action of black and Puerto Rican students who locked themselves inside the campus gates.

Kahane insisted that he was not anti-black, he was merely taking seriously what the establishment organizations refused to admit, the growth of black anti-Semitism. As Kahane later told Walter Goodman:

It bothers me strongly that Jewish groups are so ready to see anti-Semitism under every white bed and will ignore blatant anti-Semitism on the part of blacks. I know that when we started, and talked about black anti-Semitism, we were called racists. What kind of mind is it that refuses to see a danger because the person is black?[10]

There also appeared to be another aspect to Kahane's fight with black militancy. This had to do with his belief that the increasing extremity of black demands which were turning off whites and particularly white ethnics would be traced to Jewish influence, and this would ultimately lead to a more widespread and thus potentially dangerous outbreak of white anti-Semitism.

Mr. Jew is blamed for blacks—and in certain ways there is truth to it. The Jew, because of his elementary sense of fair play and decency and justice and from his own sense of what it feels to be a persecuted person—his heart went out to the black man . . . When every President of the N.A.A.C.P. was a Jew, when CORE was founded by Jews, when SNCC was half black and half Jewish it was because of that feeling for an underdog. An embittered white ethnic who sits and is out of work and is angry and worried doesn't think of it in those terms. He blames the Jew for the black man. "If the Jews hadn't started this thing, there would be no black problems."[11]

In any case, whatever the motivation for Kahane's involvement in the racial crisis, these "outrageous" activities were bringing increasing attention to the League. Kahane began to receive speaking invitations from synagogue men's clubs and Jewish civil service organizations in several sections of the nation. During 1969, JDL chapters were established in cities such as Boston, Cleveland, Philadelphia, Chicago and Los Angeles. In addition, JDL officials were active in campus recruitment, and Kahane began to tell the media of the development of Canadian and European branches. One of the League's major activities during 1969 was to engage in a campaign of harassment aimed at New York's Mayor John Lindsay who was then locked in a fierce three-way battle for re-election. To Kahane, Lindsay epitomized the struggle of the neighborhood Jew against the unsympathetic white WASP power structure. Lindsay was the type of official Kahane was thinking of when he described politicians who "run to wipe the nose of the black man when he sneezes." What was worse, Lindsay did not really have sympathy for blacks; his concessions to them were based on fear of what blacks would do if their demands were not met. As Kahane would comment after Lindsay, despite JDL opposition, was re-elected:

To me John Lindsay is the epitome of a government run by people who are not very honest and sincere but are basically using government for their own ends. Lindsay knows he has wiped out this city. This city is finished, this city is dead. It won't go under while he's Mayor but it will go under because he was Mayor, and because there are others like him who reach for a short term answer, knowing that in the long run it means disaster.[12]

The JDL Truth Squad

During the campaign the JDL "Truth Squad" baited Lindsay at his public appearances before Jewish groups and took out anti-Lindsay newspaper advertisements charging that the Mayor had been silent when anti-Semitism surfaced around the 1968 city school strike.

That these efforts may have been counterproductive was indicated in the decision of a group of seventeen Brooklyn rabbis previously opposed to Lindsay to support the Mayor. On October 10, less than a month before the election, Arthur Goldberg charged that the JDL was conducting a campaign of "hate and vilification" against the Mayor. The former Supreme Court Justice told a gathering of two hundred Jewish civic and religious leaders, "It is a great detriment to the health and welfare of our community to inject racist appeals into the campaign."[13]

After the Lindsay re-election, and the probably coincidental simmering down of overt racial hostility in New York City, Kahane began to turn his attention to the plight of the three-million-member Soviet Jewish community. Kahane had been long concerned with the situation confronting the Russian Jews. The dedication to the *Jewish Stake in Vietnam* read, "To the enslaved Jews of Russia, with the fervent prayer for redemption." However, there seems little doubt that Kahane realized that the JDL needed another more dramatic and wider ranging cause than the race problem, one with greater opportunities for "outrageous" acts, if it was to continue to command media attention and ultimately allegiance from the Jewish masses. In 1970 the League initiated a campaign in the United States of direct confrontation with Soviet diplomatic, commercial and cultural representatives. Early in January Avraham Hershkovitz, a JDL leader who was born in a concentration camp and who would later be arrested for carrying firearms and explosives in connection with an alleged aircraft hijack scheme, described one of these early incidents of anti-Soviet harassment. Hershkovitz visited the New York offices of Intourist, the Russian travel agency, and found one staff member rather uncooperative. "He tried to pull a pair of scissors from a drawer. So I slammed the drawer on his hand. I got full co-operation after that."[14]

By the following January the Union of American Hebrew Congregations in an analysis of JDL activities reported that the League had either been responsible for or had failed to disassociate itself from the following activities:

1. The driving of a car into a line of uniformed policemen standing in front of the Soviet Embassy—an act which injured seven policemen and one civilian;

2. The defacing of the property of a foreign government;

3. Physical assault by six JDL strongmen of three middle-aged officers of an organization supporting the position of the Arab viewpoint;

4. The interruption of concerts and the performances of cultural artists;

5. The falsification of documents for the purposes of boarding an international aircraft;

6. Threatening to deny the rights of free speech in houses of religious assembly because the speaker allegedly disagreed with the position of the JDL;

7. The blowing up of the tourist office of a foreign government, and in this regard, Rabbi Kahane denied

knowledge but expressed approval for those who did the bombing;

8. Disobeying the commands of uniformed police officers;

9. Libelous defamation of recognized agencies of American Jewish organizations which led to the issuance of a court order enjoining the JDL from interfering with the activities of one such organization;

10. Invasion and occupation of a New York Synagogue despite the appeal of the board and the rabbi;

11. The JDL harassment of Soviet artists in the United States had led to a Russian cancellation of the planned appearance in the United States of the Bolshoi Ballet;

12. JDL violence against Soviet embassies in the United States gave the Soviet Union the dangerous pretext to pronounce its inability to protect Americans;

13. The JDL has even demanded cancellation of the SALT talks.[15]

While one could, and many did, debate the efficacy of these activities, Kahane could boast, "Any doubts that JDL—despite the establishment's unhappiness—is firmly implanted on the national Jewish scene, were dispelled over the past few months as national publications devoted long articles to us."[16] As the JDL increased the pace of its activities, even *The New York Times,* which had refrained from getting overly excited about the JDL, carried a page-one story on the League in its January 11, 1971, edition.

Denouncements

Kahane's observation that the Jewish establishment was unhappy with him was surely one of the great under-statements of recent memory. As early as mid-1969 several Jewish leaders, particularly as a result of the Temple Emanuel episode, had issued statements denouncing the JDL. Rabbi Maurice Eisendrath, then president of the UAHC charged that "Jews carrying baseball bats and chains, standing in phalanxes, like goon squads, in front of synagogues, are no less offensive than whites wearing robes and hoods . . . standing in front of burning crosses." Eisendrath added, "The so-called Jewish Defense League violates every ethic and tradition of Judaism and every concept of civil liberties and democratic process in Ameri-can life."[17] Murray Gordon, a vice-president of the Amer-ican Jewish Congress, told Kahane in a face-to-face radio debate:

What is involved here is a very serious challenge to our American system of democracy. I believe that our democ-racy makes it possible for the synagogue to flourish, for the Jewish community to flourish, and at the same time to protect us physically. The system operates as fairly for us as it does for any others. Now, you are challenging that. You are saying that our society, and our form of govern-ment, does not afford adequate protection to the Jewish community, and that therefore we have to take the law into our own hands. I challenge that.[18]

Arnold Forster, general counsel of the Anti-Defamation League, said that the ADL would have "no part in the

Jewish Defense League's business of hysteria." The JDL, Forster concluded, "is a vigilante group and its activities are no less harmful and dangerous because it calls itself "Jewish."[19] A similar tone was struck by the National Jewish Community Relations Advisory Council, an umbrella organization representing most of the major national agencies. On September 21, 1969, the NJCRAC issued a statement which said in part:

> Jewish security—indeed the security of any ethnic or racial group—does not lie in taking the law into one's own hands. That kind of simplistic approach to the complicated problems of our times can only produce warring groups, not solutions . . . The evils of our society and the extremists in our midst must be countered through peaceful processes consistent with democratic goals. The task is to work together in a coalition of all respectable elements of the community to achieve social conditions which will eliminate the breeding grounds of rage and fear . . . Unfortunately the Jewish Defense League has fallen victim to the very tactics it claims to oppose. We consider its activities no less harmful and dangerous because it calls itself "Jewish."[20]

The JDL's policy of anti-Soviet harassment brought an even sharper denunciation from the major Jewish organizations. The American Conference on Soviet Jewry, a coordinating body for twenty-eight national organizations condemned the "actions of small groups of misguided zealots who, ostensibly on behalf of Soviet Jewry, have defaced property and performed other acts of irresponsibility."[21] The New York chapter of the American Jewish Committee, claimed that the League's actions would not "increase Israel's security nor bring a single Russian Jew out of the Soviet Union."[22] The board of governors of B'nai B'rith adopted a resolution denouncing the threats made by Kahane against Soviet personnel as "a pernicious and senseless vendetta which will only cause greater anguish for Soviet Jewry."[23] On January 9, 1971, one year after the JDL's anti-Soviet phase began, seventy-six leaders representing twenty-eight Jewish communities in the United States, sent a telegram to President Nixon, expressing outrage at the January 8 explosion of a bomb outside the Soviet Cultural Building in Washington. The telegram said in part, "American Jews strongly condemn such criminal acts because they are morally wrong, injure the cause of Soviet Jewry and undermine the cause of democracy in the U.S."[24] If Kahane received a special charge at being the target of establishment criticism, he must have had a king-sized reaction when a trio of the very top U. S. Jewish leaders condemned him in a joint statement. The three, Max Fisher, White House aide and president of the Council of Jewish Federations and Welfare Funds; Rabbi Herschel Schacter, chairman of the American Conference on Soviet Jewry and Dr. William Wexler, chairman of the Conference of Presidents of Major American Jewish Organizations said:

The handful of reckless and dangerous men guilty of attacking Soviet installations in this country stand condemned as imperilling the cause of Soviet Jewry. Their outrageous, cowardly acts do malicious harm to the courage and dignity of Soviet Jews who are speaking out for their human rights. Such desperate and criminal tactics win sympathy for the Soviet Union by the use of a mindless violence that all decent men abhor.

In holding themselves above the law, they jeopardize the very foundation of a free society that is based on the rule of law. Their actions can only repel the vast majority of Americans of all faiths and all walks of life whose generous understanding helped create the vast outpouring of opinion that won commutation of the two death sentences imposed by the Leningrad court and whose continued support is vital to the campaign to set Soviet Jewry free.

In the name of the Jewish community of America, we denounce this strategy of terror and the men who are guilty of it.[25]

The establishment which on the issue of the Soviet Jews had not set any records for efficiency or effectiveness did have the perfect right to ask whether the JDL tactics of employing violence and breaking American laws were successfully countering Russian oppression of Jews. Kahane would claim that because of the JDL "there was not a farmer in Iowa who did not know about the plight of Soviet Jewry"[26] but the fact was that the courageous acts of some young Jews *inside* Russia, who were determined to place their case before Western opinion, and the ensuing Leningrad Trials of late 1970, did more to put the issue of Soviet Jewry on the world scene, than all of the spitting, knife pulling and dynamite planting of the JDL put together. Indeed, for a five-year period prior to 1970 the American establishment was being moved toward a more active interest and involvement in the Soviet Jewish cause by its own organization, the Conference on Soviet Jewry and by the more militant but lawful, Student Struggle for Soviet Jewry.

I would agree with the conclusion reached by André Ungar in an article on the JDL in *Sh'ma,* "One may indeed charge American Jewry and its leadership with in-

eptitude but not with the sin of silence and uncaring."[27]
At the time of the Leningrad Trials the major Jewish
organizations facilitated a world outcry on behalf of the
plight of the defendants and of Soviet Jewry in general.
If there is genuine cause to doubt Kahane's claim that
the JDL put the issue of Soviet Jewry on the map, there
is also strong reason to dispute the JDL's repeated assertions of being responsible for the release of individual
Jews and for the general rise in Soviet Jewish emigration
over the last three years. There is simply no evidence that
the JDL has affected the release of one single solitary Jew
from the Soviet Union. On the other hand there is abundant cause to believe that by engaging in violence and in a
reckless and relentless attempt to gain media attention the
League has seriously distracted public attention from the
real situation of the Soviet Jewish community.

In this connection it is interesting to note that one of the
few non-JDL sponsored articles suggesting the efficacy of
the League's activities appeared in the radical Protestant
journal *Christianity and Crisis*. The authors, Jack N. Porter
and Roy Delbyck, state that though "it is too early to
judge whether JDL's tactics have been a failure or a success
. . . though the Soviet Union has certainly been agitated
by its actions. By its illegal tactics, the League raises the
important question of whether or not illegal methods should
be used to achieve a solution when respectable methods
have proved ineffectual."[28] Thus, *Christianity and Crisis*,
which has been a consistent apologist for Palestinian and
third world violence in general, and whose Middle East
position has been so one sided that Mrs. Reinhold Neibuhr
removed her late husband's name as a founder from the
publication's masthead, informs the Jewish community of
the value of the Jewish Defense League. I would much
prefer to make a judgment on the JDL's worth on the

basis of information received from recent emigrees and other informed sources. In the spring of 1971 I had the opportunity to spend the better part of several days with Rivka Aleksandrovich, a Latvian Jew who had been allowed to leave the Soviet Union after her daughter was imprisoned on a trumped up charge. Mrs. Aleksandrovich, who served as a spokeswoman for many Soviet Jewish activists, insisted in the strongest terms that the JDL was not merely a negligible force in alleviating the situation of the Russian Jews but rather was a highly counterproductive element in the total struggle.

Subsequent conversations with *Olim,* such as Rita Gluzmann and Michael Zand as well as firsthand reports from Richard Mass and Jerry Goodman, former chairman and executive director respectively of the National Conference on Soviet Jewry, have confirmed the validity of the outspoken condemnation of the JDL offered by Mrs. Aleksandrovich. And while I would be extremely cautious in accepting at face value the condemnatory assertions of American government officials regarding the JDL, I have been impressed by the critical comments concerning the JDL made by Richard Davies, current United States Ambassador to Poland, when he was Deputy Assistant Secretary of State for European Affairs. I grew to respect Davies as I observed firsthand his active and sympathetic role in helping to obtain the release from a Moscow prison of Gavriel Shapiro, a young Jewish activist who had married Judith Silver of Cincinnati. In testimony before a Congressional committee Davies responded as follows to a question concerning JDL activities:

We are convinced that the Soviet Government cannot be compelled into improving the lot of Soviet Jewry simply because Soviet housewives are spat upon in the New York streets or because fanatics shoot rifles into the playrooms of defenseless children. This kind of sick and mindless fanaticism plays gratuitously into the hands of those in the Soviet Union who oppose any easing of current Soviet policies toward Jews.[29]

A Reversal of Fortunes

In 1971 Kahane's and the JDL's fortunes took a sudden and precipitous turn for the worse. In January the League's New England co-ordinator resigned because of the "irresponsible actions of the national organization."[30] In February Kahane was denied the right to speak at the World Conference of Jewish Communities on Soviet Jewry in Brussels.[31] In May Kahane was arrested on a charge of conspiracy to violate Federal gun and bomb regulations.[32] In July Kahane, who first pleaded guilty to the charge and then declared that he would not be deterred from using explosives or other forms of violence against Soviet installations in the United States, was given a five-year suspended sentence, fined five thousand dollars and placed on five years probation by Federal Judge Jack Weinstein who declared, "it is not permissible to substitute the bomb for the book as the symbol of Jewish manhood."[33]

The developing reversal in Kahane's influence was underscored in a condemnation issued by the highly influential Orthodox authority, Rabbi Moshe Feinstein. Rabbi Feinstein's statement said:

Hereby I wish to state my opinion based on the laws of the Torah, that the actions of the Jewish Defense League directed against governments and states are contrary to the Torah.[34]

Shortly thereafter a national convention of the Union of Orthodox Jewish Congregations of America unanimously voted to condemn Jewish extremism. During the summer of 1971 *The New York Times* published an evaluative article which, while asserting that the League was gaining adherents, also concluded that the League had alienated many persons in the Jewish community.[35] In addition, the *Times* suggested the organization's strength was directly related to the degree of racial antagonism in a given community and that the JDL seemed vague about future plans and program. If the League as an entity was not certain of its long-range course, the founder was. Kahane announced plans to settle in Israel where he would become chairman of a World Jewish Defense League. In September 1971 Kahane and his family took up residence in Jerusalem although he continued to make frequent visits to the United States and remained a contributor to the *Jewish Press*. Kahane's decision to make *aliyah* must be understood in the steady movement of events that seemed to reactivate his failure syndrome. During 1971 Kahane, whose JDL experience had heretofore manifested careful calculation, began to make a series of bizarre moves. On April 28 a JDL contingent invaded the offices of the New York Board of Rabbis and demanded $50,000 in order to arrange bail for a convicted JDL member. Rabbi Harold Gordon, the Board's executive director, alerted to the entrance of the JDL, asked the building custodian to telephone the police. When a group of JDL members who had remained outside to picket heard the police coming they informed their cohorts in Rabbi Gordon's office. These individuals promptly began to destroy everything in sight telling Rabbi Gordon as they did, that Kahane had issued instructions "to take the place apart" if the police were called. The following day the Board of Rabbis who had unsuccessfully tried to initiate dialogue with Kahane a few months before accused the JDL of "stormtrooper" tactics. Rabbi Gordon with the strong support of the bulk of the Board's members and with the backing of the national organizations said:

> I think it is terribly important for those limited numbers of people, here and elsewhere, who have indicated support and sympathy for the JDL to know the kind of people and the kind of mentality they are dealing with. The New York Board of Rabbis is a religious organization serving the entire Jewish community. To disrupt our daily work on behalf of the Jewish faith, the Jewish people and the general community, is intolerable. To damage the credibility of the responsible and productive work done by the truly representative Jewish organizations in dealing with the world problems of the Jewish community is to strengthen the hands of the enemies of the Jewish people. We therefore condemn the JDL and call upon the total Jewish community to repudiate them.[36]

The destruction of the offices of the Board of Rabbis further isolated Kahane from the neighborhood leaders whose support was necessary to the health of the JDL. In any event, the sweeping nature of the Jewish condemnation of his activities evidently weighed heavily upon Kahane and was perhaps the reason for his entering into alliances with two rather unlikely organizations. In the one case Kahane found a friend in Joseph Colombo, the founder of the Italian-American Civil Rights League. Colombo who had been named by the New York State Joint Legislative Committee on Crime as the "boss" of one of the city's five Cosa Nostra families, apparently believed that association with Kahane would bring him the support of a significant portion of the Jewish community. Certainly the Brooklyn real estate salesman had no need of the services of protection offered by Kahane's minions. When questioned by Walter Goodman as to whether the association with the Italian Civil Rights League matched his vow to align with "decent non-Jewish organizations for Jewish interests," Kahane replied:

Please, let me state clearly right here, Joe Colombo may or may not be Mafia. Let's assume for the sake of this particular interview that he is with the Mafia. O.K., he's with the Mafia. And let's assume for this particular interview that Joe Colombo is not a nice guy. And I say, for the sake of this interview, and I emphasize that strongly. Our alliance was not with the Mafia. It was not with Joe Colombo, but with an organization which represents, more than any other group, the basic Italian-American . . .

We became tremendously interested in the Italian-American Civil Rights League because of the people it represents. And why? My great fear is that the wave of the future in this country—for worse, not for better, for worse —is the white ethnic. For the most part he's anti-Semitic, anti-black, and capable of doing a lot of bad things. The American Jew has had no contact with these people. The American Jewish groups, the establishment groups deal with WASP's. They play a game of musical chairs with the National Conference of Christians and Jews—"This year it's your plaque and next year it's my plaque."

If there is no Jewish contact with these people, there could be a disaster for Jews. And what we did was establish some kind of dialogue with them . . .

I'm interested here in trying to establish a dialogue between Jews and these people and in trying to temper their feelings against Jews and against blacks.[37]

The details of the Kahane-Colombo relationship are vague, but it is known that the alleged Mafioso did at one point put up $45,000 bail for Kahane.[38]

Kahane's other non-Jewish organization alliance was to some extent even stranger. In what may have been an attempt to disprove allegations of racism, Kahane joined hands with Dr. Thomas Matthew, the founder of NEGRO (National Economic Growth and Reconstruction Organization). Matthew like Kahane had troubles with various governmental agencies although he was a staunch supporter of Nixon Administration policies in the black sector. Kahane surely did not believe that Matthew represented any significant number of blacks and he must have known that NEGRO and other of Matthew's enterprises were in a crumbling state. The one interesting sidelight to their relationship occurred at a joint press conference where Matthew felt compelled to denounce the JDL tactic of harassing Soviet diplomats. The New York *Jewish Week* summed up a growing Jewish weariness with Kahane when it charged, "the JDL is focusing its publicity efforts on linking Jews and Jewish causes with unsavory elements in other minority groups. Few Jews want to identify themselves either with Colombo's rabble-rousing attacks on enemies of the Mafia or with Matthew's sabotage of the black movement for equality."[39]

A Foothold in Israel

The Colombo and Matthew episodes may also have been part of a diversionary strategy to allow Kahane time to establish a foothold in Israel. In the light of Kahane's declining fortunes in the United States, the avowed purpose of settling in the Jewish State so as to establish a World JDL simply could not hold water. Such an organization would have to rely most heavily on support from American Jews, and it was becoming increasingly apparent that such assistance would not be forthcoming. Kahane's own activities in Israel gave evidence of his desire to enter the Israeli political arena. When he first arrived in Israel there was speculation that he planned to run for the Knesset, and it is not beyond the realm of reasonable speculation to assume that his coming to Israel was a later-day attempt to fulfill his earlier dream of entering the cabinet and becoming a major personality in the life of the young nation.

During 1972 and 1973 most of Kahane's press notices had Israel datelines. These stories indicated that he was experiencing a difficult time in the supercharged atmosphere of Israeli political affairs. Even potential allies on the right wing of the political continuum were not overly delighted to have Kahane immediately at hand. Some of the more astute right-wing political figures surmised that Kahane and the JDL had peaked and reports of a growing fragmentation in American JDL ranks only contributed to this analysis. Kahane did not help himself by looking for further confrontation with American Jewish groups. On May 11, 1972, Kahane was barred from entering the ballroom of the Sheraton-Cleveland Hotel where the American Jewish Congress was conducting its annual convention. The assembled delegates characterized Kahane's tactics as "abominable, slanderous and despicable" and Rabbi Arthur Lelyveld, the organization's outgoing president, told the press, "we have nothing to learn from him."[40]

Two weeks later in an "Op-Ed" article in *The New York Times* Kahane appeared to reach a new plateau of hysteria by warning that the most critical Jewish issue of the "next decade" is the "physical survival of the Jewish community." Drawing upon an old theme Kahane insisted that frustration and bitterness over internal problems in the United States would cause American Jews to become scapegoats. Kahane's solution, not surprisingly, was simple. The only way to avert disaster in America was mass emigration to Israel.[41] Kahane's penchant for overkill—he had earlier exhibited this tendency by equating the plight of the Soviet Jews with the Holocaust—made it easy for many leaders both in Israel and the United States to summarily dismiss his comments. The last thing the Israelis wanted to hear was that the American Jewish community, which remains Israel's life line, was in its death throes. Harry Golden anticipated this Israeli reaction when he stated that U. S. Jews were living in the "golden age of United States Jewry"[42] and as such could strengthen Israel by continuing to live in America. American Jewish leaders who had suffered under the onslaught of Kahane's rhetoric for five years saw his latest outburst as an opportunity to knock him out of the ball park. Morris Abram, honorary president of the American Jewish Committee and former president of Brandeis University, answered the Kahane *Times* article with one of his own. Abram expressed his faith in the American system which contained institutional restraints against the excesses of human nature.

As long as the Supreme Court stands, as long as the ecumenical spirit of religion continues to grow, and as long as government majorities must rule by bargains struck among composite coalitions, the security of all groups in the United States will remain relatively stable.[43]

Abram surely reflected the position of the American Jewish majority when he described the unquestioned allegiance and loyalty of the Jewish community to America, "which had offered Jews democratic liberty and equality."

> To announce arbitrarily—as Rabbi Kahane does—that this contract is now about to be abrogated either by the American government or the American people is absurd.[44]

The National Jewish Community Relations Advisory Council got into the act by denouncing Kahane's "alarmist assertion that a massive wave of anti-Semitism is likely to confront the American Jewish community."[45]

Since 1973 Kahane has been regarded as something of a nuisance in Israel. His suggestion that Arabs living on the west bank of the Jordan leave the occupied territories for Jordan rankled the government and moved him into an extreme position that even right-wing politicians hesitate to assume. Of even greater embarrassment to the government has been Kahane's threatening stance toward Christian missionaries in Israel. To be sure, the actions of some of these individuals leave much to be desired from an ethical point of view and often bring dishonor upon the very religion they proclaim, but a banning of all missionary activity would surely elicit a charge of denial of religious freedom. One might hope that the Western churches that support these missionaries would finally come to the conclusion that Israel should be the last place on earth for proselytizing of Jews. Yet the activities of some Jewish extremists goaded by Kahane's rhetoric will likely only harden the Christian intention to stay in Israel.

An increasing proportion of American Jews, along with Israeli counterparts, look with disdain upon Kahane's activities since moving to Israel. To many of these individuals Kahane in coming to Israel met at first hand the real Jewish

Defense League. This was an encounter from which the Brooklyn rabbi could not possibly find success. The prognosis for the Jewish Defense League, the World Jewish Defense League and for Meir Kahane himself, is not promising. Kahane in the late 1960s had his finger on the pulse of a major segment of the American Jewish community. By seizing on the racial unrest extant in the cities, and the guilt of middle-age and older Jews over Jewish failure to ameliorate the Holocaust, Kahane found an audience receptive to his cry of "Never Again." However, the extreme character of his program, the resounding repudiation handed him by the Jewish establishment, the apparent capacity of the major organizations to deal more effectively with internal and international Jewish problems, the surface level diminution in black-Jewish tensions, and the overriding influence of the Israeli leadership combined to weaken his movement and inextricably move Kahane to yet another phase of failure and defeat. Yet Kahane helped to raise questions about the character and quality of Jewish life in America which cannot be easily dismissed. Though his predictions of doom for the Jewish community were laced with hysteria, the almost obligatory knee-jerk liberal response regarding the immortal nature of American democratic institutions indicated how far the establishment was to travel to change a philosophy more suited for the Roosevelt than the Nixon era. After all of the turmoil of the late 1960s and early 1970s the Anti-Defamation League, in a report on the JDL, could still fall back to mouthing pieties concerning the interlocking relationship between Jewish rights and the rights of others.

The social coalition is another of the tested American values at which the Jewish Defense League thumbs its nose. It is a coalition in which Jewish human relations agencies and religious and lay leaders have worked with decent, progressive people and organizations representing all religions and races toward the advancement of human rights and equal opportunity and the fruition of American democracy. This alliance could be endangered if friendships are lost and hostilities deepened through the activities of the Jewish Defense League on the American scene . . . When we all have had enough of clubs and guns and threats and confrontations, then perhaps we will come to understand that both the ends and the means of Jewish "defense" must be the defense of all men and their rights.[46]

Touching a Middle-class Nerve

It should also be stated that while Kahane's attacks upon the Jewish establishment were nearsighted and mean spirited, he did touch an important middle-class nerve. For many American Jews the national agencies are distant entities whose basic functions seem to be to issue pronouncements, release studies proving how much better things are for Jews because of their activities, constantly seek funds and provide platforms and role-playing devices for the noteworthy and affluent segment of the Jewish population. Those Jews who feel alienated from the major organizations (and they include dues-paying members of B'nai B'rith and the Jewish War Veterans) earnestly desire representation. Jews living in the front lines of the racial crisis or believing their livelihoods and security threatened by government programs to enlarge the Amercan pie, want someone to stand up for them, to articulate their fears and aspirations and to make a difference in the charting of their destinies. The fact that Kahane and his program were too shallow to meet these basic needs should not turn the establishment away from regarding communication with the unrepresented Jews as an item of the highest priority. The major organizations would do well to re-evaluate current program in light of criteria which first question the *Jewish* content of agency activity. The recent interest of these groups in the progress of the Jewish poor and the improvement of Jewish education indicates that the beginning of such a re-evaluation process may have occurred.

It is also apparent that Kahane in assuming a militant posture played upon the vicarious identification of many American Jews with Israel and her struggle for survival. The image of the Israelis as tough-talking, tough-acting *men* fully capable of defending themselves, their families and their basic interests had since the beginnings of the State, but particularly in the period following the June 1967 war, made a deep impression upon American Jews. One can recall the widespread popularity of posters depicting Moshe Dayan, whose gruff manner and all-consuming military expertise caused more than a few Jewish men to want to don eye patches. In the summer of 1967 Kahane seemed to say, if the Israelis, who are surrounded on all sides by enemies, can take care of themselves, why must American Jews always bow to the bully kicking sand in their faces. Kahane well understood that most American Jews while charmed and thrilled by the eloquence of Abba Eban defending Israel's position at the United Nations knew in their heart of hearts that in the moment of truth it would be Israeli military force and the intimidating aspects of that power that would determine Israel's fate. Thus, when you as an American Jew are dealing with an enemy who makes demands, "who is a Neanderthal type and a vicious anti-Semite," you also forgo discussion and debate and you manifest a show of force. This is exactly the treatment

Kahane claims to have applied to Sonny Carson, a leader of Brooklyn CORE, who took an intransigent position regarding the Jewish desire for a share of the anti-poverty program in the Crown Heights section.

The problem with Sonny Carson is not the problem that the American Jewish Committee has with getting an executive job for a Jew in a bank. You can sit down with the president of First National City—I don't care whether he's an anti-Semite or not—you can sit down with him and you discuss and you debate and you push and you pull—and eventually something happens. You don't sit down with Sonny Carson. Sonny Carson does not listen. With Sonny Carson, you walk in and you say, Sonny baby, you gonna get out? Or do we have to cut you up? And he says, Now man, now sit down, let's talk.[47]

Kahane advocacy of the use of force surely had a direct influence on some Jews, but there is evidence to suggest that other Jews removed from the JDL orbit were coming to a similar conclusion. A new Jewish militancy involving middle-class businessmen and upper middle-class suburban professional as well as non-orthodox rabbis and rabbinical students and featuring karate, judo, other self-defense instruction as well as training in the use of firearms sprang up at the end of the 1960s. These activities prompted Rabbi Emanuel Rackman, spiritual leader of New York's prestigious Fifth Avenue Synagogue and provost of Yeshiva University (where by late 1970 one hundred students were learning karate) and no friend of the JDL, to comment, "Jewish children have been taught to flee. I think its healthier for kids to defend themselves."[48]

Kahane also had an impact upon many affiliated Jews.

These included the individuals who flocked to synagogues around the country to hear him speak and to persons who only knew of him through the media or by way of the internal Jewish debate which surrounded the JDL. Many of these people who would not join the League or contribute funds toward its support believed that Kahane was engaged in an important mission. It must be understood that these individuals did not consider Kahane their spokesman, but in at least three ways he appeared to perform a needed service. First, although the JDL could accomplish little in the way of correcting flaws in the Jewish communal structure, the organization seemed to have succeeded in motivating leaders and followers to recognize existing faults and to work to correct them. Elkanah Schwartz in a perceptive article on the JDL in *Jewish Life* commented on this aspect of Kahane's career:

He has flung the gauntlet with undeniable force. JDL has obviously met certain unfilled community needs in a manner that is sometimes irresponsible at best. It is for those who by default created this leadership vacuum to close the gap by addressing themselves more meaningfully and intensively to these same community needs in a manner more responsible than the JDL's and more responsive to grass roots interests. Should that occur, JDL will have neither need nor source for existence, and condemnations of all sorts will no longer be necessary.[49]

Second, although many of these Jews were temple and synagogue oriented, Kahane aroused in them a new and positive sense of Jewishness. He appeared to say that it was not wrong for a Jew to look almost exclusively inward, to be primarily concerned with the security and survival of the Jewish community. This message was especially telling among those who had been exposed to years of sermons and lectures that articulated the Jewish imperative of helping the oppressed of other minority groups *even* at the expense of self-interest. The fact was that by the late 1960s more and more Jews who had absorbed the thrust of these lofty admonitions in an almost osmosislike process began listening to their leaders and in an increasing way did not like what they heard. Kahane and the JDL were neither temperamentally nor programmatically equipped to channel the feelings of Jewishness they had stirred. The gauntlet had been thrown, the question remained whether the major organizations could constructively and effectively harness the emotions Kahane had quickened. Finally, for many Jews who could not constitutionally and intellectually engage in either the appearance or the reality of intimidation and force, Kahane fulfilled a surrogate role. It was reassuring to know that Kahane and his Jewish bullies were out there in the streets protecting Jewish turf. The JDL would, according to this way of looking at things, not only actively engage Jewish enemies but also give the anti-Semites pause before they contemplated further hostile actions directed at the Jewish community. These Jews reasoned, the blacks have their Sonny Carson, we have Kahane. We really don't like either one but at least they will check each other off. Thus, to some degree, Kahane had allowed American Jews to at last achieve parity with the proponents of overt anti-Semitism.

VI

JEWS AND AMERICAN ELECTIONS

The developing inward trend of the American Jewish community has important implications for the manner in which Jews participate in the electoral process. From the election of Woodrow Wilson in 1912 through the presidential campaign of 1968 Jews overwhelmingly supported the democratic candidate in national elections. American Jews, who constitute 3 per cent of the population and 4 per cent of the electorate, made the difference between victory and defeat in 1948 and 1960 and enabled Hubert Humphrey to come within less than a percentage point of besting Richard Nixon in 1968. The political profile of the American Jewish community over a forty-year period was liberal to left, Democratic and increasingly affluent. Regardless of the issue and candidate, Jews could be counted upon to take a liberal, universalistic position and to inexorably give their votes to the Democratic standard bearer. The sheer predictability of the American Jewish voting pattern, most striking in national elections but evident also in many municipal contests, suggested that there was alive in America a distinct political phenomenon known, for want of a better term, as the "Jewish vote." The term Jewish vote did not mean that Jews automatically vote for Jews. On the contrary, this seems to be less true for Jews than for other ethnic groups.

Thus, until 1973 New York City with a Jewish electorate of 40 per cent never had a Jewish mayor, and in countless statewide and Congressional races Jews passed up voting for their coreligionists to cast ballots for candidates of many different backgrounds. The term "Jewish vote" did seem to describe a tendency for unanimity among Jews, implying that the voting statistics for Jews are in certain definable ways characteristic and distinguishable from the patterns of other groups. Thus, as suggested above, Jews vote in large majorities for Democratic presidential candidates. There are, of course, reasons to account for the Jewish predilection to favor Democratic aspirants for the Presidency and other public offices. Jews have tended to associate their safety and security with liberal social and economic policy. Such policies, they reasoned, would best promote the general prosperity and would allow for the kind of internal harmony and civility under which historically in the West, Jewish life flourished. In Europe, for example, liberals generally favored the admission of Jews as full partners into the mainstream of society while conservatives tried to inhibit Jews from achieving citizenship and equal rights. In the twentieth-century American setting, Wilson's anti-war position reflected Jewish resentment of Czarist Russia's anti-Semitic practices. In 1928 Jews felt compatible with Al Smith, a representative of another major minority group.

During the 1930s and '40s Roosevelt was the champion of almost all American Jews. FDR, whose internationalist policy, was seen as the antidote to the isolationistic posture of the Republicans, saw his vote among Jews rise to almost 90 per cent in 1944. In the first post-war election Harry Truman and Henry Wallace—one moderately liberal, the other distinctly left of center—competed for the great bulk of Jewish votes. In the Republican landslide year of 1956 Jews gave Adlai Stevenson a higher percentage of votes (60) than any other ethnic group except blacks (68). John F. Kennedy in 1960 received a proportion of Jewish votes that even exceeded his percentage among fellow Roman Catholics. Four years later, Barry Goldwater perceived by Jews as a right-wing conservative, received the smallest share of Jewish votes ever recorded in a two-man race. In 1968 Hubert Humphrey, the personification of the liberal, progressive, social democrat, garnered 83 per cent of Jewish votes while netting only 43 per cent of the general vote.

The Scenario Changed

Thus, for the better part of this century Jews believed that their fortunes were closely tied to those of the Democratic Party. This concept would be seriously questioned in the years immediately following 1968. Significant changes, mainly brought about by experience with and reaction to serious domestic and international problems, were occurring in the Jewish community. As early as September 1969 C. Daniel Chill wrote in *Jewish Life:*

. . . while political polarization among the Jews did not clearly materialize in 1968, there are steadily mounting indications that things are not the same politically with the Jews. While the evidence is inconclusive, the findings scant and the statistics confusing, it cannot be gainsaid that what was once a monolithical left of center Jewish vote is becoming increasingly fragmented.[1]

Chill, who based his analysis on the evidence of strong Jewish support in the upcoming New York Mayoralty election for the right-of-center Democrat Mario Proccacino, suggested that "careful effort by national Republican candidates could reap a rich harvest of Jewish votes in critical big city areas . . . which could affect the outcome of a close national election."[2] Thus, New York State with its forty-one electoral votes could go into the Republican column through a significant shift in the 14 per cent of the state's vote which is Jewish. In 1968, for example, Nixon, who won only 15 per cent of the Jewish vote, lost New York by only 4 per cent of the total vote.

Whether due to Chill's analysis or because of a similarly provocative scenario prepared by B'nai B'rith official Herman Edelsberg and forwarded to Nixon biographer Earl Mazo, who then communicated it to the White House, the President, by early 1971 decided to make a strong appeal for Jewish votes. In assuming this stance he evidently overruled the objections of key advisors including then chief of staff H. R. Haldeman, who utilized the conventional argument that it was fruitless to engage the Democrats in a struggle for the affection of Jewish voters. Haldeman and other Republican naysayers were apparently unaware of events taking place in the Jewish community. In a discussion of the 1972 election it is crucially important to understand that the growing indications of a potentially significant Republican gain in the Jewish vote were recognized by Chill, Edelsberg and a number of Republican politicians long before it became apparent that George McGovern would be the Democratic nominee.

The urban crisis, racial tension, increasing discussion and in some cases implementation of quotas and preferential treatment in employment and education, hostile liberal and left-wing reaction to the results of the June 1967 war and to the continued Arab threat to Israel's survival and Soviet indifference to the desire of many of her Jewish citizens to emigrate were issues that were causing more and more Jews to feel uneasy with those long-standing alliances that placed the universal over the particular on the scale of priority. The eroding links between segments of the Jewish community and organized liberalism also reflected a developing internal Jewish argument between the more Jewishly identified and religiously involved and those individuals who still viewed the health of the larger society as more important than the security and stability of Jewish life within that society. These important and potentially far-reaching changes were already being manifested in Jewish voting patterns. As early as 1966 heavily Jewish middle-class neighborhoods of New York City voted down by a 2 to 1 margin the establishment of the Lindsay-liberal supported Civilian Police Review Board. In 1969 Mario Proccacino received about 50 per cent of the city's Jewish votes to roughly 42 per cent for John Lindsay. The Proccacino vote, incidentally, was significantly higher in the working-class Jewish areas of Brooklyn and the Bronx. In 1970 James Buckley, the brother of well-known right-wing columnist William F. Buckley, running for the U. S. Senate on the conservative line, got almost 20 per cent of New York State's Jewish votes in a race against two liberally oriented opponents. Similar results obtained in the 1969 Los Angeles and 1971 Philadelphia Mayoral elections. In these two races the conservative candidates, Sam Yorty and Frank Rizzo, ran

well in lower middle-class and middle-class Jewish precincts.

The Conservative Shift

The conservative shift in Jewish ideological position was
also manifested in the writings and statements of a growing
number of professionals and intellectuals. *Commentary*
magazine, under the provocative leadership of Norman
Podhoretz, condemned most of the new wave of left-leaning
movements (Panthers, Counter-Culture, Women's Liberation) while articles by highly regarded Jewish academicians
began to appear in right-wing journals. A Jewish move
away from traditional liberalism could also be detected in
the action of the Oakland chapter of the Anti-Defamation
League who designated establishment defender S. I. Haya-
kawa its "Man of the Year." The president of embattled
San Francisco State College was cited for conduct which
"manifests the true spirit of America in its finest hour."
Several Jewish organizations sought out political conservatives for speaking assignments, the Religious Zionists of
America for example were favored by the oratorical talents
of Vice-President Agnew. After 1968 the Republicans, or
at least Mr. Nixon, made a number of important personal
conquests. William Wexler, a leading figure in B'nai B'rith
and chairman of the World Conference of Jewish Organization, Sam Rothberg and Louis Boyar, both affiliated with
the Israel Bond Organization, and Rabbi Herschel Schacter,
former chairman of the Conference of Presidents of Major
American Jewish Organizations, jumped the Democratic
track and signed on with the Committee to Re-Elect the
President.[3] Perhaps the most interesting convert was Rabbi
Seymour Siegel, professor of theology at the Jewish Theological Seminary and a widely influential figure in the con-

servative religious movement. Siegel, a member of the New York City Democratic Committee, who had supported Robert Kennedy in 1968 and was the lone Jewish name on the National Clergy for Senator Kennedy list, would play an active role in the 1972 Nixon effort.

Rabbi Siegel announced his conversion in the Jewish monthly *Sh'ma*. "I have never voted for a Republican presidential candidate. This year I shall vote for President Nixon. I have enlisted as an active worker in the campaign for his re-election."[4] Siegel further stated that his support of Nixon was predicated on the President's approach to foreign policy, the possibilities of an open society and "the values that form a national life style." According to Siegel, Nixon's foreign policy "had been spectacularly effective." His combination of realism and flexibility had resulted in a breakthrough in our dealings with the other major powers. Nixon's view of the just society rewarded "ingenuity, energy and natural endowment" regardless of who possesses them. This principle not only made for an open society, it was also most beneficial to Jews and other "high achievers." Similarly, Nixon would hold the line on those values espoused by a concensus of the national community. Siegel pledged to work for Nixon because the President would uphold:

the venerable liberal ideas of achievement through effort; restraint; a recognition of the importance of structure and tradition; and the value of giving everyone a chance to start at the same place without guaranteeing that they will end up in a dead heat.[5]

To his credit, Rabbi Siegel remained loyal to the President in the difficult period following the election and was the most well-known and influential Jew to join in a public defense of Mr. Nixon over the Watergate situation.

By mid 1971 the Committee to Re-Elect the President had set up a Jewish desk to be ably manned over the next eighteen months by Larry Goldberg, a fortyish lawyer from Providence, Rhode Island. Much of the policy-making responsibilities for Nixon's Jewish apparatus came from Max Fisher, a major Jewish communal leader and long-time Nixon fund raiser, and Rita Hauser, former United States Ambassador to the U. N. Commission on Human Rights. Mrs. Hauser, one of the most astute Republican politicians in the nation, devised the neighborhood-level strategy that would prove so effective in November 1972. It was her idea, for example, to print up several million Nixon for President buttons in Hebrew. This attempt to mix it up with the Democrats at the grass-roots level horrified establishment Jewish Republicans like New York Senator Jacob Javits who appeared in Brooklyn and the Bronx only during the last year of each six-year electoral cycle. Javits and the Manhattan Jewish Republicans must have had a difficult time adjusting to the presence of *yarmulke*-garbed young men at CRP's sedate Roosevelt Hotel headquarters. My stereotypic image of a Republican campaign office was jolted when, while waiting for Mrs. Hauser to appear for a luncheon engagement, I counted the impressive number of observant Jews working in the CRP suite.

The Republican Jewish strategists did not hesitate to give interviews to the national media outlining their program. These officials appeared to vie with each other in predicting the percentage of the Jewish vote Nixon would pick up. Max Fisher consistently placed the President's strength with Jewish voters at 50 per cent while Rita Hauser offered to bet *New York* magazine's Richard Reeves that Nixon would garner at least 35 per cent of New York State's

Jewish vote.[6] By the summer of 1972 a steady flow of stories and articles had appeared calling attention to the importance of Jewish votes for the outcome of the presidential election. One edition of *New York* magazine, obviously widely circulated and read in the seat of Jewish organizational headquarters, contained three articles headed, "McGovern, Nixon and the Jewish Vote," "The Chosen Party" and "Is Nixon Kosher?" In addition, the magazine featured a cartoon saying "OI! Will Jews Dance to Nixon's Tune?"[7] *Time* and *Newsweek*[8] carried several articles describing Republican activities vis-à-vis the Jewish community, and *The New York Times,* often considered the second Testament for Jewish organizations, featured a growing number of stories on the Jewish vote. Thus, Terence Smith had a long article in the July 7, 1972, edition headed, "Nixon Aides, Seeing Big Gains, Plan a Drive for Jewish Votes."

These dispatches often stressed the functions of Jewish-oriented special-intent committees and endorsements given the President by recognized Jewish communal leaders. Several Jewish organizations reacted sharply to the attention being given such committees and endorsements.

The board of governors of the half-million-member B'nai B'rith adopted a resolution that viewed with "disfavor the formation of Jewish committees on behalf of any candidate for public office."[9] Seymour Graubard, the national chairman of the Anti-Defamation League, a B'nai B'rith satellite, charged that the "reaction of some Jews who have been flattered and romanced by the politicians is damaging to the image of the American Jewish community."[10] The endorsement issue caused eight major national organizations including the American Jewish Committee, the American Jewish Congress, the Jewish War Veterans and the National Council of Jewish Women, to issue a joint statement declaring it an error to assume "that political endorsements by individuals identified as officers or members of an organization reflect the views of that organization or its membership."[11]

The Jewish organizations that employed similar endorsement techniques to facilitate fund raising and that had not in past elections, when most Jewish leaders supported Democratic candidates, seemed terribly concerned with the question of personal endorsement were justified in their concern over the media's exploitative treatment of Republican interest in garnering an increased share of Jewish votes.

There is no question but that the media put an undue and at times hysterical emphasis on themes such as "Jewish money," "Jewish interests" and "Jewish influence." Rational reflection would have indicated that a group as numerically small as the Jews in comparison with other minority groups and the white Protestant majority could under normal circumstances hardly influence the outcome of a national election. The millions Max Fisher was raising from heretofore Democratic givers could not begin to match the enormous financial contributions of individual non-Jewish Republican donors nor, as it would later turn out, the funds supplied by gentile-controlled major corporations. The suggestion of Jewish influence raised the specter of a clique that could move events along a Jewishly programmed path. Such careless media assertions could only assist the professional anti-Semites who traditionally used every national election to propagate their paranoid theories concerning a sinister Jewish conspiracy. In the light of the fact that these operators had been joined by Arab students in disseminating the Protocols of the Elders of Zion and other suggestive materials concerning Jewish plans for societal domination, the concerns voiced by the Jewish organizations were understandable and in order.

The Jewish Influence Issue

The ease with which the media seized upon the "issue" of Jewish influence, and their highly exaggerated coverage of the impact Jews would have upon the campaign, clearly signaled the widespread and pervasive existence of anti-Jewish stereotypes in American society. Unfortunately, however, the organized Jewish community in an attempt to combat and dispel the notion of Jewish electoral influence tended to overreact by suggesting that Jews would vote on the basis of an idealism that put aside all considerations of self-interest. Thus, the statement on the election issued by eight major organizations stressed that Jews would "vote as individual Americans, according to their individual judgments on controversial and complex issues that are at stake in any election."[12] The Jewish establishment despite all the genuine threats to Jewish security and well being that had surfaced since the election of 1968 would still insist that Jews would not examine an issue on the basis of that classic and valid, "Is it good for the Jews?" It may have been true for the greater part of the twentieth century that, as sociologist Irving Louis Horowitz suggests, the Jews were a unique force in American politics, "despite their class backgrounds or interests they have the capacity to vote and act beyond their class and beyond interest group constraints."[13] But anyone who had been in the communities, who had spent any time at all talking to Jews and gauging their reactions to recent unpleasant events and who took the trouble to make even a cursory study of recent municipal election returns would have had to conclude that Horowitz' theory of Jewish electorial universalism would not hold up in 1972.

The reaction of the Jewish organizations to the rightward shift in the community demonstrated the capacity of these groups to engage in self-delusion. Between 1968 and 1972 a vast outpouring of articles and memoranda flowed from the major communal bodies attempting to rationalize the electoral statistics or disprove allegations of their significance as did information challenging the Jewish move away from the liberal and left-of-center current. All the establishment attachment in the world to democracy and liberal political theory as it was perceived in the communal organization boardrooms and executive suites would not convince many Jewish storekeepers in the ghetto to vote against a law-and-order candidate or Jews with a strong religious commitment or sense of identity to support a nominee identified with the new left, the third world, the developing rejection of traditional morals and the turn toward personal anarchy. The establishment's argument against an appeal to Jewish self-interest was flawed in at least two important ways. First, from a pragmatic perspective, the history of American political life clearly illustrated the long-standing nature of such appeals. The Republican Party benefited from the Lincoln image among black voters up to the Roosevelt era. In the post-World War II period Democratic candidates sought black support on the basis of civil rights actions taken by FDR and Truman. By the mid 1960s every political analyst and the majority of informed lay people assumed that blacks believed the Democrats to be the political party especially concerned with their problems. In a similar fashion the Democratic Party made special appeals to white ethnic groups such as Poles, Czechs and Slavs and usually received impressive pluralities among these voters. If Jews could be expected to vote Democratic, then Episcopalians and other affluent and middle-class WASPs would predictably pull the Republican lever. It was no dark or embarrassing secret that Republican support for Taft-Hartley, the oil depletion allowance and legislation favoring big business was expected to and did produce a favorable climate at the polls by like-minded individuals in the general society. Second, on a more philosophical plane, if Jews were full partners in the American system, why should they be excluded from special-interest pleading on behalf of the political parties? If there was a farm vote, a labor vote, a Catholic vote, why could there not be a Jewish vote? Herman Edelsberg, who recognized the developing political shift in the Jewish community, raised this question with regard to Jewish interest in the well being of Israel:

If wheat farmers make no apology for voting in reaction to the price of wheat, and labor leaders make no apology for voting in reaction to the wage price policy, why should a Jew feel self-conscious about hinging his vote on an issue he devoutly believes involves the security of his family, particularly when it is consistent with America's national interest?[14]

The fact was, and the Jewish organizations certainly were aware of it, that Jews in the past, *even in America,* had voted their self-interest before the group interests of the larger society. This led some observers to believe that an ingrained anti-Nixon bias formed the better part of the establishment's opposition to the activities of CRP's Jewish desk. Combined with the intense personal dislike of Mr. Nixon was the view of many Jewish social action professionals that the President had failed to confront those issues that were of paramount importance in the Jewish mission to accomplish the redemption of the larger society.

This position was neatly summed up by Rabbi Eugene
Borowitz, a professor at the Hebrew Union College-Jewish
Institute of Religion. In an article in *Sh'ma* Borowitz
wrote, "What America needs today is more democracy . . .
without this I do not see America attaining the social stability and maintaining the national power which will permit
us to exercise international leadership."[15] Specifically, Mr.
Nixon was to be rejected because he had not effectively
dealt with civil rights, urban decay, unemployment and
other like issues which had become the litany of universal-
minded Jewish social actionists.

Support for Israel

In his *Sh'ma* article Borowitz also touched on what had
become the single most significant issue of Jewish interest in
the campaign. That issue involved American governmental
support for Israel. Indeed, Nixon's demonstrated support
for the beleaguered Jewish state appeared to be the foundation upon which CRP's Jewish strategy was built. As
Herman Edelsberg had written in his famous letter to Earl
Mazo, Nixon might never be a hero with the Jewish population but "they like what he's doing on Israel and Soviet
Jewry."[16]

It is most interesting to note, however, that candidate
Nixon who promised in 1968 to increase military shipments
to Israel so as to "tip the balance in Israel's favor" was until
mid 1970 at odds with President Nixon who gave every
indication of seeking a Middle East solution not compatible
with Jewish interests. No sooner had Nixon been elected
than he sent former Pennsylvania governor William Scranton to the Middle East as a special envoy. Scranton who
after reaffirming American concern for Israel's security

caused Jewish hackles to rise when he publically called for a "more even handed" U. S. Middle East policy. Scranton concluded that by over-identifying with Israel, the Johnson Administration had undermined American influence with the Arab states. Though Nixon had declared at his first press conference that the Middle East problem would receive attention second only to Vietnam, he did not mention Israel at all in his initial foreign aid message. In February 1969 Nixon startled the Jewish community by announcing that the United States would engage in bilateral and four power talks to achieve a Middle East settlement. Secretary of State Rogers seemed to underline the new American policy by stating that while the Nixon Administration did not intend to impose a settlement, "if the world community should agree on a certain formula," the governments in the area "would want to think long and hard before they turned it down."[17] In late October a detailed American proposal for a draft agreement between Israel and Egypt was submitted to the Soviet Union. This draft, which became known as the "Rogers Plan," was made public on December 9, 1969. The Rogers Plan, which called for Israeli withdrawal from the occupied territories, was a distinct shift from the policy of the Johnson Administration, which had insisted that there could be no return by Israel to the pre-existing boundaries.

The Israel Government reacted sharply to the new American proposal. On December 29 Prime Minister Meir informed the Knesset that adoption of the Rogers Plan would present "a grave threat to our very existence." In an attempt to pressure Israel into acceptance of the new border suggestions, the United States withheld shipments of military hardware including the crucial F-4 Phantom Jet aircraft. Anyone who was active in the Jewish community during the early months of 1970 can well remember the crisis atmosphere that prevailed. A major American Jewish effort was launched to channel public opinion toward a favorable position on the Phantoms. So tenacious was the Nixon commitment to the terms of the Rogers Plan that the President cut off friends and associates who attempted to articulate the Israel argument concerning the necessity of the jets. To fully understand Max Fisher and Rita Hauser's tireless activity on behalf of Nixon, one must realize the depths of despair they had experienced in early 1970.

Fisher's position was especially compromised by the administration's policy of arm twisting the Israelis and the American Jewish community on the border and military assistance questions. The Detroit industrialist was in the unenviable position of trying to straddle two conflicting worlds, and even as astute an individual as Max Fisher could not accomplish this prodigious feat. Fisher increasingly came under fire from Jewish communal leaders and the Anglo-Jewish press who demanded that he use his influence to change the administration's stance. Fisher's dilemma was that he had little if any real influence. In a White House where the President was constantly shielded from members of his own staff, Fisher had almost no opportunity for direct conversation with the Chief Executive. The fast-developing Jewish apprehension over Nixon Middle East policy was a constant source of embarrassment to Fisher, who during much of the winter of 1969–70 was unreachable by telephone on his yacht in the Caribbean.

The June events in the Middle East caused a dramatic turnaround in United States policy. In the first six months of the year, Soviet military involvement intensified. Russian pilots were detected by the Israelis in flight over the Suez Canal and the Sinai. This increased and active Soviet presence in Egyptian affairs posed the threat of a great power confrontation. As a result of the new crisis, the administration's Middle East portfolio was transferred from the State Department to the National Security Council staff. From this setting the considerable expertise of Dr. Henry Kissinger could be utilized to greater advantage. The Soviets then compounded their initial indiscretion by providing Egypt with sophisticated surface-to-air missiles. These weapons were to be deployed in the area bordering on the Suez Canal. This act was regarded by Nixon and Kissinger as a betrayal of an unwritten agreement to ease up on the shipment of advanced military hardware. Nixon reacted to the Soviet moves by agreeing to supply Israel with not only tanks and the Phantoms but also with equipment to neutralize the effect of the missiles. The administration began to stress the need for maintaining the balance of power in the Middle East, an assertion that was interpreted in Jerusalem and New York to mean that Israel would receive the weapons needed to secure her defense.

So great was the impact of the release of the Phantoms that many Jews soon forgot the difficulties encountered by Israel during the initial stages of the Nixon Presidency. Suddenly Nixon became known as a friend of Israel, and Fisher, now off the hook with the Jewish community, began receiving positive responses to his feelers concerning contributions and support for the next Nixon Presidential run. When the preference primary season began in March 1972 many Jews had already decided to vote for the President.

A good proportion of those Jews who still remained in the Democratic camp initially split their support among three U. S. Senators, Edmund Muskie, Hubert Humphrey and Henry Jackson. The considerable Jewish enthusiasm shown the Jackson candidacy appeared to most clearly attest to the importance of Israel as an issue in 1972. The Washington Senator was the staunchest defender of Israel in the upper chamber and in recent months had emerged as the leading proponent of American support for the Soviet Jewish community. Unfortunately for Jackson, his staff did not include an experienced Jewish professional who could exploit the sympathy being expressed for his candidacy at the grass-roots level. I was very much aware of this failing in the Jackson campaign organization during the December 1971 weeks I spent in Florida as an advisor on Protestant middle America. I couldn't help but be interested in the progress of the campaign in the Miami area although I was careful to refrain from active involvement with the Jewish community, since this was not my assignment. The individuals who were charged with winning Jewish votes were simply outclassed by the Humphrey operatives. My non-political travels into several regions of the country in the late winter and early spring of 1972 confirmed the earlier impression that Jackson was perceived by many Jews as the most solid and trustworthy candidate on Israel. I have no doubt that should the Washington Senator choose to make a 1976 race, his candidacy would engender an even greater interest on the part of Jewish voters.

The early failures of both the Jackson and Muskie campaigns acted to focus the bulk of Jewish interest in the effort being made by former Vice-President Humphrey. Indeed, the Jewish voters of California almost pulled the Minnesotan to victory on June 6. However, when Humphrey lost the crucial California Primary by 5 percentage points it was obvious that Senator George McGovern would be the Democratic standard bearer. The McGovern Cinderella story made no group happier than the people who were responsible for CRP's Jewish desk. Of all the potential Democratic candidates, McGovern was the candidate the Republican Jewish strategists most wanted to succeed. By the summer of 1972 several old-line Nixon backers in the Jewish community would have the experience of Taft Schreiber, executive vice-president of the powerful show business conglomerate MCA. As Schreiber told *Time,* "I used to have trouble finding any supporters when I walked into the Hillcrest Country Club [the favorite Jewish fat cat hangout in Los Angeles]. Now it's like everyone has had a revelation. People come rushing up to me and say, 'I just want to tell you how I'm going to vote.'"[18]

McGovern's history of questionable support for Israel, his support of quotas and other policies construed by many Jews as threatening their livelihoods and eventual security, his identification with the new left and his national defense posture rendered him in terms of potential Jewish support the most tenuous Democratic Presidential candidate of the last fifty years. Many careful observers of the Jewish community can recall the sympathy they felt for Richard Cohen when it was announced that the highly competent assistant director of the American Jewish Congress had taken a leave of absence to supervise McGovern's Jewish operation. By the time the unruly Democratic convention ended, all Cohen could hope to do was to hold the Nixon inroad into the Jewish Democratic pattern to a degree where the major states would not fall into the Republican column through the impetus of newly won Jewish votes. This in itself was viewed by many Jewish professionals as an impossible task. It was apparent that Nixon would significantly increase his percentage of the Jewish vote, the only question was by how much.

In addition, the fumbling attempts at communication by

the McGovern Jewish backers were in sharp contrast to the very professional efforts of Lawrence Goldberg, Rita Hauser and Max Fisher. It might be true, as the rumor suggested, that John Mitchell was ordering Mogen David at "21," but even without such acts of heroic self-denial and team play, the Republican message was getting across. This message was simple but highly effective: Stick with Nixon and do not risk a fundamental change in United States policy toward Israel by opting for McGovern.

Israeli Intrusion

The articulation of this message was grealy facilitated by the activities of the Israel Government. The apparent desire of the Israelis to play an active role in the campaign surfaced in early June when Ambassador Yitzhak Rabin told a radio interviewer that President Nixon in his recent Moscow summit had made the strongest commitment to Israel of any American President. Rabin concluded that "Israel should reward men who support it, in deeds rather than words."[19] These comments coming from Israel's highest official in the United States appeared to articulate an official Israel Government endorsement of Nixon. The *Jerusalem Post* in a front-page editorial urged Rabin's recall for remarks which "have been construed as unwarranted interference in American politics,"[20] and many American Jews took less than seriously Prime Minister Meir's disclaimer that "Israel's policy—past, present and future—is never to involve itself in the domestic policies of any country."[21] While Messrs. Fisher and Wexler were delighted with the Rabin statement, the Ambassador's remarks caused intense consternation among American Jews, many of whom would vote in November for Nixon. Albert

Arent, chairman of the National Jewish Community Relations Advisory Council, articulated the growing concern over Israel's interference in the American electoral process in an address to the organization's plenary:

How damaging to Israel's interests it would be if members of either political party became concerned that Israeli officials were trying to influence American Jews in favor of the other party. How disruptive it could be to the united humanitarian efforts of the American Jewish community to raise incredible sums each year for the needs of the people of Israel if Jewish Democrats or Jewish Republicans thought that Israeli officials were undermining their favored candidates for public office.

Thank goodness, in the coming Presidential election, as in all Presidential elections in the past quarter century, all candidates are fully committed to our now traditional national policy in support of Israel: and the sophisticated American Jewish community is fully capable of evaluating the ability and determination of the respective candidates to deal effectively with this issue and with all other issues which concern us as Americans and as Jews.[22]

Rabbi Eugene Borowitz conceded that "the Israelis have a right to indicate which candidate better suits their interests," but concluded that in this instance, "the heavy, unrelenting pressure the Israelis have put on American Jewry to vote for Richard Nixon is utterly inappropriate to the issue and thoroughly demeaning to American Jewry."[23]

This thoughtful analysis provided a needed philosophic corrective to the Israeli activities but could have little impact upon the reality of the situation. There is no question but that the Israeli intrusion in the 1972 election was a distinct help to Richard Nixon. It must be recognized that Rabin's statement and the other Israeli indications of support for Nixon could not, in and of themselves, cause significant numbers of Jews to vote for the President, but the Israeli imprimatur did capitalize on an existent set of circumstances and was for many Jews who were leaning in the Republican direction the final factor that moved them into the Nixon camp.

It is easy to become self-righteous and sermonic over the determined imposition of the Israel Government's views into the American political process. It is important to retain a perspective, and one should avoid the self-serving and intentionally hostile reactions of some in the Jewish and non-Jewish communities to the Israeli stance. But having said this I believe the action of the Israel Government to be unconscionable and self-defeating. Israel put undue strain on the American Jewish community which was forced into issuing disclaimers concerning the importance of the Middle East as an issue in the campaign. Professor Mark Krug of the University of Chicago was correct when he suggested that if a candidate's support for Israel was the only criterion for the Jewish voter, "we will be branded by the American public as parochial, narrow partisans of a foreign state who lack interest in the fate of this country and who in turn do not deserve much public attention."[24] The Israelis with their typical shortsightedness concerning life in the Diaspora, overreacted and gave American anti-Israel forces the opportunity to raise questions concerning dual loyalty and outside influence. In the final analysis, the Israeli imposition in 1972 resulted from a faulty perception of the American scene. For all of their expertise displayed in defense and in their internal political experiences, the

Israelis seemingly cannot understand the inner workings of American society—despite the presence of a galaxy of public relations men and advisors. From a pragmatic standpoint, the overriding fact is that Mr. Nixon simply did not need the assistance of the Israel Government to significantly increase his share of the Jewish vote.

The Israel question was not the only issue that would tax the ingenuity and resourcefulness of McGovern's Jewish advocates. Their candidate's stand on quotas, income distribution and law and order would have likely precipitated a Jewish move toward Nixon even if the Israel issue did not exist. One of the first pledges made by McGovern after the convention (which in itself was the product of a quota system) was to say he would appoint women, blacks and chicanos, to his cabinet, the Supreme Court and other Federal offices in proportion to their percentage of the general population. This pledge was actually a reaffirmation of an earlier statement made during a meeting in San Francisco in the fall of 1971. There McGovern had been hard pressed by a black listener to indicate what measures he would adopt to increase black representation in government.

McGovern's plans for increasing "minority" employment opportunities were rightly construed as an attack on the merit system of appointment. Jews, who in the American context had fought for over one hundred years to break down the system of negative quotas, saw their jobs and promotion rights achieved through competitive examinations and seniority put in jeopardy. Where would the quota system, in which a man's rights depended on the group he belonged to and the relative size of that group, leave American Jews who number about 3 per cent of the population?

The McGovern quota position was particularly galling

to the Jewish communal organizations who had in an earlier period fervently supported civil rights legislation. These groups now advocated that government and private industry should adopt affirmative action programs to enable blacks to move into the mainstream. Such programs involved remedial education, job training and special recruitment techniques. The introduction of quotas would take the society far beyond the aims desired through affirmative action. Jews were well aware of what the quota system could do. To cite just one example, if the McGovern quota-based guidelines employed at the Democratic National Convention were applied to the general society, there would never again be a Jew on the United States Supreme Court. The McGovern position on quotas was to many Jews symptomatic of his basic outlook, which appeared to be grounded in the new political left. In recent years it was this faction that had mounted a determined attack upon those traditional American values and institutions that facilitated Jewish advancement.

McGovern's income redistribution plan would also have an adverse affect upon the Jewish community. Though there are about 800,000 American Jews at the poverty level, Jews probably have the highest average income of any American ethnic group. The net effect of McGovern's program would have been to redistribute income away from the Jewish community. On the issue of law and order McGovern appeared to again reflect the new left position of being soft on the criminal and explaining away his behavior in often torturous sociological terms. To the 87 per cent of the Jewish population who live in cities of a quarter of a million people and larger, the rise in crime had a special impact. These Jews were as frightened and nervous about violence as any other ethnic group. Their leaders might assign them a position above the urban battleground, but many Jewish city dwellers would take Irving Louis Horowitz' advice:

> It behooves the Jews to be at least as candid as the rest of the American middle class and ethnic working class and not make believe that they are making voting decisions on the basis of abstract foreign policies, the substance of which they are as ignorant of as the rest of the American population, rather than concrete street-level deviance, the substance of which they are as knowledgeable of as the rest of the American population.[25]

For those Jews who were deeply troubled by crime and who had demanded—as in East Flatbush and Crown Heights, Brooklyn—increased police protection, the obvious candidate was Mr. Nixon.

Kosher and a Glass of Milk

In addition to opposition to McGovern based on his international and domestic positions another level of hostility was at work in the Jewish psyche. McGovern was too much the outsider. He represented the type of WASP who never had expressed a genuine interest in understanding what it meant to be Jewish. On one of his first campaign visits to New York City he stopped at a hot dog stand. "Kosher?" asked the counterman. McGovern looked blankly at his guide, Queens Democratic boss Matthew Troy. "Kosher," Troy whispered. "Kosher and a glass of milk," said McGovern.[26]

One might argue that McGovern's unfamiliarity with Jewish culture was to be expected. After all he came from a state with less than six hundred Jewish residents. But there were also few blacks and chicanos in South Dakota, and he seemed to have little trouble understanding and articulating their concerns.

McGovern's all-consuming self-righteousness, his predilection to preach, his diffuse and effete social gospelism, rendered him a remote figure to many Jews. There was little of the *mensch* in him. I also believe the comportment of his followers at the Democratic convention turned some Jewish voters off. The media-oriented posturing of Friedan and Stenheim, Jackson and Singer, Chavez and Abernathy, the long hairs, the slick, extra-size lapel-suited aides, the frivolous vote for the Vice-Presidential nominee made for a circuslike atmosphere thoroughly inconsistent with the high degree of seriousness Jews place in the electoral process. McGovern himself in the nationally televised debate with SDS representatives did not look and act like a President. His flowery open-necked sport shirt and his insipid response to the hysterical blandishments of a female SDS member simply did not fit the image of the Chief Executive held by many Jews and other Americans. The SDS confrontation in the Fontainebleau Hotel lobby and the several political and ethnic minority-group conflicts on the floor of the Convention Center seemed to prefigure the shape and character of the McGovern administration. What McGovern and his staff would never realize and what the major Jewish agencies were having a terrible time comprehending was the apprehension of conservative values by an increasing number of Jews. In 1972 Jews would vote in more substantial numbers for Richard Nixon than had seemed possible only a few years before. Jews had become, as Nathan Glazer and Daniel Moynihan suggest, "far more aware of conservative working class values, which they always practiced but refused to celebrate."[27] In doing so they would join in the new political coalition keyed to the traditional American middle-class virtues of religion, family, morality and patriotism. To these Jews the American Dream with its promise of success through sacrifice and hard work was worthy of retention even if it meant crossing long held political lines.

On November 7, 1972, almost three times as many Jews voted for Richard Nixon as voted for him in 1968. This staggering reversal of a fifty-year pattern in Jewish voting habit became the almost immediate subject of a raging controversy within the Jewish community. Predictably, several major organizations such as the National Jewish Community Relations Advisory Council and the Union of American Hebrew Congregations attempted to minimize the effect of the Jewish vote for Nixon. The NJCRAC in a report prepared for the January 28, 1973, meeting of its executive committee called the shift in the Jewish vote an accident—"an aberration attributable to the fact that many Jews, like many of their non-Jewish fellow citizens, were simply uncomfortable and uneasy about George McGovern."[28] The report while stating that "it may be too soon to make a sound judgment" (if anything it was too late) concluded:

the shift to Nixon does not represent any major long-term trend, nor any swing by Jews toward economic conservatism or away from a basic and traditional commitment to economic and social justice of the kind represented by the Roosevelt-Truman-Stevenson-Kennedy-Humphrey-Johnson tradition.[29]

The UAHC, in a memorandum prepared by Marvin Braiterman, director of the organization's Washington-based Religious Action Center, would demonstrate "that the widespread notion of Jewish abandonment of ethical concern and social liberalism is a myth."[30] This would be accomplished by the employment of a device utilized by both pro- and anti-Nixon forces, the precinct analysis of the Jewish vote. It must be understood that in the winter of 1972 every Jewish commentator had his favorite Jewish precincts. Thus, while some Jewish areas gave McGovern only 52–54 majorities, the UAHC with the help of NBC was able to find "selected Jewish voting areas" that "developed an aggregate Jewish vote for McGovern of 63 per cent." Braiterman could even find a precinct in the overwhelmingly Jewish section of South Miami Beach that scored over 67 per cent for McGovern. The fact that the UAHC analyst could not come up with too many other like examples was probably the reason behind his caveat that "the best way of polling for various kinds of voter classification is *not* by precinct, but by a *survey of voters at the polls immediately after they emerge after voting.*" Such polling might "indicate that the Jewish vote for McGovern was substantially higher than the figures coming out of sample precincts would indicate." This device was needed by Braiterman to explain "the deficiencies of precinct analysis which may account for some sample Jewish precincts that showed, even for 1972, an uncharacteristically high Nixon vote." The problem that the NJCRAC, the UAHC and other establishment organizations faced was centered in the 40 per cent of the Jewish vote received by Nixon. This striking reality would lead Marvin Braiterman to make the following preposterous and self-deceptive observation:

Over-all, the Jewish supporters of McGovern claim an overwhelming Jewish victory despite the shrinkage—a 60 to 63% Jewish vote for McGovern, after all is said and done, is a larger "landslide" for McGovern among American Jews than was the Nixon landslide in the election as a whole.[31]

The establishment's rush to assure itself that Jews still worshipped at the shrine of liberalism and remained transfixed by the pantheon of yesterday's heroes, inhibited these bodies from recognizing both the immediate and long-range implications of the Jewish vote for Nixon. Nixon ran best among middle and lower middle-class Jews and in neighborhoods that had experienced racial tension. He also did remarkably well in Michigan where busing, an issue fraught with racial overtones, was predominant and in Ohio where race vied for Jewish attention with international issues and the state of the economy. Nixon's ideological inroads into the Jewish community were revealed by his strong vote among Orthodox and Conservative Jews. Nixon ran up an incredible margin of 75 per cent of the Jewish vote in the Hasidic sections of Williamsburg and Crown Heights, Brooklyn.

The Ice Has Been Broken

These results provide evidence that in the future significant numbers of Jews will react in terms of self-interest on problematic issues. After 1972 no serious politician, the Jewish establishment notwithstanding, can afford to take Jewish voters for granted. As the Nixon partisan Victor Lasky points out, "the ice has been broken. Jewish hands did not fall off when they pulled Republican levers in the polling booths." Next time around voting for a Nixon-type candidate will not be a traumatic experience.[32]

Nevertheless, Jews must take stock of their political position in America. There is little doubt that Jewish representation in the House of Representatives will show a decline over the next decade due to the shift in urban population. Jews, along with other identifiable groups, are in an increasing manner leaving the cities to settle in the surrounding suburbs. Heretofore, Jews lived in distinct neighborhoods and exercised electoral control over several House seats. This is especially true in Brooklyn, Queens and in certain areas of Chicago. In Brooklyn, the Thirteenth and Sixteenth Congressional districts have sent Jews to Congress for over fifty years. The Sixteenth District, which was served by Emanuel Cellar for most of this period and is now represented by Elizabeth Holtzman, will likely have a black majority before 1978. Jews moving out of the Sixteenth and other like districts will be diffused in the suburban setting and simply will not have the capacity to automatically elect one of their co-religionists. While some may argue that it is narrow and parochial for Jews to be concerned about losing political representation, I would suggest that a continuing drop in the number of Jews in Congress will have a negative impact upon issues of particular concern to the Jewish community. Each specific group in America requires advocates who are experientially as well as philosophically familiar with its life style, aspirations and problems.

Of more serious impact to the Jewish community is the possibility that a McGovern-type candidate will win the Presidency in 1976. Many of the new left liberals and radical churchmen, who have been shut out of the White House and excluded from any semblance of influence during the Nixon years, may again surface in a liberal Democratic administration. There are already signs that mainline Protestant bureaucrats are prepared to support a liberal-oriented candidate in the hope that success in the 1976 election will propel them into positions of consequence in a new administration. Some of these officials exude an air of confidence that a McGovern-type candidate will prevail in the next presidential contest.

The Jewish community should be alerted to the potential deleterious effects of such a return to influence by liberal churchmen. To recall recent events, one can only wonder how the United States would have reacted to the Soviet arms build-up during the Yom Kippur war if George McGovern had been President. A similar question could be asked as to how McGovern would have viewed the Soviet intention to unilaterally send troops to police a cease-fire. There is little doubt in my mind that the liberal Protestant establishment close to McGovern would have moved heaven and earth to inhibit a positive U.S. reaction to Israel's plight. In the light of the history of the past twenty-five years, one can safely conclude that there will be another Middle East crisis before the end of the decade. American Jews should begin to give careful thought to who they would want to be resident in the White House should such a circumstance occur. Similarly, Jews must, on the basis of liberal disinterest in the domestic Jewish agendas, recognize that a McGovern-type candidate will likely not have any genuine feel for issues of concern to the Jewish community.

I believe the circumstances of the 1976 presidential race will make necessary the most careful and soul-searching electoral analysis ever undertaken by American Jews. I fully expect and strongly hope there will be a "Jewish vote" when the nation elects a new Chief Executive.

VII

SURVIVAL IN AMERICA

Jewish Identity

The question of identity is perhaps the most important of the many problems that at any given time concern the Jewish community. From the biblical period to the present Jews have wrestled with the problem of self-identification. More often than not the desire to fully define and comprehend what it means to be Jewish has been left unsatisfied. Although Jewish legal tradition emphatically states that one is a Jew if he is born of a Jewish mother, a perennial argument rages over the definition of what constitutes a Jew. Thus, while orthodox Jews would insist on the halachic definition, other Jews would describe their Jewishness in terms of peoplehood, adherence to a particular set of ethical principles and values and identification with specific cultural patterns.

The question of Jewish identification has also been influenced by outside forces and events. Even a cursory examination of Jewish history indicates that Jews have often been hard pressed to maintain their distinctiveness as a people. In pre-Christian times Jews who left Palestine encountered cultures that encompassed religious, ethical and cultural values far different from those developed in the Hebrew nation. The powerful pull toward assimilation and absorption was evidenced by the ready adoption by Jews of Greek modes in the Hellenistic period. The coming of Christianity presented a new and more dangerous challenge to Jewish continuity.

The nascent Christian church saw itself not only as the agent of salvation for the pagan world but also as the successor to Judaism. Indeed, the earliest Christian missionary activities were in large part directed specifically toward the Jewish community. The gospel was to be extended from Jerusalem to Judea to the entire known world. When the apostle Paul came to a new city, he would first seek out the Jewish population and attempt to preach in the synagogue and Jewish quarter before turning his attention to the gentile community. The intense efforts of Paul and other early church officials to win the Jews over to Christianity were marked by failure. Perhaps due to their disappointment over Jewish resistance or because of an inherent triumphalism, Christian teachers and authorities, specifically the Greek and Latin church fathers, developed a theory that suggested that the continued existence of Judaism was a scandal to Christianity.

After the fourth century and the political triumph of Christianity, the continued presence of Judaism as a religious faith was an especially bitter pill for the Church to swallow. From this period canonical legislation began to be marked by a series of measures aimed at restricting Jewish religious life and in general inhibiting normal social and economic interchange between Jews and Christians.[1]

In addition to the difficulties imposed by legal action, Jews were also psychologically battered by the growing tendency within Christendom to regard them as God killers who were assigned by divine fiat to endure the role of outcasts and wanderers. When one considers the disabilities Jews suffered under and the tentative nature of their existence in any nation at almost any given period up to the French Revolution, the very survival of Jewishness was a near miracle. The simple fact is that for the mainstream of Jews, those who were either not extremely wealthy (and very few were) or extremely inward in philosophic approach, life was at best quite difficult. Many Jews were baptized either forcefully at the hands of others or voluntarily as a result of reflection on the unpromising future awaiting them and their children. Others who could not make this radical move were gradually absorbed into the larger Christian-oriented society.

The French Revolution, while providing a respite from the oppressive conditions under which Jews were forced to live, further aided the disintegration of Jewish community by providing opportunity for assimilation. The removal of social and economic barriers brought Jews into close contact with the non-Jewish world. In addition, the philosophical underpinning to the Revolution suggested a new vision of fraternity and equality which would act to break down the divisions that tended to separate varying groups of people. The tension between particularism and universalism implied in this new and enticing world view would continue until the present to disturb Jewish life. Prior to the French Revolution outside pressures made Jewishness a liability, after the Revolution, enlightened minds had to struggle with retaining their Jewishness at the expense of newly won freedoms and the vision of a society where distinctions would be eventually eradicated. Jewish identification was, to an increasing number of individuals, a negative phenomenon which one either completely disavowed or compromised with.

In the American setting, despite the presence of covert, and at times overt, manifestations of anti-Semitism, Jews have had unprecedented opportunities to dilute or drastically alter their religious and group affiliation. The American climate seemed especially conducive to absorption and assimilation. The almost hallowed beliefs of the immigrant generation concerning America as the melting pot also made for a breakdown in allegiance to what were considered old-fashioned and even undemocratic group identifications. The American Jewish community, eager to please the gentile majority and thoroughly taken with a political system that allowed Jews greater freedom than ever before experienced in any nation, made a special effort to integrate into the American mainstream. Many of the cautions exercised by Jews in other lands regarding adaptation were discarded in the American setting.

The American Path

America was a land of promise where one could look to the future with hope and not despair, a nation where one could be a Jew and yet share in all of the benefits of society. That is, of course, if one's Jewishness was not too noticeable in dress and demeanor or too rigid in belief and practice. In many regions of the United States, Jews took special pains to blend in with the surrounding culture. Even today there are Jews, particularly in the South, who would probably be more at home in a social sense in the Episcopal church than in the Temple or Synagogue. To be sure, there were those Jews, particularly in the largest cities, who clung to an inward-oriented life style based on the Eastern European experience. However, most of these individuals could not expect to travel the American path of upward socioeconomic mobility. There were, of course, some strong Jewish identifiers who did achieve considerable success in business or in the professions, but such persons tended to build their fortunes or reputations in close proximity to the Jewish community. The canons of social acceptability in America demanded that the individual adopt the prevailing mores developed and codified by the majority community. The drive for acceptance might necessitate a name change, cosmetic surgery, new speech patterns, a shift in neighborhoods or even estrangement from parents and family. For the greater part of Jewish experience in America, Jewish identity was thus interpreted in negative terms.

The American way did not allow for group identity of solidarity. This foundational principle was suggested during World War I by the quintessential WASP President Woodrow Wilson. "There are no minorities in the United States. There are no national minorities, racial minorities, or religious minorities. The whole concept and basis of the United States precludes them."[2] A similar articulation of this theme was evident in an article written by Dorothy Thompson for the predominately Jewish readership of *Commentary*

You cannot become true Americans if you think of yourself in groups. America does not consist of groups. A man who thinks of himself as belonging to a particular national group in America has not become American, and the man who goes among you to trade upon your nationality is not worthy to live under the Stars and Stripes.[3]

There will be, of course, many persons today who marvel at the *Chutzpah* of Miss Thompson's admonition, but the fact remains that in terms of identity Jews have struggled with the tension inherent in a democratic society for almost all of the history of their experience in America. A graph projection of Jewish life in the twentieth century would show many shifts in the identity curve. In the period between the two World Wars overt anti-Semitism was a common phenomenon in America. Jews were discriminated against in housing and employment and were subject to an unofficial quota system in the universities and professional schools. During this period over one hundred and twenty anti-Semitic organizations were active in the United States. This was also the era when millions of Americans faithfully listened to Father Charles Coughlin's anti-Jewish radio tirades. As the Second World War approached, Jews were blamed by isolationists for plotting to bring the United States into the European hostilities. That the Jews were fair game during these years is illustrated in an editorial which appeared in the *New York Daily News:*

> The Bill of Rights means only that our government shall not officially discriminate against any religion. It does *not* mean that Americans are forbidden to dislike other Americans or religions or any other group. Plenty of people, just now are exercising their right to dislike the Jews.[4]

Not Melting Pot but Orchestra

As the war drew near the stigma attached to Jewishness undoubtedly motivated many persons to opt out of the organized Jewish community. At the same time some individuals came under the influence of a new theory of group life in America first expounded by Horace Kallen and his intellectual mentor Henry James. This thesis suggested that rather than being viewed as a melting pot, America should be regarded as an orchestra of diverse cultures. This ideological position, known as cultural pluralism, would allow members of racial, ethnic and religious minorities to retain particularities common to the specific group while acting as contributive members of the general society.

Although the tenets of cultural pluralism enabled numbers of Jews to shift their sense of Jewish identification from negative to neutral it remained for World War II and its aftermath to provide the impetus for individuals to confront their Jewishness in a new and more positive context.

The Holocaust and the dramatic founding of the State of Israel had a most profound impact upon the American Jewish community. From the Holocaust one learned that Jewish identification could not easily be shed even through conversion and assimilation. The National Socialist regime fully intended to track down every last person on the continent who had a Jewish ancestry. The Jewish tragedy in Europe also elicited feelings of guilt and self-recrimination among many American Jews who realized that only the accident of birth in the United States had enabled them to escape the fate of their brethren in Europe. If it had heretofore been difficult for American Jews to understand that there was indeed something unique in Jewish identification, the Holocaust enabled many persons to confront the specificity of Jewishness. The establishment of Israel as a free and democratic nation allowed all but the most ardent anti-Zionist Jews to take pride and satisfaction in the return to the national homeland. Israel's success in transforming the land into a setting conducive to the development of a viable social and economic state and her achievements on the field of military encounter further intensified the new sense of positive Jewish identification.

Ironically, this sense of positiveness has led to the development of a new and troubling complication to the problem of Jewish identity in America. An increasing number of Jews exhibit anxiety over the extent and degree of their Jewishness. Many Jews, perhaps due to comparison with the Israelis, feel inadequate for the task of being assertively Jewish. Earl Raab, executive director of the San Francisco Jewish Community Relations Council, describes a meeting where an Israeli told a large American Jewish gathering that it was "weak, incompetent and probably doomed." The members of the audience greeted this statement with wild applause. On the basis of this reaction Raab concludes that: "Many American Jews may still commonly suffer from something called self-hatred but these days they more commonly hate themselves not because they are Jews, but because they consider themselves *inferior* Jews."[5]

Undoubtedly many Jews feel especially inferior to the Israelis. Ever since the founding of the State, but particularly in the period following the June war, the Israeli experience has acted to set the pattern for Jewish life in other nations. This emulation factor can lead to endless group and personal frustration. The American Jewish organizations for all their resources, professional expertise and public relations competence can hardly develop policy and conduct programs commensurate with that of a sovereign state. The American Jewish establishment will always be limited in terms of options, potential strategy, and tactics and realizable goals. Despite a pronounced penchant for involvement with decision makers at the highest levels of government, the Jewish establishment cannot conduct foreign affairs and must fight its battles with press releases rather than Phantom jets.

Similarly, in the personal sphere most American Jewish grandmothers, even those from Milwaukee, can never equal Golda Meir, the majority of middle-age Jewish men would not look sexy wearing an eyepatch, and even the most attractive American Jewish young women suffer by comparison with a smartly dressed female member of the Israeli defense forces. If Jewishness is to be defined in accordance with Israeli standards, then the American Jewish community faces an impossible task in attempting to develop a more intensive positive Jewish identification. Raab's inferior Jews cannot find the answer to their sense of inadequacy by seeking to replicate the Israeli Jewish experience. It should be readily apparent to anyone who gives even a second thought to the situation that the Israelis live in a much different context than their American brethren. Factors such as anti-Semitism, intermarriage, absorption and assimilation into a majority culture, which have traditionally made for a weakening in positive Jewish identity, are totally irrelevant in the Israeli milieu.

The American Jew in search of identity can neither look to Israel nor to other Diaspora nations for a role model. To be sure, he may gain strength and encouragement from the positive experiences of Jews in other societies, but he can resolve his personal and group dilemma only within the framework of Jewish life in America. This is why the many youth-oriented programs that attempt to duplicate the Israeli experience in America are doomed to failure.

It is foolish and patently self-defeating to expect that a society that is highly tentative and still in a development stage can provide answers to the problem of continuity facing the American Jewish community. Also, if the Israel experience can be so instructive and instrumental in building positive Jewish identification in America, why is it that the overwhelming majority of American Jews of all ages and socioeconomic and religious backgrounds simply are not interested in pulling up stakes and permanently settling in Israel. Israelis, and there are many of them, who criticize the American Jewish community and stridently predict its soon demise make no contribution toward a solution of the identity problem. In the light of the tensions in the relationship between Israel and American Jewry and the many serious internal issues that trouble Israeli life, it would be better for all concerned if representatives of the Israel Government and other "spokesmen" exercised circumspection in their evaluations of American Jewish life.

Intermarriage

The increasing incidence of intermarriage presents one of the most serious challenges to Jewish continuity in America. For several years Jewish religious authorities as well as communal leaders and social scientists have called attention to the extreme severity of the problem. In 1968 the Rabbinical Council of America declared that intermarriage has reached "catastrophic proportions" among Jewish college youth.[6] Rabbi Pesach Levovitz, a former official of the Orthodox organization, urged Jewish religious leaders to use their influence to stem the tide of marriages between Jews and non-Jews. Rabbi Levovitz claimed that Jews who marry Christians "disappear" into the Christian religious and cultural community.[7] In the same vein, Rabbi Judah Nadich, an outstanding leader of the Conservative movement, warned in 1970 that the survival of Judaism in the United States was seriously threatened by the accelerating degree of intermarriage.[8] In April 1973 a major blow against mixed marriages involving Jews was struck when the Central Conference of American Jews, co-ordinating body for the Reform rabbinate, voted to oppose intermarriage.[9] This action was especially noteworthy in the light of the fact that heretofore a significant minority of Reform rabbis had officiated at mixed marriages.

The CCAR resolution came just weeks after the New York Board of Rabbis, the nation's largest rabbinical body, heard its president, William Berkowitz, assert that marriage between Jews and non-Jews endangers "Jewish survival."[10] The Board at an uproarious session narrowly defeated a move to bar rabbis who perform intermarriages from membership in the organization. At about the same time the Rabbinical Council of America announced a policy aimed at "the elimination from leadership roles in Jewish public life of all those who marry out of their faith." In accordance with this position, the Council's President, Rabbi Louis Bernstein, declared that his organization would oppose the appointment to office of any lay or rabbinic leader "who violates these rules in any of the organizations with which the Rabbinical Council is affiliated."[11] This foreshadowed a potentially serious split in Jewish communal ranks since the RCA is a constituent member of several major umbrella organizations including the Synagogue Council of America, the Chaplaincy Division of National Jewish Welfare Board and the Joint Advisory Committee of the National Jewish Community Relations Advisory Council. In support of the RCA move, Rabbi Bernstein asserted that mixed marriages "have become so grave a peril" to Jewish survival in America, "that drastic measures must be taken."[12] If the Rabbinical Council's position were to be adopted by the National agencies and in local communities, the ranks of Jewish leadership would be severely depleted. No one, of course, expects such a development to occur, and it is certain that the communal bodies would prefer an orthodox walkout to the unhappy prospect of chopping heads on the basis of an individual's marital situation. Yet the fact that such an extreme measure could even be rationally suggested and discussed indicates the sense of frustration and concern that intermarriage has elicited in the Jewish community.

A recent study conducted for the Council of Jewish Federations and Welfare Funds has apparently confirmed the worst fears of those concerned with the phenomenon of Jewish intermarriage. The study found that the rate of intermarriage among Jews reached 48.1 per cent during the period 1966–72.[13] This represents a dramatic rise from earlier figures which placed intermarriage among Jews at 13 per cent in 1960 and at 29.7 per cent in the years 1961–65.[14] The CJFWF survey compiled data based on approximately seven thousand interviews conducted throughout the United States. The CJFWF findings are especially distressing in the light of earlier studies which indicated that in at least 70 per cent of mixed marriages involving a Jewish partner, the children of the union were not identified with the Jewish community.

A further discordant note lies in the declining Jewish birthrate in the United States. Milton Himmelfarb, director of research for the American Jewish Committee, considers the low Jewish birth rate to be the single greatest threat to Jewish survival in America.[15] In support of this argument, Himmelfarb, himself the father of seven children, points to projections that suggest that in the not too distant future there simply will no longer be a significant Jewish component in America. Compounding the low birth rate factor is the absence of the possibility of large-scale Jewish emigration to the United States in either the present moment or foreseeable future. The only important segment of world Jewry who wish to emigrate today reside in the Soviet Union. The hundreds of thousands of Russian Jews who wish to leave the U.S.S.R., provided an implacable government will grant them permission to do so, will in all likelihood journey to Israel rather than to the United States or other Western nations. This would be the case even if restrictive American immigration laws could be changed or circumvented.

If the fact that Jews are intermarrying at a greater rate than ever before is statistically obvious, the reasons behind this phenomenon are varied and complex. Most contemporary Jews are far removed in time, status and attitude from the immigrant generations. The social, cultural and religious bonds that tied the immigrants together have through the influence of American civilization become loosened. There has also been a pronounced diminution in the power of religious tradition to influence the acts of American Jews, particularly young Jews. The prevailing spirit of the age is eclectic and ecumenical, and barriers to communication and direct contact between individuals of differing backgrounds have come down. Edward Fiske, religion editor of *The New York Times,* points out that the very concept of intermarriage has won growing acceptance within the American context.[16] Gentile parents are less likely to be as unalterably opposed to intermarriage as their predecessors who often fought a mixed marriage even more vociferously than their Jewish counterparts.

Jewish young people who a generation or two ago would have been totally anathema to prospective Roman Catholic or Protestant in-laws are today more acceptable if not entirely welcomed into the bosom of the family. The breakdown in parental authority is surely another factor in the ready adaption of parents to the reality of mixed marriage involving their children. The willingness of many Jews to drop Jewish affiliations and their ready acquiescence to demands that the children of the union be raised in the non-Jewish faith has also contributed to greater acceptance of intermarriage by the non-Jewish partner. There are also deep-seated personal causes for intermarriage.

Dr. Mortimer Ostow, a practicing psychiatrist and chairman of the New York Federation's task force on Mental Health and Judaism believes that many Jews enter into mixed marriages because of compulsion stemming from severe emotional problems.[17] Dr. Ostow cites three categories of mixed marriages—marrying down, marrying up and marrying across. An individual marrying down, chooses a partner who is "clearly unsuitable because of lower social status, inferior background or both." The person who marries down usually "betrays a fairly severe personality disorder," is plagued by low self-esteem and feels that he "cannot live up to the high standard imposed by his parents and the Jewish community." The Jew who marries up prefers a union with a non-Jew of higher social status. Marrying up enables the individual who feels excluded from parental intimacy and the aristocracy of the Jewish community to take revenge by "stepping up in the social scale of the broader community." The Jew who marries up often will be more sensitive to anti-Semitism than others because he attributes his rejection to being Jewish rather than to being "personally objectionable." Marrying across, represents less of an emotional disorder than marrying up or down. Here there is seldom any attempt to reject Jewish values, indeed the non-Jewish partner is expected to embrace Judaism. Dr. Ostow claims that an increasing number of mixed marriages involving Jews, fall into the marrying across category. This has occurred because of an effort by young Jews to "overcome the central isolation which is created by living in the Jewish community and which is part of the phenomenon of being Jewish." The non-Jew takes on the fascination of the stranger for the Jewish young person. Intermarriage on this basis has increased in proportion to the breakdown in the internal cohesiveness of the Jewish community.

Whatever the motivation for intermarriage involving Jews, a recent study seems to dash earlier expectations that by imposing religious conditions Jewish continuity would not necessarily be vitiated by a mixed marriage. Thus, in the past Reform rabbis have often demanded that the partners in a mixed union must agree to establish a Jewish home and raise their children as Jews. The survey conducted by Rabbi Marc Raphael focused on members of 114 mixed marriages solemnized by rabbis in Los Angeles between June and September 1970.[18] Rabbi Raphael found that after one year of marriage 111 of the 114 couples claimed the same religious affiliation as at the time of the marriage. Less than one third of the couples attended a synagogue on either High Holy Day. Similarly, less than one fifth attended a synagogue on any other occasion during the year and only fourteen couples attended a synagogue on both a High Holy Day and one other occasion. Even more discouraging was the finding that a majority of the couples attended a church service on at least two occasions during the year. Likewise, more couples exchanged presents on Christmas than on Chanukah. At Passover not one couple conducted a Seder in their home, although thirty-seven couples attended a Seder somewhere else. This finding was not terribly reassuring in the light of the fact that more than half the couples spent part of Easter Sunday in church. In his analysis of the data Rabbi Raphael noted that some observers "will fall back on the hope that things may improve after children are born and demands for choosing a religious tradition for the children increase."

However, the findings of another study by Rabbi Raphael suggest that this is an unlikely occurrence. Of the children of thirteen Columbus, Ohio, area mixed marriages, only one currently attends a synagogue religious school while four are in church schools and six express either indifference or indecision regarding religious education. Rabbi Raphael does hold out some hope for those couples who have extensive experiences such as counseling sessions, adult study classes, worship attendance and visits to the officiating rabbi's home prior to the marriage. He claims that "the relationship between exposure to Jewish experiences before and after the wedding seem quite suggestive." Thus, while promises to the rabbi by couples seeking his services for marriage "are meaningless, participating in Jewish life immediately prior to an intermarriage is more likely than not to encourage Jewish experiences immediately after the marriage." Rabbi Raphael concludes for the officiating rabbi to demand any less, "is to commit Jewish suicide."

While intermarriage continues to raise Jewish hackles, it must be noted that the Council of Jewish Federations and Welfare Funds survey, which statistically described the rapid rise in mixed marriages involving Jews, also found that there appears to be less difference than previously believed between the attitudes and behavior of Jews who intermarry and those who marry other Jews. In an analysis of the study, George E. Johnson, research director of the Institute for Jewish Policy Planning and Research, stated "intermarrying and non-intermarrying Jews alike, to a great extent, have already assimilated and that identifying oneself as 'Jewish' is increasingly less meaningful."[19] In terms of Jewish men, the likelihood of intermarriage was 55.1 per cent among those whose Jewish background was minimal compared with only 2.5 per cent who had a strong Jewish foundation. The implications for Jewish continuity are obvious. As Johnson concludes, "If intermarriage is viewed as the outgrowth of leaving the fold rather than the essence of it, then one can better focus on the need to inform parents of their crucial role in the transmission of Jewish behavior and values."[20]

The enormous problem created by intermarriage cannot be solved by education alone or through the creation of task forces or by the purge of intermarried Jewish communal leaders. What is necessary is a change in the prevailing Jewish attitude concerning the manner in which Jews are perceived in the general society. There continues in America a Jewish fear of being different. The universalistic liberal position with which so many American Jews identify does not allow for particularity and distinctiveness.

Jewish leaders realize that intermarriage will, if not checked in the next several years, mean the disintegration of the Jewish community, yet the major communal organizations will not directly speak to the mixed marriage menace. To do so would be to confuse the non-Jewish liberal establishment, which likes its Jews to be of the Amos and Micah variety rather than the Moses type.

The Jewish establishment must somehow summon the courage to speak out directly and forcefully against intermarriage. What is also required is a program to provide the rationale and means for encouragement of marriages between Jewish partners. This does not suggest an emotional or nostalgic articulation of the life style of the Jewish home or the often asserted dominant role of the Jewish mother. The urgent need for Jewish marriage must be keyed to the realities and demands of life in contemporary society.

A systematic, co-ordinated and well-funded effort, involving all the pertinent major national and community agencies, aimed at enriching the quality of Jewish marriage and developing positive role models for prospective marriage partners should be immediately launched. This initiative should be geared to all age levels and could begin with preschool-age children. In conjunction with this campaign, a program should be developed to interpret Jewish objections to intermarriage to the non-Jewish community. This activity need not be defensive in nature but should stress the vital need for Jewish continuity and the positive contributions Jewish marriage can make to the survival of Jewish experience in America.

The Young People

Today's college-age Jewish person has been greatly influenced by the events and forces of the last decade. The civil rights revolution, the war in Vietnam, political assassinations, urban violence, the environmental crisis and the general trend toward dehumanization in America, have combined to create doubt in students' minds concerning the viability of liberal institutions. This disillusionment with the secular order has carried over into a growing impatience with and alienation from the Jewish communal institutions. These organizations are increasingly regarded by young people as faceless, unfeeling, amorphous bureaucracies, incapable of comprehending the basic needs and aspirations of youth.

Some Jewish young people focus their dissatisfaction with the organized community in what they regard as the failure of the major institutions to effectively grapple with the social problems confronting American society. These young people view the major Jewish organizations as being "socially irrelevant to the issues of life and death in our time." The following description of the feelings of such young people concerning the religious institutions offered by Dr. Albert Jospe, an official of the B'nai B'rith Hillel Foundations, would surely conform to opinions viewed by young people concerning the communal structure as a whole:

> They turn their backs on the Jewish community because they have the uneasy feeling that our Synagogues are all too frequently economically conservative, that they are fearful of social change, that they pay lip service to social ideals but shy away from redemptive action and that they are preoccupied with trivialities and irrelevancies at a time when they ought to be more relevant than ever and speak out courageously on the issues.[21]

Another observer suggests that these young people cannot align themselves with Jewish organizational life because in doing so they would be "compelled to choose between Jewishness and concern for mankind." Such young Jews tend to be universalistic in approach and criticize the major agencies for not taking a more aggressive Jewish-oriented prophetic stance vis-à-vis black-Jewish relations, busing to achieve racial integration, the continued American presence in Southeast Asia and the Watergate aftermath. Some of the universalistic-oriented young people worked in the Presidential campaign of Senator George McGovern in the belief that the McGovern effort represented a last-ditch attempt to restore liberal values to the position they had once occupied in America. Other universally minded Jewish youth form a small but militant faction in support of radical movements and causes ranging from the Patet Lao and Vietcong, to the Tupammaros and, not surprisingly, to the Palestinian guerrillas. Some of these individuals engage in selling Al Fatah stamps and in disseminating literature that characterizes Israel as a racist, establishment-supported state.

It would be a serious miscalculation, however, to suggest that the majority of Jewish students currently manifest significant interest in the political and social spheres. The fact is that many students are passive and even indifferent, a situation that also pertains to life on the campus, much to the relief of administrators. In the 1960s, social critic Dorothy Rabinowitz could write, "When the history of the last decade's campus imbroglios has finally been written, it will be an inadequate historian indeed who does not take into account the curiously large role assigned to the Jews."[22] However it is quite likely that this observation will not apply to the Jewish student generation of the mid and late 1970s. As early as 1971, Hillel Foundation directors reported that Jewish students had dropped the confrontation tactics employed so ardently if not successfully in the late 1960s. The Hillel staff asserted that many Jewish students had turned to "mystical quests for personal salvation" and were resisting the "air of fraternalism" associated with the synagogue and establishment of religious organizations.[23]

The reaction of the Jewish communal organizations to the disaffection expressed by Jewish youth has been quite predictable both in terms of diagnosis and suggested treatment. Some commentators view alienation as stemming from a failure of Jewish education to nurture youth in traditional Judaism, or call attention to the negative influence of the new left and political radicalism or blame parents and teachers for permissiveness or talk of the failure of the suburban synagogue which is "too closely associated by youth with the caterer and not with Judaic ethics and values" or suggest that the traditional role of the institutional bodies in fighting anti-Semitism and providing social services is not correctly understood by youth.

The treatment prescribed by the various Jewish organizations to deal with alienation involves "reordering priorities," "crash programs," the use of "experimental" religious services, the establishment of "networks of institutions for youth" where they could enter into dialogue with distinguished Jewish authorities, meeting youth "where they are at," creating "task forces" to visit campuses, energizing cadres of scholars to develop "lines of communication" with Jewish youth on campus. There are, of course, other suggested devices, but I leave it to the reader to complete the remainder of the blanks. The intended recipients of this largesse generally react with skepticism to the press conferences and publications that announce the inception of such programs. The students are wise enough to know that in the first instance the adoption of new programmatic approaches usually either creates new jobs for Jewish professionals or provides security for those individuals who were about to be terminated for lack of productive assignment. The students also realize that the mere impression given by a major agency that a new youth-oriented program exists has important fund-raising implications. As with so many other phenomena, the appearance of a program is often more important than the reality. Indeed, it may be more profitable to announce a new program and gain financial support for it rather than follow through in terms of execution. Many such "paper" programs exist within the Jewish communal world and will continue to do so until the stockholders more closely scrutinize the actual operation of the organizations they support. This is not to say that young people knowledgeable in the way of Jewish institutions will not accept funds and other material assistance connected with youth-related programs from these bodies. They will and do and no one should be surprised to learn that positive results often accrue from such arrangements.

The basic point, however, is that the present student generation understands that the Jewish establishment will not and really as currently situated cannot fundamentally change. Press releases and symposia aside, there will be no major breakthroughs facilitated by the communal institutions in alleviating the problem of alienation so long as power and decision-making responsibility continues to be wielded by affluent middle-aged and older individuals. There exists in the Jewish community a profound generation gap that is rooted in differences in life style, political outlook, sexual mores and religious commitment. One may of course believe that this situation will be redressed as today's young person becomes tomorrow's adult. This may prove to be true insofar as the current crop of college-age persons is concerned, but what of today's teen-agers and sub-teens? On the basis of the inadequate communal response to alienation among this generation can one really expect that the situation will be different five, ten or twenty years from now? Recent evidence concerning the experiences of young people "converted" to the Lubavitcher Hasidic movement paradoxically suggests that the deeper any alienated young person from a non-observant or low-identifier background gets into Jewishness, the greater problem he will have in relating to his family. Some of the young devotees of the Lubavitcher have been described by their parents and friends as being too Jewish. A young man who became active in the Lubavitch-sponsored Chabad house at UCLA described this parental reaction to his new sense of Jewishness:

My becoming *so* Jewish bugs my parents, especially my mother, and I'm glad! They're all a bunch of phonies and they know we know it! I don't want any part of that Temple stuff, where my mother's always running to meetings and my dad falls asleep! These Chabad guys aren't hypocrites and I'll buy their bag. It's making me do a lot of thinking about this Jew bit, and that's good.[24]

The Chavurah or Fellowship Movement

The Lubavitch situation points to that side of the Jewish alienation question that suggests that for an increasing number of young Jews the problem of alienation is not related to their Jewishness but rather to their disaffection from the institutional establishment. It is more than ironic that at exactly the time the Jewish organizations were manifesting alarm and chagrin at the alienation of youth an impressive number of Jewish young people were coming together to search out the possibility of developing new forms in which their Jewishness could be expressed and intensified.

In a 1971 study prepared by Rabbi Oscar Groner for the Hillel Foundation, a new type of "ethnically conscious and committed" Jewish college youth was identified as emerging.[25] These Jews were strongly anti-establishment but firmly assertive about their Judaism. One of the most striking developments emanating from this new type of Jewish student was the appearance of the Chavurah or fellowship movement. The Chavurah is organized on or close by a college or university campus. Its members include undergraduates, graduate students and individuals who had recently attended school but for the moment have opted out of the formal educational setting. The typical Chavurah has from ten to thirty members and is characterized by communal cooking and cleaning assignments. The goal of the

Chavurah is to foster Jewishness in accordance to the manner in which that concept was understood by the particular group or each individual member. Not all Chavurot are alike. Some are explicitly Zionist and *aliyah* oriented; others are committed to enriching the life experience of Jews in the Diaspora. Some Chavurot contain only observant youth while others are quite heterogeneous with a membership running the gamut from atheist to Hasid. Jon Groner, a member of the Beit Ephraim Chavurah at Columbia University describes the motivations behind Chavurah membership:

It is impossible to generalize about our motivations for forming a Chavurah. Some came primarily to feel comfortable observing *mitzvot,* others primarily to learn, others to improve Jewish life on campus. Beyond all this, however, is an unspoken root feeling which none of us can express or needs to express. We are longing for a home. We feel instinctively that being Jewish is not something you do in a synagogue or a Jewish organization or even a classroom. We want to be *haimish,* not out of a vaguely counter-cultural striving for authenticity but out of a desire to experience Judaism as it was meant to be experienced. We are no longer adapting the form of another culture, but returning to one of our own. It's hard to light *Shabbat* candles or compose a creative service or have a Talmud *shiyur* (lesson) in a dormitory room; some of us have tried. Our *bayit* is a place where nothing Jewish is alien.[26]

The initial experiences of two Chavurot, one in New York City the other in Chapel Hill, North Carolina, are instructive in allowing one to catch a glimpse of this new form of

Jewish communitarianism. The New York Chavurah was formed by a group of young people who originally came together at a conference sponsored by the World Union of Jewish Students to determine whether a radical Jewish community in America was in the embryonic stage.[27] These individuals did not find a definitive answer to the question but did experience a growing sense of community as they continued meeting in the months following the conference. Their initial sessions were devoted to an exploration of the possibility of creating a community-living project, but these discussions had no tangible result. Then an event occurred which crystalized for the group the need to come together in a communal setting. The event centered around a day of prayer, study, song and fellowship spent in the chapel of the Jewish Theological Seminary to express solidarity with Burton Weiss, a draft resister. The fact that Weiss, who had sought sanctuary in the chapel, was arrested by Federal authorities, did not dampen the sense of community generated by the experience of being together for a common purpose.

The Chapel Hill Chavurah[28] had its beginnings in a series of discussions among a group of five students who expressed a common need to better work out the Jewishness that had been "profoundly instilled within us since childhood." This Chavurah felt a special need to raise the level of Jewish consciousness on a campus where Jewish students were in a distinct minority. The Chavurah has formed a kosher co-op and has been instrumental in having a course in modern Hebrew established at the University of North Carolina.

The Chavurah movement as might be expected has its critics. One of the most articulate of these is Rabbi Wolfe Kelman, executive vice-president of the conservative aligned, Rabbinical Assembly. Rabbi Kelman offered this evaluation of the Chavurot in *Conservative Judaism:*

> This observer tends to believe that the significance of the Chavurot has been highly exaggerated, partly by the need of some Jews to convince themselves that like the Church, Judaism has also produced radical dissenters. I am inclined to suggest that this artificially inflated dimension of the youth culture will prove to be a passing fad remembered nostalgically by those who are easily seduced by slogans and fashions which promise instant eschatology, and by schools where students and teachers are interchangeable, love is God, and the greening of America is inevitable.[29]

James Sleeper, co-author of *The New Jews* and a member of the Havaruth Shalom of Boston, asserts that the involvement of the Chavurah in youth culture is not an end in itself but a means toward directing young people into an intensified Jewish experience. According to Sleeper, Chavurah members "embrace youth culture in order to transform it" and are thus "excellent meeting points between the young and the tradition."[30]

Other critics suggest that the Chavurah serve only to further shatter the already disunited Jewish community. Bill Novak, an early Chavurah devotee dismisses this criticism with the argument that the Chavurah cannot fragment the Jewish community any more than it is currently divided. On the contrary, he says, "the new movements in Jewish life are actually bringing together various alienated segments of American Jewish life."[31] Jon Groner would likely answer the charge of fragmentation by stating that the Chavurah is not intended to replace an existing structure with a new institutional device. Rather, the Chavurah provides a variety of experiences, some highly meaningful, some mundane, which will shape and encourage the individual member's Jewishness long after he has left college.

> What we, and many other *chavurah* members, will take with us will be the spirit and the feeling of the community rather than its day-to-day details. A moving *Shabbat* service, an exciting late-night rap session, a solid study group, a house-cleaning for *Pesach*—these will serve as guideposts for our future Jewish existence. On this level—by influencing and inspiring individuals, not by remaking our communal structures—the *chavurah* movement will have its effect on American Jewry.[32]

George Johnson, of the Institute for Jewish Policy Planning and Research, enlarges on this theme in an analytic critique of the Chavurah movement:

> These young Jews are consciously looking for a life style that will take them through life—not just through college. As this self-consciousness of young Jews builds they will want to continue to express it wherever they live. They will want close, tightly knit, communities, rather than huge synagogues. They will want to study in small groups—and will prefer to pay for three teaching rabbis, rather than for one administratively overburdened rabbi and a huge, highly mortgaged building. They will weave their Jewishness into the fabric of their lives, rather than saving it for a few days a year, and will define it in terms of knowledge and behavior, rather than through organizational programs, lox and bagels, and fund raising drives.[33]

A less sympathetic critique comes from Jon Levenson, a Harvard graduate student:

There is more to American Jewry than can be served by small conventicles of mystics, all in their twenties, huddling in proximity to major universities. There comes a time when graduate school must end, when Daddy (inevitably an establishment Jew) stops footing the bill, and when the contradiction of *chasidim* without a *rebbe* becomes too painful to ignore any longer. In short, the Jewish counter-culture is a desirable protest against the easy conscience and genteel agnosticism of our contemporary Jewish in-stitutions, but it cannot be the basis for an enduring community.[34]

These criticisms notwithstanding, it is probably too early to assess the long-range significance of the Chavurot. The move toward Jewish communitarianism came at the time when much of the campus unrest of the 1960s was reced-ing. At the end of that decade young people, fatigued by the constant tensions, marches, petition campaigns, and demonstrations of the period and frustrated over their failure to make a dent in the armor of establishment in-transigence, turned inward and became preoccupied with self rather than with the major societal issues. For some Jewish young people this meant a headlong plunge into the drug culture; for others it led to a search for transcendental reality. In the late 1960s and early '70s it was not uncom-mon to find that the bulk of the latest "in" Eastern guru's followers were young Jews. Even today a good share of the disciples of the sixteen-year-old "perfect master" are Jewish, and it is safe to predict that the next teacher who suddenly appears from the hinterlands of India or Burma will be assured of a significant number of Jewish supporters. Other students not taken by the OM chants of Hare Krishna or other forms of Eastern "truth" opted for the Jesus movement. The Jews for Jesus owes its origin to the initial surge of Jewish student interest in the Jesus trip. The individuals who initiated the Chavurah movement were contemporaries of these students who looked to ideologies and practices foreign to Judaism as a *raison d'être* for life in a complex and troubled time. In the light of the many recent defections from Judaism, the Chavurah movement should have been welcomed if only because its practitioners remained within the Jewish camp. Much of the early establishment criticism directed at the Chavurot was in the form of an unthinking reflex action which responded to what appeared to be a challenge to traditional institutions. To an important degree these criticisms exacerbated the situation and intensified the desire of the persons involved in the Chavurot to go it alone outside of any existent organized structure. As a result, the Jewish community lost a marvelous opportunity to relate to and learn from a new and dynamic form. The stilted and defensive response of the establishment was predictable and testified to the American Jewish community's inherent fear of losing control of its young people. In a perverse way the individuals involved in the Chavurot were more of a threat to the organized Jewish community than those young people who had completely defected to Maharishi and Jesus.

In the last two years, however, some Jewish leaders have begun to discern value in the Chavurah movement. Dr. Gerson D. Cohen, chancellor of the Jewish Theological Seminary, in an apparent reference to the Chavurot has said:

. . . young people today are in the vanguard, leading their elders in a common search for religious roots. The elders have sensed from time to time that elements in some of our services or in some of our communal institutions are out of step with our time. But it is our young people who have had the courage to remind us that some of these forms were merely habits, and that re-examination of classical tradition might reveal forms more relevant to our immediate needs.[35]

It should be noted that Dr. Cohen, who made this remark to a group of conservative lay leaders, tried to assign credit for the creative achievements of the young people to activities related to the Jewish Theological Seminary. Dr. Cohen's claim raises the specter of co-option, and it may be that the major Jewish institutions will attempt to buy in to the Chavurot movement in the near future. It is likely that the will and determination of the Chavurim to "do their own thing" will be severely tested over the coming months. The greatest problem facing the movement is haphazard growth. Without proper planning and safeguards the Chavurot may find themselves in the position of having to appeal to the major institutions for funding and personnel services. This could be disastrous to the ongoing need for experimentation and innovation within the Jewish community.

It must also be added that even if the Chavurot are able to survive on a more or less permanent basis, they will only attract a limited audience of Jewish youth. The great bulk of Jewish young people will remain outside the intimate confines of a communal fellowship and will only marginally identify with the synagogue or other organized communal structure. The Jewish establishment has not evidenced the capacity to successfully deal with the aspirations, demands and confusions of Jewish youth and there is little likelihood that a drastic change in this pattern is forthcoming. The major organizations appear to echo the parental hope that the "kids" will eventually come to their senses and shape up into responsible adults. In the majority of cases this expectation will probably be realized. However, the tendency of some of the ablest Jewish youth to opt out of the community on the one hand and to engage in radical social and political activity on the other hand, should give pause to those parents and organizations who are concerned with the role of youth in preserving Jewish continuity.

Jewish Studies

One of the more interesting developments of recent Jewish life has been the remarkable growth of programs of Jewish studies in American institutions of higher learning. A recently published catalogue of Jewish Studies in American Colleges and Universities lists 324 colleges in the United States offering at least one course in Judaica.[36] The same report mentions forty schools with undergraduate majors and twenty-five institutions with graduate programs in Jewish studies. This represents a dramatic increase from the period prior to World War II when only a few colleges and universities offered course work in Judaica. It should be noted that much of this increase has come in the last five years.

There are of course a variety of factors that account for the rise of interest in Jewish studies. Edward Fiske, religion editor of *The New York Times* suggests that the proliferation of courses in Judaica stems from a new openness to Jews resulting from the climate created by Vatican Council II and the victory of Israel in the Six Day war.[37]

University administrators, who heretofore had only regarded Jewish history as a backdrop for comprehension of
Christianity, now began to accept Jewish experience as a
legitimate area for academic inquiry. Dr. Albert Jospe, an
official of the Hillel Foundation, cites the Holocaust and
the founding and development of Israel as catalysts in gen-
erating Jewish self-awareness and self-assertion.[38] This
new wave of self-understanding came just at the time
when Jews had substantially increased their college enrollment and were in general more visible than ever before
in the general society. Also helping the acceptance of
Judaica as a college and university area of study was the
trend toward specialized regional and area studies. In this
regard the introduction of black studies into the curriculum
had a major influence on the adoption of courses and
academic departments of Judaica. One should not be so
naïve, however, to imagine that administrators took it
upon themselves to foster the growth of Jewish studies.
In almost every instance the introduction and deepening
of Jewish study programs resulted from the active efforts
of Jewish students and faculty members.

The pattern of Jewish studies varies widely. Many institutions have full-scale Judaica departments. At Ohio
State and the University of Texas, students may earn a
doctorate in Jewish studies. At other institutions the approach is interdepartmental. Columbia offers Jewish courses
in the departments of history, linguistics, religion, Near
Eastern studies and sociology. The University of California at Berkeley offers an undergraduate major in the
department of Near Eastern languages, a Jewish studies
major in religious studies, courses in Hebrew literature in
the department of comparative literature and a graduate
program in Hebrew studies in the department of Near
Eastern languages. Dr. Jospe reports that the funds for

the support of Jewish studies come from several sources. About two thirds of the support comes from the institutional budgets; others are funded by Jewish agencies such as the B'nai B'rith, Hillel Foundation, the American Jewish Committee and the Hebrew Culture Foundation. At present there are ten fully endowed chairs of Judaica in American institutions. In addition to these sources, support for Jewish studies comes in directly from the Jewish Chautauqua Society and the National Foundation for Jewish Culture who underwrite individual courses taught by rabbis and visiting scholars.

The field of Judaica is rapidly becoming organized. Uniform standards and procedures are currently being developed and an academic guild, the Association for Jewish Studies, was formed about five years ago. The American Association for Jewish Education publishes a model curriculum and bibliographies to assist administrators of public institutions in setting up Judaica programs.

As recent critiques of black studies programs have indicated, there are philosophic problems involved in the development of specialized courses in Judaica. The basic problem revolves around the question as to whether such programs will tend to isolate the Jewish student from his immediate institutional environment and thereby inhibit him from having the opportunity to interact with peers representing different backgrounds and viewpoints. Some critics of Jewish studies argue that the seminaries and other specialized institutions of Jewish education rather than the public institutions are the proper setting for Jewish studies. Some observers fear an overemphasis on Jewish life and experience in the public institutions will eventually have a negative impact upon the manner in which the non-Jewish majority views the Jewish community. These critics generally oppose all public expressions of Jewish distinc-

tiveness. Other commentators question what vocational opportunities will be open to the increasing number of graduates with Judaica majors. There is already a dearth of
positions available in academia, and recent retrenchments
in the communal organizations (even if many of this current generation of young people would consider working
within the establishment) give little encouragement that a
significant number of positions will be available in the
Jewish bureaucracy. It is obvious that young people with
majors in Jewish studies are not going to be able to compete in the general job market with Jewish peers who have
prepared for careers in business, government and the professions. A recent study issued by the Bureau of Labor
Statistics indicated that even highly qualified young Jews
will experience "relatively greater" job-hunting difficulties
in the 1970s. Herbert Bienstock, New York regional director of the Bureau urged Jewish youth to give serious
consideration to the areas of non-professional employment.
Bienstock also called upon the Jewish organizations to place
more emphasis on vocational guidance and "attitudinal re-
conditioning particularly in terms of value structures relating to non-professional opportunities."[39]

If Bienstock's prognosis is valid, and there is firm evidence to indicate that it is, the Jewish agencies currently
funding Jewish study programs at institutions of higher
learning should probably re-evaluate their support. There
is, of course, no harm and perhaps even benefit in individual Judaica courses, but serious consequences may
result from an acceleration of Jewish study majors at both
the undergraduate and graduate level. One can simply
have too much of a good thing. There are already growing
signs that the rabbinical training centers are turning out
too many students for too few available pulpits. The Jewish
community, which understandably hailed the interest in

Jewish studies as a panacea for alienation and the problem of continuity, must diligently and systematically confront the probability that an increased emphasis on Jewish studies will lead to frustration and bitterness on the part of students who emerge from the cocoon of Judaica to find that there is no viable market for their knowledge. For the Jewish organizations to do less than recognize this unhappy circumstance would be to exacerbate an already explosive situation.

An apparently concomitant development to the growth of programs in Judaica has been the emergence of "Free Jewish Universities" at a number of colleges and universities during the last few years. Many of the same factors that resulted in the establishment of Jewish studies within the curriculum of public institutions have been at work in the development of the free universities. Jewish self-awareness stemming from the Holocaust, the experience of Israel and the growing tendency in America toward ethnic identification and the searching out of one's roots have all contributed to the establishment of educational forms outside of the official jurisdiction of the colleges and universities.

The free university provides the opportunity for a less-structured setting and gives the students a role in determining the curriculum. The free university is thus student-centered in that it assigns him the primary role in decision making. One of the strengths of the free university is that it offers courses not contained in the regular university curriculum. Another strength is the opportunity it affords the Jewish faculty member to serve as a role model for students. The free universities have also provided the opportunity for the Jewish academician to apply his secular expertise in a Jewish setting. As might be expected, course format and content differ from situation to situation. The

Free University of Judaica at the State University of New York in Albany has offered courses in "Jews and Revolution," "Roots of the Middle East Conflict," "History of East European Jewry," "Radical Jewish Experience," "Jews and Pacifism." The curriculum of the Free University at the University of Iowa has included, "The Jew and the Black," "Judaism and History—A Dissenting Voice," "Jewish Identity in Transition." The tendency for the curriculum to reflect contemporary concerns is also evident in the following courses offered at the Free University of Judaic Studies at Boston University: "On the Disillusion of Self," "Judaism and the Counterculture," "The Art of Godmanship." The last-mentioned course is subtitled "Approaches to the Holocaust" and consists of readings and discussions based on "Wiesel, Fackenheim, Camus, Rubenstein, Schwarz-Bart, Alan Watts, and some Hasidic masters." The open-ended nature of the free university has enabled it to be utilized for the development of weekend study programs, institutes and other learning experiences normally unavailable within the college or university structure. Dr. Albert Jospe, who along with colleagues at the Hillel Foundations actively involved with the Free Universities, notes the strengths of the movement:

They involve the student in activities that reflect many of his interests which are not met by the traditional university curriculum, in a setting independent of what is rightly or wrongly considered the "establishment." They challenge him to assume responsibility for his own education and involve him in the planning, administration and sometimes even in the teaching aspect of the program. And they involve faculty members as significant models of Jewish knowledge and commitment.[40]

On the other hand, Dr. Jospe lists several of the risks and dangers inherent in the Free University setting,

> . . . many students, in their zeal and enthusiasm, may set up Free Universities in which instructors may not have adequate academic qualifications, standards of instruction may be unprofessional and even dilettantish, few readings are required or expected, students attend not with a measure or regularity but as the mood dictates; and the constantly emphasized quest for "relevance" threatens to degenerate into a few bull sessions on current events.[41]

The very lack of structure or centralized authority may also lessen the potential positive impact of the free universities. The fact that there are no attendance requirements means that only student interest and sense of responsibility and the quality of the instructor's presentation can keep a particular class together. There is also the possibility that some students will neglect their regular university course work in favor of the free university offerings.

The proliferation of Jewish studies, the introduction of free Jewish universities, and the formation of Chavurot give evidence of a new and in some ways dramatic interest in Jewishness by college-age Jews. In large measure this has been a spontaneous development in the sense that it evolves from historical events and social forces rather than through the conscious and systematic efforts of the Jewish communal bodies. That such a development could occur testifies not only to the capacity of youth for growth and change but also to the turgidity and sterility of the major communal institutions. The organized Jewish community faces the challenge of either coming to terms with the new and diverse turn of Jewish youth or eventually fading from the active scene as internal and external forces combine to erode its power base and *raison d'être*.

Education

During the late 1960s many Jewish professionals regarded Jewish education as the *sine qua non* in the struggle against the growing alienation and disaffection of young people. The panacea of education was constantly raised in conferences and colloquia despite the fact that it was during this very period that enrollments in Jewish religious schools were already well into a precipitous decline. Today as one travels the convention circuit it becomes clear that in terms of Jewish continuity, more contributions are hoped for and results are expected from Jewish education than from any other institutional arm of the Jewish community. The unhappy reality is that Jewish education is in a state of almost complete disarray.

A questionnaire distributed by the American Association for Jewish Education to administrators elicited the following causal factors which help to account for the drastic decline in Jewish religious school enrollment: Fewer young couples in the community, reduced Jewish birth rate, lack of parental interest, Jewish population movement to the suburbs.[42] It is interesting to note that the composition of the curriculum and the quality of instruction, obviously important factors to parents and students, do not appear in this list.

At one time Jews sent their young people to religious schools out of instinct for the preservation of the species or because they saw education as a useful tool in the encounter with anti-Semitism.

Today the great majority of young people who do attend religious school are there for one reason, to prepare for Bar or Bat Mitzvah. Once they have reached this milestone, few young people continue their religious education. The parents who have agonized over their children dropping out before the age of thirteen or fourteen usually have neither the strength, patience or desire to urge their offspring to remain in the religious school.

Despite the numerous calls for "crash programs" and the formation of seemingly endless task forces to consider the crisis in Jewish education, not a great deal has actually been accomplished in recent years to upgrade the quality of Jewish religious education. Jewish teachers in relation to public school peers continue to be underpaid, have fewer fringe benefits and are given less inducement to undertake advanced training. Many teachers in the afternoon schools hold two jobs, a situation often encouraged and in some cases arranged for by the school officials. School personnel also quite generally suffer from a lack of security, and few individuals outside of supervisors have pension rights. There are, to be sure, variations in the normally bleak pattern of Jewish religious education. Several educators such as Dr. Lawrence Myers of San Diego and Rabbi Fred Eisenberg of Cleveland are involved in exciting and creative projects. But the bulk of the afternoon and once-a-week educational settings are characterized by the problems elucidated by Rabbi Irving Greenberg:

We must reckon [with] student and teacher latenesses and absences; the ballet lesson and dentist appointments that receive first priority; the host of distractions and interruptions . . . the fact that [such schools] are generally of marginal concern to rabbis upon whom congregations place . . . a host of other rabbinical obligations . . . the frequent lack of commitment of teachers and administrators . . . the frequent absence of standardized and/or properly evaluated curricula . . .[43]

In view of the serious deficiencies manifested by the afternoon and once-a-week religious schools it is not surprising to learn that there has been a remarkable growth in the Jewish day school movement over the past decade. In 1960 there were 237 such institutions in operation in the United States; by 1972 this figure had climbed to 372.[44] While Jewish day schools continue to be a large-city phenomenon (the New York metropolitan area has two thirds of the 75,000-member day school student population), there are at present day schools in all but eight communities with a Jewish population of 5,000 or more. The greatest number of day schools are Orthodox in orientation, but there is a growing segment of Conservative schools, and in the last few years the Reform movement—long an implacable foe of Jewish day schools—has organized several such schools of its own.

There are several factors that account for the growth of the day school movement. We have already mentioned the weakness and relative ineffectiveness of the afternoon and once-a-week schools to provide young people with a solid Jewish foundation. In addition, the Jewish day school is regarded by many suburban-oriented parents as a counterpart to the secular or Christian "country" day school or prep school. This factor has been described by Milton Himmelfarb as the "trading-up" aspect of day schools. Also the Jewish day school is viewed by parents who are concerned with the crisis in Jewish continuity as having the best potential for instilling in their children a positive sense of Jewish identity. Finally, the rapid rise in the number of day schools is also due to parental dissatisfaction with the public schools. To an enlarging group of Jewish parents the Jewish day school is a viable alternative to public education. In this connection it should also be noted that the growth of Jewish day schools has to some degree been related to the urban crisis and the racial revolution. In some communities, particularly the larger cities, Jewish parents are fearful for the safety of their children. An acceleration in incidents of a violent nature and the omnipresence of drugs in many junior high and high schools has frightened Jewish parents and caused more of them to enroll their offspring in a private setting. The controversial and difficult issue of busing has also aided the expansion of the Jewish day school movement. This especially pertains to medium-size cities where busing has become a fact of educational life. Nashville, Tennessee, provides the best illustration of how busing has affected Jewish day school enrollment. Prior to the advent of busing the lone Jewish day school in Nashville struggled to keep its doors open. When plans for busing were announced by city officials, the Jewish day school was flooded with applications. Some blacks and their sympathizers in the Jewish community were quick to direct the charge of racism at the Jewish parents who decided to remove their children from the public schools. There is, of course, the possibility that these assertions were correct, but it also may be true that the Jewish parents, acting in similar fashion to white and black peers, were disturbed by the distances children were forced to travel to achieve racial integration of the schools. In any case, the introduction of busing had immediate impact upon the Jewish day school in Nashville, and evidence from several other communities indicates a similar pattern at work.

David Singer in a concise *Commentary* article identifies the several types of contemporary Jewish day schools. The first and most common are the traditional yeshivas. These institutions, which account for about 35 per cent of day schools serving Orthodox constituencies, are basically past-oriented. The student is taught to master the classical Jewish texts. The language of instruction, though, is either Yiddish or English since Hebrew as a holy tongue is not suitable for such a mundane purpose. The other common form of Orthodox day school is modern in its pedagogical approach. This school attempts to teach Torah in conjunction with secular knowledge. Singer notes that while this is the educational ideal, it still awaits "translation into reality." This is due to a failure of the modern Orthodox school to inform the student how he may serve God in his chosen calling. Thus, while the student is encouraged to excel in general studies, he is also made conscious of the fact that his role model should be the *Lamdan* or master of classical Jewish sources. Singer observes that many graduates of these schools experience guilt feelings and lead lives "as accomplished, religious observant secularists." The phenomenon of guilt is similar to feelings engendered in the traditional Roman Catholic and fundamentalist-oriented Protestant day school. The dichotomy in the Orthodox day school between the sacred and the secular is quite striking. The school day is divided into two time segments with the morning devoted to the traditional Jewish curriculum and the afternoon given over to general subjects.

The Conservative day school system (named after the great savant Solomon Schecter) puts less stress on the mastery of Jewish texts and more emphasis on the comprehension of essential Jewish values. Whereas the Orthodox school struggles with the problem of how to come to grips with general studies, its Conservative counterpart has difficulty in determining what constitutes ideal Jewishness. Singer suggests that the Conservative philosophy of "tradition and change" results in confusion in the student's mind as to the purpose of Jewish studies. He cites as an example the situation that pertains in one New York City Schecter school where "Bible is taught by an instructor who makes frequent use of the findings of modern biblical criticism, while Talmud is taught by a rabbi who regards the Jewish legal tradition as binding."

In contrast to the day school authorities who claim their institutions can instill Jewish consciousness, Singer is not very sanguine about the importance of the day school as a factor in Jewish continuity. He states, "It is not so much a question of whether or not the day school is able to shape attitudes, but rather whether its influence is powerful enough to counteract the apathetic Jewish environment the student encounters outside the classroom, particularly at home."

Many of the same critiques directed at Jewish studies and the Chavurot movement could, concerning the danger of inwardness and isolation, also apply to the day schools. Whether or not these criticisms are ultimately valid, the proponents of day schools should give serious thought to the manner in which the movement has developed over the past decade. The Topsy-like growth of these institutions is due more to external pressure and internal anxiety than to a belief or commitment on the part of parents that day schools represent the best possible or even practicable educational experience for their children. As with so many other Jewish reactions to contemporary problems, the recent response to the day school has been characterized by impulsiveness rather than systematic thought. The long-range danger is that the major organizations will jump on the day school bandwagon because it appears to be the wave of the present. The several approbative consultations on the day school movement sponsored in recent months by the establishment organizations give evidence that the national agencies are already appropriating turf upon which angels should normally fear to tread.

A sign of the times can be read in a recent comment of Dr. Alvin Schiff, consultant to the Jewish Education Committee of New York. Dr. Schiff described the Jewish day school as "the most effective instrument for transmitting the Jewish heritage to our youth."[45] Another educator, Dr. Isaac Toubin, executive director of the American Association for Jewish Education, perhaps with a more realistic conception of what education can accomplish says: "It is illusory and frustrating to expect that Jewish education alone can preserve the old or help create a new Jewish community in America."[46]

Religion

It will come as little surprise to anyone acquainted with contemporary Jewish religious experience to learn that organized Judaism in America is in serious trouble. The major religious institutions are under constant attack for their lack of relevance, their outmoded administrative machinery, their failure to come to grips with new trends and movements (such as women's liberation) and their inability to attract and hold young people.

In recent years the religious bodies have not been powerful enough to counter the onslaughts of intermarriage, the Jesus movement, the lure of Eastern cults, secularism, and the overwhelming sense of boredom, apathy and frustration that seem to characterize the religious response of significant numbers of young and middle-aged Jews.

A growing number of critics, both from within and without the religious establishments have called attention to the failings of the synagogue, the rabbinate and the national religious organizations. Rabbi Levi Olan of Dallas, a former president of the Central Conference of American Rabbis, declared that the steadily declining influence of the synagogue is due to its having become "secularly motivated" with the rabbi relegated to the role of an "institutional functionary."[47] A study panel organized by the Union of American Hebrew Congregations asserted that the synagogue is playing the role of a "service station" that simply dispenses rites and ceremonies instead of providing a sense of Jewish community.[48] Writing in the respected quarterly *Judaism,* Michael P. Lerner, a philosophy professor at the University of Washington, expressed his distaste for the religious establishment in these terms:

Anyone who is familiar with the internal politics of the United Synagogue, the Union of American Hebrew Congregations, the Synagogue Council of America, etc., knows that they are sewers which allow of no significant reform. The demands of the Jewish radical must be: Shut down the synagogues so that Judaism may have a chance.[49]

Rabbi Hershel Matt in an article in *Conservative Judaism* described the failure of the synagogue to come to terms with:

. . . the reality of Jewish life today that multitudes of Jews are outside the synagogue and multitudes of those nominally inside the synagogue consider themselves to be outside its authority and discipline . . .[50]

Dr. Charles Liebman, a noted Orthodox scholar in a study of rabbinical education concluded that Jewish seminary training does not seek to make rabbis or their message relevant to modern man. Dr. Liebman also registered doubt as to whether many congregants would be receptive to their rabbi speaking relevantly. On the basis of his data, Dr. Liebman also found that the three major Jewish seminaries in the United States have failed to develop an image of what the American Jewish society should be.[51] Rabbi Joachim Prinz, chairman of the governing council of the World Jewish Congress warned in 1973 that spiritual Judaism in America is headed for extinction. Rabbi Prinz suggested that intermarriage, the preoccupation of American Jewry with Israel and the diminution of "liberal tradition" could lead to the disappearance of American Jewry in two generations.[52]

Rabbi Philip Schecter, an articulate advocate of alternatives in Judaism, has deplored the "spiritual vacuum in Judaism which leads to the neglect of individuals and to spiritual hunger."[53] Rabbi Murray Saltzman, of the Indianapolis Hebrew Congregation, writes in the *Christian Century* of his "unhappy vision of the 70's . . . that the Jewish people's own internal weakness, compounded by external circumstance, critically threatens a self-image that can sustain them and their Judaic faith."[54]

While some of these criticisms may be overdrawn, this is certainly the case in Professor Lerner's ill-tempered article, they are illustrative of a growing conclusion within the American Jewish community that a serious and perhaps irreparable breakdown of the religious establishment has occurred.

The critical decline in influence and authority of the major religious organizations has enormous implications for the question of Jewish continuity and survival. Rabbi

Hershel J. Matt rightly suggests "though religion is not the basis of Jewish identity, it supplies the basis for understanding that identity." Religion, according to Rabbi Matt, provides the concept of covenant, the Covenant between God and the People Israel. This covenant began with Abraham, was confirmed at Sinai with the giving of the Torah and has always been regarded by Jews as eternal in nature. Rabbi Matt explains the relationship of the covenant to the Jewish people:

Thus, religion is not the definition, but *provides* the definition of the Jews: Jews are those who, normally by descent and occasionally by conversion, are within the Covenant. Sociologically, the Jews remain a puzzle; psychologically, they are a problem; theologically (in conception) and religiously (in existential affirmation) they become a mystery and a miracle: the unique and supernatural—but very real—Covenant People Israel.[55]

The overriding question confronting the religious bodies in their attempt to facilitate Jewish continuity is how to maintain Jews in an existential relationship to the covenant. A search for the answer to this question is complicated by the profound crisis of faith that has characterized much of Jewish religious thought in the period following the Nazi Holocaust. Jewish theological response to the European tragedy ranges from Richard Rubenstein, a Reform rabbi who as a result of the Holocaust can no longer hold to a theistic position,[56] to Rabbi David Hartman, an Orthodox leader, who denies the presence of a religious sign in the Holocaust[57] to Rabbi Joel Teitelbaum, the spiritual leader of the ultra-Orthodox Satmar Hasidic sect, who explains the death of the six million as due punishment for their sin.[58]

A search for religious meaning appears to be taking place among some of the most influential Jewish religious philosophers and authorities. Some individuals within the Orthodox movement are engaged in an attempt to apply Jewish law in a more flexible manner to current personal and social issues such as divorce and marriage and birth control. Rabbi Emanuel Rackman, speaks for the "new left" of orthodoxy when he says:

Orthodoxy sought to guarantee its survival by freezing the *halacha* and its theology. As a result it now cannot realize its full potential in an age when more and more intellectuals are prepared for the leap of faith but hardly for a leap to obscurantism.[59]

While some Orthodox leaders have moved to the left, a number of Reform authorities have shifted to the right on matters concerning observance of the dietary laws and the Sabbath. Reform theologians such as Emil Fackenheim and Jacob J. Petuchowski are using the *halacha* as a basis of criticizing secular cultural values. Rabbi Arnold Jacob Wolf suggests that "Jewish theology is developing its own dynamics for the first time in years. Classical German Reform theology was the Jewish version of German Protestantism. Now we are going back to our own sources."[60] One of the most provocative American Jewish theologians, professor Ellis Rivkin of the Hebrew Union College, sees Jews creating new forms to meet the challenges posed by "the new creativity and the new individuality of man." Dr. Rivkin insists "Jews must create a fresh religious value system for their new age. It should be a feature of Judaism to be the first religion of this new age."[61]

A number of lay people, believing the traditional synagogues to be "sterile" and "depersonalized," have initiated informal communities that feature experimental forms of worship. Rabbi Everett Gendler, who has served as a source person to one such group, describes the motivation of the drop-outs from the organized religious bodies. "Jews like other Americans, are becoming skeptical about the promises of post industrial society and are seeking to re-establish sources of spiritual sustenance. They are finding that there are options in their traditions that have never been fully appreciated."[62]

The major religious institutions are of course making attempts to cope with the developing pattern of alienation and defection. In 1972 Reform and Conservative leaders agreed on an immediate co-operative effort to confront the problems of intermarriage, Jewish education, Jewish identity and the future of the synagogue.[63] This unprecedented national move toward joint program reflected both the feeling of many young people and adults who are not very concerned with theological differences or labels and the ominous fact that establishment of new Conservative and Reform congregations had come to a nearly complete standstill.[64]

One of the most serious challenges to the stability of the religious establishment is the growing uneasiness of Jewish women concerning their role in the life of the synagogue and the Jewish community. In 1972 an organization calling itself *Ezrat Nashim* (with the help of women) composed of Orthodox and Conservative women issued a "Call for Change" that claimed that the Jewish tradition concerning women, which once was far ahead of other cultures, "has now fallen disgracefully behind in failing to come to terms with developments of the past century."[65] The *Ezrat Nashim* manifesto which was presented to the Rabbinical As-

sembly, the collegial body of Conservative rabbis, asked
for full participation by women in religious observances,
and in the synagogue and community decision-making
process. In 1973, perhaps in response to the women's demand, a special committee of the Rabbinical Assembly
voted to permit women to be considered part of the Minyan,
or group of ten persons required by Jewish law for the
conduct of a religious service.[66] This action was sharply
criticized by Orthodox bodies who are struggling to hold
the line against encroachments by women on long-held
male prerogatives. The Orthodox groups also lobbied
against the Equal Rights Amendment on the basis that the
proposed legislation was harmful to morals as well as injurious to the Orthodox Jewish life style.[67] A few women
have broken through to positions of leadership within Judaism, but almost all of these persons are organizationally
related to the Reform and Reconstructionist movements.

The Hasidim

While Reform, Conservative and modern Orthodox Judaism are confronted with increasingly severe problems related to theological position, organizational style, diminution of financial support and alienation of membership,
Hasidism, the fourth major division of American Judaism,
is flourishing. The Hasidic movement was born in Poland
in the eighteenth century. Hasidism aroused a response to
the intellectually narrow religious conservatism that characterized much of organized East European Judaism in the
early modern era. The Hasidic movement originated at a
time of great Jewish misery and suffering and provided the
poverty-stricken and unlettered Jewish masses with a faith
centered in simple piety and mystical delight in nature.
While Hasidism began and developed as a reaction to a

stilted and exclusivist religious world view, it has come to be identified in recent years as a symbol of rigid orthodoxy. The Hasidim consider themselves a group apart from the remainder of Jewish religious bodies who, according to the movement's leaders, have all in one way or another made serious compromises with modernity and secularism. There are several Hasidic groups in the United States, but the two largest, the Satmar and the Lubavitch, dominate Hasidic life in America. The Satmar contingent live mainly in the Williamsburg and Borough Park sections of Brooklyn and represent Hasidism in its most fundamental parochial sense. This group follows the spiritual direction of Rabbi Joel Teitelbaum, who as the Satmar Rebbe has great influence over the daily lives of his constituents.

The Lubavitch sect is significantly different from the Satmar in philosophy and approach. The underlying ideology of the Lubavitch movement can be determined from the acronym "Chabad" which summarizes its three main principles, *chocma* (wisdom), *bina* (intelligence), *deat* (knowledge). Chabad was founded in the latter half of the eighteenth century as a means of reconciling Hasidism with the more intellectual Judaism prevalent at the time. The Lubavitch movement is world-wide in scope, and most of its American devotees dwell in the Crown Heights section of Brooklyn. Lubavitch is led by Rabbi Menachem Mendel Schneerson, a direct descendant of the sect's founder and a graduate of the Sorbonne and the University of Berlin. Like other leaders of Hasidic groups, the Lubavitcher Rebbe is accorded the greatest respect and adoration by his followers. Rabbi Samuel Schrage, a Lubavitch member who has made his mark as a competent official of the Lindsay administration sums up the awe in which Rabbi Schneerson is held, "We regard the Rabbi as a saint, . . . his beliefs are very important."[68]

Unlike almost all other Hasidic groups, the Lubavitch movement actively seeks to win converts among the ranks of secular Jews. To achieve this goal the sect has set up Chabad houses near major university campuses, to play host to Jewish young people seeking a greater understanding of Judaism, and has instituted a Jewish "Peace Corps" to bring American Jews the message that traditional Judaism can and should be their way of life.[69] Peace Corps members travel in pairs and often co-ordinate their activities in a given community with the non-Hasidic religious leadership.

Lubavitch has met with considerable success in motivating Jewish young persons formerly involved with drugs, Eastern religions, left-wing political activity, and in some cases the Jesus movement, to adopt a distinctively Jewish life style. A nineteen-year-old convert to the movement described the change Lubavitch had made in his life in these terms:

My life, if one can call it that, in the past, was drugs, beliefs of the Orient, college dropout. Here at Hadar Hatorah [a movement school located in Brooklyn] is the essence of life—a Jew leading a Jewish way and finds truth, self-respect, purpose and peace in love of Torah.[70]

In listening to accounts of change and renewal articulated by other Hasidic young men and women, I have been struck by the similarity in form if not, of course, in substance, of these testimonies to the stories told by Christian evangelical youth after they have experienced a sense of personal salvation through Jesus. The movement has also been a factor in intensifying the spiritual experiences of Jewish young people who have not opted out of the organized community but who find little substance in the normative religious institutions. In an increasing manner Lubavitch is being called upon by the established organizations to apply its unique approach to the widening universe of alienated Jewish youth.

Lubavitch, with its peculiar blend of emotion, tradition and rationalism has special appeal to young people searching for personal meaning and human values in a complex and difficult period. The movement also provides roots and connection with a Jewish past often neglected by the contemporary and future oriented leaders of the other branches of Judaism. Rabbi Israel Jacobson, the founder and director of Hadar Hatorah underscores the appeal of the movement in this description of his school's aims:

> We have an aim—to re-orient the uprooted and alienated academic Jewish youth, those who have lost contact with our faith, to return them to Torah and genuine Judaism through restored Jewish identity, religious revival, study of our lore, devout prayer, scrupulous practice of the prescribed tenets and conduct of an ethical way of life.[71]

Yet one must not become overly enthusiastic concerning the capacity of the Lubavitch movement to "save" this generation of Jewish youth. In evaluating the ultimate effect of Lubavitch, the question of whether the sect will be able to retain the young people entering its ranks from non-Hasidic backgrounds must be considered.

Traditionally, the Hasidic sects have maintained their identity through the vehicle of the family with religious instruction initiated at the earliest possible age. Rabbi Daniel

Goldstein, an official of the Skvirer Hasidic sect, explains why boys are taught to read the Old Testament at age three. "You start a boy reading the sacred books at the age of three, he doesn't have time for any type of foolishness."[72] But the new devotees have not had the background and long years of training normally identified with Hasidism. What will happen to the typical Lubavitch convert five or ten years after his initial encounter with the movement is quite unpredictable.

It is also true that despite the significant success of Lubavitch, there are multitudes of young Jews to whom Hasidism as well as all other forms of Judaism have no appeal. In the long run, the other major branches of Judaism would seem to have the greatest potential for serving as a catalyst for Jewish identity and continuity. The question remains whether these bodies can adapt themselves to the needs of young and adult Jews who at present find little value in the activities of the organized religious community.

The prognosis for the future of Jewish religion in America is not promising. A recent survey of Reform rabbis found that only one in ten believe in God.[73] One wonders how many of these individuals share the experience of their colleague Richard Rubenstein who has found "ancient earth gods and the realities to which they point extremely meaningful." Rubenstein's gloomy articulation of faith is suggestive of the views undoubtedly held by many within the rabbinate:

It is my faith after Auschwitz that we are children of Earth, that all of us are destined eventually to be consumed by our original progenetrix, that we have nothing to hope for beyond our bodily lives, and that our religions

with their impressive rituals are but the distinctive ways
we share and celebrate a condition entirely enclosed within
the fatalities of an absurd earthly existence.[74]

The Future of the Communal Organizations

The capacity of American Jewry to successfully respond
to its many internal and external problems is seriously
compromised by the loosely knit organizational structure of
the Jewish community.

To fully comprehend the manner in which this structure
operates it is necessary to trace the various stages in the development of American Jewish organizational life. In the
early period the small and relatively homogeneous Jewish
population achieved unity on the local level through a system of congregations. The individual congregation provided all the necessary religious, social and educational
communal services. This system was modified in the mid-
nineteenth century as a greater diversity of population and
multiplicity of congregations resulted from the wave of
Jewish immigration from Central Europe. The final phase
of communal organizational development occurred after
the enormous influx of East European Jews in the early
1900s. Dr. Daniel J. Elazar, professor of political science
at Temple University asserts that this vast tide of immigration "created the largest and most diverse Jewish community in history, scattered over the largest area ever considered as embracing a single countrywide community."[75]
This unprecedented situation resulted in an almost total
lack of unity at the local level. The new organizational
structure of American Jewish life, which arose to replace
the older pattern, was developed along the lines of American voluntarism and was thus associational in character.
The associational basis of American Jewish life is expressed

in a variety of local and national organizations. The most successful of the bodies (in terms of memberships) combine national and/or international scope with local attachment based on the social needs of the individual Jew.

While there are a number of national organizations, some involved in defense and community relations, others representing the three major synagogal divisions, the center of gravity for Jewish communal life in America is to be found at the local level.

The major national religious organizations—the Union of American Hebrew Congregations, the United Synagogue of America, the Union of Orthodox American Congregations—are confederations of independent local congregations. These national bodies are linked together by the need for co-ordinated services such as professional placement, inter-congregational program and the production of educational materials, but they have no direct influence on the policy of the individual congregation.

Similarly, the community relations agencies, American Jewish Committee, American Jewish Congress, Anti-Defamation League of B'nai B'rith, conduct programs on a national scale but cannot in any sense claim to speak for the entire Jewish community on any particular issue. And while it is true that the leaders of these organizations often issue statements on matters of concern to the whole community, these officials exercise no real power or control over either the local community or the individual Jew.

The national agencies are currently locked in a power struggle with the more than two hundred local Jewish Federations and Welfare Funds. These Federations not only determine the allocation of financial resources at the local community level but also are increasingly becoming involved in community relations program. The issue of Federations vs. national organization is compounded by the reliance of the national bodies on the Federations for supplemental fund raising to support their branches in local communities. Anyone who has ever had the dubious opportunity of representing a national agency at a Federation allocation session knows of the grass-roots impatience with the national bodies. One of the most often heard charges made against these groups is that of duplication of program and services. Questions are asked as to why there is a need for the Anti-Defamation League and the American Jewish Committee to both have staffs working in the area of interreligious affairs, or why the Committee and the American Jewish Congress are both involved in the urban crisis. Underlying the specific concerns is the question as to whether the Jewish community needs several national community relations agencies or could not get along with just one super defense organization.

This query is not new, it has been raised for many years and became the subject of a major study by a Columbia University social scientist in the early 1950s. The Columbia expert recommended that the agencies remain in operation but that they each assume responsibility for a specific program area. This suggestion was not greeted with enthusiasm by the groups involved who all cited important reasons for their continued involvement in multifaceted program. Generally, the major community relations agencies justify their existence on the grounds of differing style, contacts, areas of expertise and effectiveness. Notwithstanding the strong desire of the individual agencies to remain in operation, there are times when the major groups do come together in a common front. This usually involves a specific issue of overriding concern which has a reasonable expectation of time limitation. Thus, the National Conference on Soviet Jewry brings together the major national Jewish community relations, synagogal and social-service bodies. However, the very serious funding problems currently being experienced by the National Conference vividly suggests that the first priority of any particular agency is self-survival. The continuation of independent programs in the Soviet Jewish sphere by the national groups clearly indicates their reluctance to fully surrender program prerogatives to any other body, even to a co-operative effort.

The Federations Have the Jump

The Federations also have the jump on the national agencies in terms of leadership. The fact is that in most cities the Federations attract more of the top echelon of affluent and capable leaders than the chapters of the national organizations. These individuals express a loyalty to the Federation and its goals and program far exceeding whatever interest they might have in the local and perhaps national activities of the major community relations bodies. In the years ahead this crisis of leadership will have dire consequences for the national bodies in terms of program and financial support.

In former years a cadre of rather wealthy, highly skilled and extremely dedicated laymen played important leadership roles in the national organizations. Self-made men, such as Jacob Blaustein and Abraham Sonnabend, not only contributed significant personal resources but also gave generously of their time and aided in the solicitation of funds from business and social peers. Today, individuals of this rank, who could command respect from the three constituencies vital to the ongoing program of American Jewish agencies, Israel, American Jewry and the non-Jewish political and economic establishment, are relating more to the Federations and the Federation's co-ordinating umbrella organization, the Council of Jewish Federations and Welfare Funds. The CJFWF, which has recently become more active in the program arena, evidenced its growing clout with the establishment in 1972 of the Institute of Jewish Life, a million-dollar three-year project whose purpose was "to encourage, support and create innovative experiments, demonstrations and new models to strengthen the quality of Jewish life in North America by reaching local communities."[76]

Despite its grandiose projections there is little likelihood that the Institute of Jewish Life will usher in the millennium, but its existence as a creation of the CJFWJ gives it important influence over the direction taken in the current community-wide struggle with the issue of Jewish continuity. The apparent ease with which the CJFWF funded the Institute for Jewish Life stands in sharp contrast to the increasing fund-raising difficulties encountered by the major community relations agencies. These groups are struggling to keep at an even keel in the face of stiffened local competition for the fund-raising dollar, and rapidly accelerating administrative costs. In the last few years the fund-raising department of the national bodies have been hard-pressed to keep up just with the rate of inflation and overhead expense. The pressure on fund raisers sometimes makes for shortsighted campaigns which in the long run can only prove to be counterproductive. Thus, the American Jewish Committee in 1973 seriously contemplated giving a human relations award to Donald Kendall, chairman of Pepsico, even though it was universally known in the Jewish community that Kendall was one of the most ardent supporters of United States-Soviet trade, and perhaps the single most vociferous industrialist voice opposing the Jackson/Mills-Vanik legislation. Fortunately, the AJC changed its mind but not before a wave of protest swept through the Jewish community.

The Jewish organizations also face serious competition for the fund-raising dollar from Israel-oriented causes. In a genuine sense the national bodies are in the unenviable position of being caught between the needs of Israel and the requirements of the local community. In the period since the June 1967 war Israel-connected giving has been pre-eminent among American Jews. While one can, of course, justify the truly huge sums of money contributed to the United Jewish Appeal and Israel Bonds, it must be recognized that these gifts have seriously inhibited the fund-raising efforts of the national Jewish organizations. Despite the mythologies of Jewish wealth and financial power there is after all only so much money available for charitable purposes. The Yom Kippur war again proved the dominance of Israel in Jewish fund raising and precipitated a major financial crisis within the ranks of the organized Jewish community. In the first days of the war a massive campaign aimed at raising 750 million dollars was launched by the United Jewish Appeal. Such a volume of giving is truly staggering and in large measure represents genuine sacrifice on the part of many individuals. The UJA action came at the worst possible moment for the national Jewish organizations who were then in the initial stages of their own fund-raising campaigns. The emergency needs of Israel as outlined by the UJA and as detailed by the visiting Israeli Finance Minister, Pinhas Sapir, totally overshadowed the already scheduled fund-raising events of the national defense agencies and other major communal organizations. In some cases the national bodies were forced by community pressure, often with the active support of their own lay leadership, to postpone or cancel dinners, receptions and other sessions normally utilized to secure funds. By the second week of the war terms such as "hysteria" and "panic" were increasingly employed to describe the mood of the Jewish community's response to the UJA's blandishments.

The typical UJA meeting was characterized by an extraordinary donor reaction with many individuals significantly increasing their previous pledges. One man in Chicago, after hearing Minister Sapir at a noon meeting went immediately to his bank and borrowed fifty thousand dollars to contribute to the UJA. Four hours later he attended another session where Sapir spoke and he pledged another fifty thousand dollars. The extremely high level of giving to Israel-oriented agencies would probably in and of itself have inhibited further support for the national organizations. Added to this, however, was the suggestion that at a time of crisis to Israel all communal bodies should totally suspend fund-raising operations. This combination of adverse circumstances placed the national organizations in a serious cash imbalance and threatened to erode staff and program. Yet despite the war-related factors which seemed capable of overwhelming them, the national agencies performed in an exemplary manner during the crisis. Each of these bodies went on an emergency footing and allocated substantial funds to accomplish those tasks that the Israel Government could not undertake within the American context.

There is simply no question but that the first thought in the minds of the key executives of the national defense organizations was the survival and well being of Israel. The major agencies were backed against a fiscal wall, but they made every possible effort to contribute to Israel's ultimate success. I have been highly critical of the style and program of these agencies in other areas, and I am certain that these criticisms will hold over the long run, but as far as the war is concerned I have nothing but praise and admiration for the self-sacrificial role played by the national bodies. It must be understood that these groups were in an especially difficult position since they could hardly criticize the fund-raising techniques of the UJA and local Federations. There is little doubt in my mind that the UJA and the Federations exploited the deep and genuine concern generated by the war for their ongoing fund-raising purposes. The major national agencies had to stand by and allow this to happen; first because the Federations provide significant resources to them, and second because the rank-and-file Jewish community was not in a mood to question the nuances of Israel-oriented fund-raising appeals. There is also evidence to indicate that the local Federations used the emergency to again question the necessity for several rather than one national defense agency. If anything, however, the war indicated the value of several bodies, each with its own contacts, style of operation and communication system. The charges of duplication of program and institutional aggrandizement can legitimately be raised in connection with several aspects of the operations of the national agencies, but the experience of the Yom Kippur war will not allow for their total validation. All of the national bodies made specific and important contributions to the Israel-oriented effort, a factor that must be considered in discussions concerning the viability of the multi-agency approach.

The Yom Kippur war clearly outlined the important role national organizations can assume in the building and maintenance of positive public opinion vis-à-vis Israel. The community relations bodies provide interpretive services that the Israel Government and its U.S.-based missions cannot possibly offer. The increased pressure of the active Arab lobby in America, now oriented toward the energy crisis, graphically suggests the crucial contribution the American Jewish organizations can make to the survival of Israel.

Survival or Martyrdom?

The experience of the war period should take on added significance to a community that is prone to problem and crisis. I would suggest that the Yom Kippur war also confirms my general proposition that as helpful as the national organizations can be to Israel they cannot allow themselves to be overly preoccupied with an Israel orientation. The survival of these groups, and despite my persistent criticisms I trust they will survive, depends on their carving out a distinctive role that will contribute to Jewish continuity in America while recognizing an ongoing responsibilty to Israel's survival and development. To accomplish this mission, the national bodies must initiate significant administrative and programmatic changes. But these changes will have little positive effect until the Jewish establishment is prepared to adopt a basic policy that places Jewish concerns above other interests and that is dedicated to Jewish survival rather than to Jewish martyrdom. Such a commitment to Jewishness must be foundational to every strategy and program that brings Jews into relationship with Christians, blacks and other ethnic and racial minorities.

It must also be recognized that to a sometimes significant degree, many of the problems currently confronting the Jewish community are exacerbated by the actions of individual Jews. This seems to be particularly true with reference to the entertainment and publishing industries. In recent years an increasing number of books written by Jewish authors filled with anti-Semitic caricatures and stereotypes have risen to the best-seller lists. Philip Roth's *Goodbye Columbu*s and *Portnoy's Complaint* are examples of works of this genre. The negative impact of these books has been compounded by their adaptation to the film medium.

Lew R. Wasserman and Taft Schreiber, the two top executives of MCA, Inc., made the film *Jesus Christ Superstar* without seriously taking into account cautionary advice from responsible parties concerning the anti-Jewish tendencies of the *Superstar* vehicle. These same film executives are now distributing the movie on a world-wide basis despite the charges of anti-Semitism directed at the movie by almost every major Jewish community relations and defense agency.

One of the most ironic aspects of Jews hurting Jewish interests involves the late impresario Sol Hurok, who emigrated from Russia during the great wave of East European Jewish movement to America. Hurok regularly brought Russian entertainers to the United States and in doing so provided enormous public relations mileage to the Soviets, while his brethren in Russia struggle to obtain the same basic human right that allowed Hurok to leave the nation of his birth.

This phenomenon also pertains in the economic and political realm. Armand Hammer, president of Occidental Petroleum and a strong supporter of unrestricted trade with the Soviet Union, is a Jew, and the two key House Ways and Means Committee aides who worked assiduously to delete the Mills-Vanik bill from trade legislation related to the Soviet Union are also Jewish, as is the Assistant Secretary of State who supplied misleading information to the Ways and Means Committee on the question of Israeli-Russian trade.

No one, of course, should expect total solidarity from any group, and the Jewish community is no more a monolith than any other racial, ethnic or religious body, but at the very least some sort of internal discipline could be applied to those Jews whose actions may inhibit or make more difficult Jewish continuity and survival in America and elsewhere. Should movie magnates who willfully produce and distribute an anti-Semitic film be allowed to continue in good standing in the synagogue and in the various communal bodies? Should writers whose works reflect a total disregard for the aims and objectives of the Jewish community be invited to book club luncheons, lectures and other remunerative sessions organized under Jewish auspices? Should Jews patronize productions of Jewish entrepreneurs who allow themselves to be tools of governments manifesting policies inimical to basic Jewish interests? These are difficult questions and must be considered on an individual basis. Yet I would hope that the time is at hand when the major institutions of the Jewish community will deal decisively with persons who consciously permit enterprises under their control to become vehicles for anti-Jewish propaganda and behavior.

A more complex disciplinary problem is suggested by the activities of Jews who are supportive of movements and organizations whose ideologies and practices are or contain the potential of being injurious to Jewish concerns. Many Jews have been involved with planned parenthood and have strongly supported the principle of abortion on demand, despite the continuing decline in the Jewish birth rate. More critical in terms of this issue has been Jewish advocacy of Zero Population Growth. Dr. Daniel Elazar, a renowned political scientist and a leader of the Sephardic community, states that "even with zero population growth coming in the United States as a whole, we will be a smaller percentage of the total population and less able to defend our legitimate interests as Jews." Dr. Elazar enlarges on this projection in these ominous terms:

While I do not believe that American Jewry will disappear, I think that the Jewish population in the United States is going to fall rapidly in the next generation. Between disappearance of people through assimilation and the drop in the Jewish birth rate we are likely to lose two million Jews, "off the top," over the next sixty years. Many will just fade out of the picture as Jews; we will not even know about it. While the "saving remnant" will remain, we will be that much weaker internally and externally. We will have less in the way of human and economic resources to draw upon and our influence in the larger society will diminish.[77]

In the light of this prognosis, I would call upon the Jewish-establishment organizations to immediately take steps to discourage their constituents from involvement in any plans or schemes to further reduce the Jewish birth rate. In addition, I would advocate the allocation of special educational and communal service subsidies for Jewish families of three children or more. This and other like programs should be implemented in a concerted attempt to significantly raise the Jewish birth rate over the next ten to twenty years.

Beyond this the Jewish agencies must find a way to channel the genuine humanitarian universalistic impulses of many Jews into more particularistically Jewish channels.

The universalist bent of significant numbers of American Jews can only result in harm to Jewish continuity and survival. Although it may be difficult to accept, these Jews must, in the coming months and years, come to realize that concern for the problems of other groups can to varying degrees inhibit or even damage Jewish civilization. This is not to say that Jews must be so totally single-minded and parochial that they can have no legitimate interest in the plight of others, but such interest must be tempered by the realities of Jewish problems and concerns. One of the most distressing manifestations of Jewish universalism has been the support extended by considerable numbers of Jews to the United Nations. For years many of these persons have heralded the U.N. as the world's most viable mechanism for the achievement of peace and social justice. These hopes have of course never been realized and there is currently no indication at all that the United Nations can ever serve in this utopian capacity. What is more pertinent to the issue of Jewish survival is the decidedly anti-Israel and I would suggest anti-Jewish tone of the world organization. Thus, not only is the U.N. an unlikely vehicle for the fulfillment of Jewish and other universalist dreams, it is also a threat to the survival of Israel and to the stability of Jewish life. The contempt shown Israel by many members of the Security Council during the Yom Kippur war debate clearly articulated the bias of this allegedly objective world forum. The hostility directed at the Israeli delegation caused one Western delegate to remark after a tense session, "At times I thought I was in the middle of a lynch mob." Many representatives by their applause indicated agreement with an anti-Jewish diatribe delivered by Jacob Malik of the Soviet Union:

Like savage, barbaric tribes, in their mad destruction, they [the Jewish people] have annihilated, destroyed and tried to remove from the surface of the earth, cities, villages, the cultural heritage of mankind. They have ravaged entire civilizations.[78]

These remarks were totally consistent with other Malik comments concerning Jews as "the chosen people" and the "size of Jewish noses." The problems faced by Israel in the Security Council are compounded in the General Assembly where an enormous pro-Arab bloc holds sway. It has been apparent from June 1967 to any but the most pollyannish observer that Israel was in a no win position in the U.N., but the October 1973 fighting detailed the anti-Jewishness of the world organization in an almost ghoulish manner. As a result of the U.N. activity related to the October war, I would hope that every major national Jewish organization and local federation and community relations agency would completely cease support for any direct or indirect U.N. program. I include UNICEF in this category, and especially urge individual Jews who have worked for UNICEF to desist in these efforts.

The Jewish communal bodies should immediately investigate the possibility of providing relief to children and others in difficult and unfortunate situations outside the framework of the United Nations. Such funds and services should be provided, however, *only* after it has been determined that Jewish needs in America, the other areas of the Diaspora and Israel can be met. I would urge the Jewish community to engage in a total boycott of the United Nations and its affiliates and I would suggest that community discipline be applied to any Jews who continue to lend assistance to the U.N. itself or to groups such as the United States Association for the United Nations.

The willingness of some rabbis and other identifiable Jewish communal leaders to sign newspaper advertisements and petitions calling for President Nixon's impeachment at the very moment during the Yom Kippur war when the Chief Executive was providing the material assistance needed to enable Israel to successfully counter Arab aggression is another cause for concern. If the Jewish community had the capacity for internal discipline, these individuals would have thought twice before lending their support to an effort that not only threatened the President personally but may also have provided the impetus for the Soviet Union to believe that the United States Government was in such a state of disarray that unilateral activity in the Middle East would, by default, be countenanced.

The Jewish establishment must develop a methodology to cope with the significant incidence of negative and potentially destructive actions of individual Jews related to issues of Jewish continuity and survival. In addition, the communal organizations need to do a more effective job in membership recruitment and retention. These groups should also broaden their base by reaching out to Jews in the streets. These individuals can contribute energy and enthusiasm while providing a balance to the upper middle-class dominated life style of the establishment groups.

The major Jewish agencies are currently engaged in a struggle for institutional survival. I would suggest that this struggle is inextricably linked to the larger battle currently being waged over the question of Jewish continuity in America. It is safe to predict that only those organizations that commit themselves to a thoroughgoing and all-inclusive concentration and preoccupation with *Jewish* concerns and issues will continue to be in active operation at the close of this decade. In the light of the tremendous problems and challenges facing American Jewry, no Jewish organization can responsibly continue on the path of coalition with hostile or indifferent non-Jewish forces, and no agency can justify a program that supports the aspirations of others at the expense of the rights of Jews.

I surely trust that the universalist-minded segment of the Jewish establishment will be prepared to accept the fundamental change in orientation that is demanded by the contemporary situation of Jews in America. It is crucial that all persons in positions of communal responsibility recognize that the time has passed when the Jewish community could marshal the resources, expertise and program to pull everyone else's chestnuts from the fire while Jerusalem, Torah and the Jewish people are pushed toward the developing inferno.

New Tests on the Horizon

The capacity of the American Jewish community to effectively respond to the problems already lying on the near horizon will soon be severely tested. In the light of the Jewish establishment's reactions to manifestations of anti-Semitism in the late 1960s and early 1970s, I am not particularly sanguine about the possibilities of both a realistic assessment of the problem and the development of an effective program to deal with the threat to Jewish security in America.

Again and again I have been struck by the failure of many Jewish leaders to come to grips with the deepening crisis confronting American Jewry. I can painfully recall a conversation held with the president of a Jewish Federation in a major city during the second week of the Yom Kippur war. One of my colleagues told of an incident in which a gentile youngster had warned a ninth grade Jewish classmate, "You Jews are not going to keep us from driving our car." To this the Federation leader responded, "You professionals are always oversensitive about anti-Semitism." Another lay leader added that one should not take the boy's remark seriously since "he was obviously put up to it by an adult." I am afraid that these reactions, which represent an almost pathological unwillingness to face reality, are only too typical of a significant segment of Jewish leadership at both the national and local level. These individuals fail to recognize that the Christian establishment's antagonism to Israel, the spread of anti-Jewish attitudes from extremists to rank-and-file elements of the black community, the trend toward quotas and away from the principle of merit in employment and educational opportunities, the diminution of Jewish political clout, the renaissance of ethnic identification among groups traditionally hostile to Jewish experience, the joining together of a great industrial force with the Arab lobby and the general tenor of domestic uneasiness and instability resulting from Watergate are all factors pointing toward serious trouble for the Jewish community.

When such phenomena are analyzed in the light of the particular Jewish crisis involving youth, education, identity and the cohesiveness and stability of the communal structure, the inescapable conclusion must be reached that the age-old question concerning the status of Jewish life would have to be answered by the emphatic statement, "It's not good for the Jews!" In such a time institutional rivalries, community jealousies, competitions over prerogatives and turfs, along with barriers to effective action resulting from class and religious distinctions must give way to a new, radical and universally operative commitment to Jewish continuity and survival. Now as perhaps never before American Jews must make their very lives a testimony to that most powerful of all Jewish affirmations, *Am Yisroel Chai!*

AFTERWORD

This book has been written from the perspective of one who though intellectually and professionally familiar with the Jewish community, has lived, for much of his adult life, outside the context of active Jewish experience.

I was born of Jewish parents and lived for my first eighteen years within a Jewish milieu. At age eighteen, a personal spiritual experience, prompted by reading the New Testament, resulted in my conversion to Christianity. My decision to become a Christian, was not frivolous, nor was it arrived at in a sudden flash of revelation. I embraced Christianity only after extensive study upon the life and ministry of Jesus. The seriousness of my intentions were manifested in Christian baptism and in identification with a local Baptist congregation. Three years after my conversion, I entered the Moody Bible Institute to prepare for a career in Christian service. After a year at Moody, I transferred to Gordon College and graduated from that institution in 1961. While in college I pastored a church in rural New Hampshire and I continued with church-related activity when enrolled in graduate studies at New York University. In 1964 I began a two-year assignment as a history instructor at Barrington College, an evangelically oriented school located in Rhode Island. In 1966, I returned to New York to complete work toward a degree in Jewish studies.

During the middle 1960s, as a reflection of a shift in theological position from a conservative to a more moderate stance, I changed denominational affiliation from Baptist to Presbyterian.

In 1967 I joined the staff of the National Conference of Christians and Jews as director of a research project aimed at analyzing the image of Jews and Judaism in Protestant church school curricula. One year later I accepted a position as consultant to the Interreligious Affairs department of the American Jewish Committee. For the past five years I have enjoyed a close personal and professional relationship with both AJC colleagues and with a wide range of persons in the Jewish community. I hope that in my activity with the AJC I have at least in small measure, made a contribution to the development of mutual respect and understanding between Jews and Christians.

During these past several years I have had the opportunity to observe at first hand, the strengths and weaknesses of the organized American Jewish community. In this book I have attempted to both outline the problems confronting American Jewry and to offer some suggestions for coping with the many serious issues that currently trouble Jewish life in the United States. I have also been critical of those aspects of the organizational style, philosophy and program of the major Jewish communal agencies which appear to me to be inconsistent with the demands of Jewish continuity and survival. I have also been at least implicitly critical of individual Jews who manifest a universalistic rather than a particularistic approach to issues of concern to the Jewish community.

While it would be quite proper for a non-Jew to ob-jectively examine Jewish life in America and draw critical conclusions, it would be an act of gross hypocrisy for some- one of my background to talk of the vital need for Jewish continuity while retaining a personal non-Jewish identifica- tion. It is therefore my intention to return to the Jewish community. This decision comes after long and careful re- flection. As one who has been greatly influenced by the writings of the twentieth-century Jewish philosopher Franz Rosenzweig, I can find theological justification for regard- ing Judaism as eternally valid and meaningful a faith system as Christianity. I can also cite support for a return to Judaism in the demand of Emil Fackenheim not to allow Hitler any posthumous victories. As important as these con- cepts are, the basic reason for my "coming home" is the existential reality of Jewish birth and a consuming desire to rediscover personal and group roots. There is in this de- cision nothing of martyrdom or self-denial or the sense of zealousness so often associated with conversion. I know from personal experience how fraught with peril is the way of the true believer. Instead, I feel joy and freedom in taking up that which I never really perceived or appreciated as a young person.

I am certain that those Christian brothers and sisters who manifest a profound theological and human appreciation and love for Israel and the Jewish people will comprehend the desire of a son of Abraham, Isaac and Jacob, to return to the house of his fathers. I am also convinced that my Jewish brethren with whom I have labored and lived will extend the hand of fellowship and welcome. To all these friends and co-workers and to my wife and children, I ask for understanding and the opportunity to join together with them to enhance Shalom.

NOTES

CHAPTER I
ISRAEL AND THE AMERICAN JEWS

1. Arthur Morse, *While Six Million Died: A Chronicle of American Apathy* (New York, Random House, 1968).
   Henry Feingold, *The Politics of Rescue: The Roosevelt Administration and the Holocaust, 1938–1945* (New Brunswick, New Jersey: Rutgers University Press, 1970).
2. Nora Levin, *The Holocaust: The Destruction of European Jewry, 1933–1945* (New York: T. Y. Crowell Co., 1968).
3. Raul Hilberg, *The Destruction of the European Jews* (Chicago: Quadrangle Books, 1961), p. 728.
4. Emil L. Fackenheim, "The People Israel Lives," *Christian Century*, May 6, 1970, p. 567.
5. Jacob A. Rubin, *Partners in State Building: American Jewry and Israel* (New York: Diplomatic Press, 1969), Foreword.
6. Robert Silverberg, *If I Forget Thee O Jerusalem: American Jews and the State of Israel* (New York: Morrow, 1970), p. 479.
7. Marshall Sklare, "Lakeville and Israel: The Six Day War and its Aftermath," *Midstream*, October 1968, American Jewish Committee Reprint.
8. Ibid., p. 13.
9. Ibid., p. 18.
10. Memorandum written by Jacob Blaustein and sent to members of the American Jewish Committee, August 1970.
11. Ibid.
12. Ibid.
13. Silverberg, op. cit., p. 471.
14. Blaustein, op. cit.
15. Silverberg, p. 474.
16. Ibid.

17. *The New York Times,* January 31, 1972, p. 7.
18. Ibid.
19. Ibid.
20. Judah J. Shapiro, "The Assignment Was the Future," *Jewish Frontier,* December 1972, p. 10.
21. *The New York Times,* November 7, 1969, p. 30.
22. Religious News Service, August 12, 1970.
23. Ibid.
24. *The New York Times,* August 9, 1970, p. 5.
25. *London Jewish Chronicle,* February 9, 1973, p. 4.
26. Albert E. Arent, "The Partnership Between the Jewish Communities of Israel and the United States," *Plenary Session Papers,* National Jewish Community Relations Advisory Council, June 28, 1972, p. 12.
27. *Jewish Post and Opinion,* December 8, 1972, p. 6.
28. *Jewish Post and Opinion,* January 19, 1973, p. 3.
29. *Jewish Post and Opinion,* April 6, 1973, p. 6.
30. Allen Pollack, "American Jewry and Israel: Partners in the Struggle for the Jewish Future," *Assembly Papers,* Council of Jewish Federations and Welfare Funds, November 1970, p. 9.
31. *The New York Times,* August 6, 1972, p. 13.
32. Ibid.
33. *Jewish Post and Opinion,* July 21, 1972, p. 6.
34. *London Jewish Chronicle,* February 9, 1973, p. 4.
35. *The New York Times,* May 8, 1973, p. 5.
36. Ibid.
37. *The New York Times,* February 14, 1972, p. 4.
38. Jewish Telegraphic Agency, May 3, 1973.
39. Abba Eban, "Substance of the American-Israeli Dialogue," *The American Zionist,* January 1972, p. 8.
40. Los Angeles Times Syndicate published in the *New York Post,* October 24, 1973.
41. Daniel J. Elazar, "Kinship and Consent in the Jewish Community," *Assembly Papers,* Council of Jewish Federations and Welfare Funds, November 1972, p. 7.

CHAPTER II
THE SOVIET JEWS

1. Allen Pollack, "The Soviet Union and the Jewish People," *Assembly Papers,* Council of Jewish Federations and Welfare Funds, November 1971, p. 11.
2. For the discussion of the post World War II period I am indebted to Arieh Tarktower, "The Jewish Problem in the Soviet Union," *Jewish Social Studies,* October 1971.
3. Shmuel Ettinger, "Russian Jewish Relations Before and After the October Revolution," in Richard Cohen, ed., *Let My People Go* (New York: Popular Library, 1971), p. 165.

4. Maurice Friedberg, "The Plight of the Soviet Jews," *Problems of Communism,* November–December 1970, p. 21.
5. Steven Bauman, "Soviet Jews, Human Rights and the U.N.," *Vista,* September–October 1972, p. 34.
6. Elie Wiesel, *The Jews of Silence* (New York: Holt, Rinehart and Winston, 1966), p. 44.
7. Cohen, op. cit., p. 80.
8. Text of the Brussels Declaration quoted in Cohen, pp. 141–42.
9. Memorandum from Richard Maass to members of the National Conference on Soviet Jewry, July 23, 1973.
10. From the writer's notes taken at Washington, D.C., June 17, 1973.
11. See Report of Consultation, National Interreligious Task Force on Soviet Jewry, April 1972.
12. Ibid.
13. *The New York Times,* September 14, 1973, p. 39.
14. See William Korey, "A Century Old Tradition of American Initiatives on Behalf of Oppressed Minorities," distributed by National Conference on Soviet Jewry, 1973.
15. See budget reports for 1971–73, National Conference on Soviet Jewry.

CHAPTER III
AMERICAN JEWS AND THE CHRISTIAN COMMUNITY

1. Quoted in Saul Friedlander, *Kurt Gerstein: The Ambiguity of Good* (New York: 1969), p. 38.
2. See Leon Poliakov, *Le Breviare de la haine* (Paris: 1951), pp. 242–44.
3. Assemblies of God, *Romans,* 1962, pp. 78–80.
4. Hertzel Fishman, *American Protestantism and the State of Israel,* Ph.D. Dissertation, New York University, 1971, p. 339.
5. Robert Alter, "Zionism for the 70's," *Commentary,* February 1970, p. 50.
6. Franklin H. Littell, Excerpts from remarks delivered to National Emergency Conference on Peace in the Middle East, January 25, 1970. See also *Congress BiWeekly,* February 20, 1970.
7. Writer's notes NCC governing board meeting, New York City, October 12–15, 1973.
8. See *The New York Times,* October 15, 1973, p. 21.
9. This conversation also included Rabbi A. James Rudin, Associate Interreligious Affairs Director, American Jewish Committee.
10. Religious News Service, October 18, 1973.
11. *The New York Times,* October 15, 1973. p. 21.
12. Report prepared by Sister Rose A. Thering, Seton Hall University, October 1970.
13. *Washington Post,* June 19, 1971.
14. See Arnold T. Olson, *From Israel to the National Association of Evangelicals,* Evangelical Free Church of America, May 1973.

15. See *The New York Times*, June 8, 1972, p. 50.
16. *Adult Student*, July–September 1968 (Scripture Press), p. 38.
17. Manny Brotman, "The Abundant Jewish Life," *Power*, July 15, 1973, pp. 6–7.
18. Ibid., p. 6.
19. American Board of Missions to the Jews, *Pray for the Peace of Jerusalem*, October 1971.
20. American Board of Missions to the Jews, *The Chosen People*, May 1972, p. 15.
21. *The New York Times*, April 2, 1971, p. 1.
22. *The New York Times*, December 10, 1971, p. 33.
23. *Newsweek*, April 17, 1972, p. 60.
24. *Moody Monthly*, June 1972, p. 10.
25. *Christianity Today*, September 28, 1973, p. 43.
26. Roslyn Lacks, "Moishe Sees the Light," *Village Voice*, September 14, 1972.
27. Ibid.
28. Samuel Fishman, "Comment from the Campus: The Jesus Freaks," May 8, 1972 and "Jewish Students and the Jesus Movement: A Follow-up Report," December 15, 1972.
29. Moishe Rosen, "Why Are Young Jews Turning to Christ?" *Christianity Today*, November 10, 1972, pp. 12–13.
30. Fishman, op. cit.
31. Moishe Rosen, *Christmas Is a Jewish Holiday*, Jews for Jesus.
32. Writer's notes taken at Explo '72, June 16, 1972.
33. Writer's notes NCC governing board meeting, March 1, 1973.
34. Statement issued by Dr. Graham from Montreat, N.C., March 2, 1973.
35. Writer's reconstruction of conversation between Dr. Graham, Rabbi Marc H. Tanenbaum and himself, Montreat, N.C., February 26, 1973.
36. See Report of Solidarity Day Activities, National Interreligious Task Force on Soviet Jewry.
37. *Event*, February 1972, pp. 4–8.

CHAPTER IV
THE BLACKS, THE JEWS AND THE URBAN CRISIS

1. Student Non-Violent Coordinating Committee, *Newsletter*, June–July 1971.
2. Earl Raab, "The Black Revolution and the Jewish Question," *Commentary*, January 1969, p. 30.
3. *The New York Times*, September 3, 1967, p. 1.
4. *Time*, January 31, 1969, p. 59.
5. See Leonard J. Fein, "The Negro Revolution and the Jewish Community," an address published by the Synagogue Council of America, 1969, p. 9.

6. Ibid.
7. *The New York Times,* September 10, 1968, p. 73.
8. Jewish Telegraphic Agency, July 1, 1968.
9. *The New York Times,* October 23, 1968, p. 32.
10. Ibid.
11. *Time,* January 31, 1969, p. 58.
12. *The New York Times,* February 1, 1968, p. 26.
13. Ibid.
14. Ibid.
15. *The New York Times,* October 23, 1968, p. 32.
16. See *ADL Bulletin,* June 1967.
17. *The New York Times,* October 23, 1968, p. 32.
18. *The New York Times,* January 26, 1969, p. 1.
19. *The New York Times,* December 20, 1968, p. 20.
20. *The New York Times,* January 26, 1969, p. 1.
21. Ibid.
22. Ibid.
23. *The New York Times,* October 23, 1968, p. 32.
24. *Time,* January 31, 1969, p. 62.
25. *The New York Times,* January 26, 1969, p. 1.
26. Allen Schoener, ed., *Harlem on My Mind: Cultural Capital of Black America* (New York: Random House, 1968).
27. *The New York Times,* January 19, 1969, p. 61.
28. *The New York Times,* January 26, 1969, p. 1.
29. Ibid.
30. *The New York Times,* January 18, 1969, p. 1.
31. *The New York Times,* January 31, 1969, p. 21.
32. Religious News Service, February 21, 1969.
33. *The New York Times,* April 13, 1969, p. 35.
34. *The New York Times,* March 16, 1969, p. 35.
35. See Remarks by Rabbi Arnold J. Wolf in "The Negro Revolution and the Jewish Community," Synagogue Council of America, March 1969, p. 22.
36. *The New York Times,* January 29, 1969, p. 22.
37. *The New York Times,* January 26, 1969, p. 1.
38. *Time,* January 31, 1969, p. 57.
39. *The New York Times,* February 7, 1969, p. 29.
40. Henry Lee Moon, "Of Negroes, Jews and Other Americans," *The Crisis,* April 1967.
41. Earl Raab, "The Black Revolution and the Jewish Question," *Commentary,* January 1969, p. 26.
42. Richard Rubenstein, "The Politics of Powerlessness," *Reconstructionist,* May 17, 1968, p. 12.
43. Raab, op. cit., p. 30.
44. *The New York Times,* October 14, 1971, p. 22.
45. Religious News Service, February 22, 1971.
46. Joseph Robison, "Affirmative Action and Reaction," *Reform Judaism,* October 1972, p. 6.

47. Bernard Weinberger, "The Interracial Crisis: How Should Jews Respond?" *Journal of Jewish Communal Service,* Fall 1969, pp. 38–44.
48. Ibid., p. 39.
49. *New York Amsterdam News,* September 29, 1973, p. A-1.
50. Ibid., p. B-5.
51. Richard Rubenstein, "Jews, Negroes and the New Politics," *Reconstructionist,* November 17, 1967, p. 15.

CHAPTER V
THE JEWISH DEFENSE LEAGUE

1. *The New York Times,* January 24, 1971, p. 51.
2. Ibid.
3. W.S., "Catching Up with Kahane," *Jewish Currents,* September 1971, p. 6.
4. *New York Journal-American,* July 4, 1965.
5. Walter Goodman, "I'd Love to See the J.D.L. Fold Up But—" *The New York Times Magazine,* November 21, 1971, p. 33.
6. Jack Luria, "In Place of Numbers," *The Jewish National Monthly,* February 1971, p. 33.
7. *Newsweek,* January 25, 1971, p. 32.
8. *The New York Times,* April 29, 1971, p. 51.
9. *The New York Times,* June 24, 1969, p. 31.
10. Goodman, op. cit., p. 116.
11. Ibid., p. 115.
12. Ibid., p. 116.
13. *New York Daily News,* October 9, 1969.
14. *Newsweek,* January 12, 1970, p. 35.
15. Memorandum of Commission on Interfaith Activities, Union of American Hebrew Congregations, January 13, 1971.
16. See American Jewish Committee, *Fact Sheet-Jewish Defense League,* January 1971, p. 15. See also Henry Iancovici, "The Jewish Defense League," *Patterns of Prejudice,* July–August 1971, p. 11.
17. *Newsweek,* January 12, 1970, p. 35.
18. Roy Bongartz, "Three Meanies: 2. Superjew," *Esquire,* August 1970, p. 128.
19. See statement issued by Arnold Forster, November 20, 1969, ADL Press Release.
20. Quoted in "Fact Sheet-Jewish Defense League," Trends Analyses Division, American Jewish Committee, January 1971.
21. *Facts,* February 1971, p. 527.
22. Ibid., p. 526.
23. See American Jewish Committee, Fact Sheet on the JDL, p. 17.
24. Ibid., p. 17.
25. *Facts,* February 1971, p. 527.

26. Goodman, op. cit., p. 33.
27. André Ungar, "A Phenomenon called Kahane," *Sh'ma,* May 14, 1971, p. 108.
28. Jack N. Porter and Roy Delbyck, "The Jewish Defense League: New Tensions in the Old Melting Pot," *Christianity and Crisis,* April 17, 1972, pp. 89–90.
29. Goodman, op. cit., p. 33.
30. *The New York Times,* January 19, 1971, p. 42.
31. See *Current Biography,* October 1972, p. 23.
32. *The New York Times,* May 13, 1971, p. 1.
33. *The New York Times,* July 24, 1971, p. 26.
34. Jewish Telegraphic Agency, June 9, 1972.
35. *The New York Times,* June 28, 1971.
36. Quoted in memorandum distributed by the National Jewish Community Relations Advisory Council, April 30, 1971.
37. Goodman, op. cit., p. 121.
38. *London Jewish Chronicle,* September 17, 1971, p. 8.
39. *Jewish Week,* May 20, 1971.
40. *The New York Times,* May 12, 1972, p. 9.
41. *The New York Times,* May 26, 1972, p. 35.
42. *The New York Times,* June 12, 1972, p. 34.
43. *The New York Times,* June 2, 1972, p. 37.
44. Ibid.
45. *The New York Times,* July 1, 1972, p. 24.
46. *Facts,* February 1971, pp. 524–25.
47. Goodman, op. cit., p. 117.
48. *Time,* January 11, 1971, p. 15.
49. Elkanah Schwartz, "Notes on the JDL Experience," *Jewish Life,* April 1972, p. 19.

CHAPTER VI
JEWS AND AMERICAN ELECTIONS

1. C. Daniel Chill, "Changing Jewish Voting Patterns," *Jewish Life,* September–October 1969, p. 15.
2. Ibid., p. 20.
3. See Rowland Evans and Robert Novak, "Nixon Woos Jewish Voters," *Washington Post,* June 21, 1972, p. A-23.
4. Seymour Siegel, "A Vote for President Nixon," *Sh'ma,* September 1, 1972, p. 123.
5. Ibid., p. 124.
6. Richard Reeves, "McGovern, Nixon and the Jewish Vote," *New York* magazine, August 14, 1972, p. 28.
7. *New York* magazine, August 14, 1972.
8. *Time,* August 21, 1972; October 16, 1972
Newsweek, August 21, 1972, pp. 14–15.

9. Seymour Graubard, "The Jewish Vote," *Comment,* September 1972.
10. Ibid.
11. *The New York Times,* September 2, 1972, p. 7.
12. Ibid.
13. Irving Louis Horowitz, "The Jewish Vote," *Commonweal,* October 13, 1972, p. 32.
14. Herman Edelsberg, "For Myself or Not For Myself Alone," *The National Jewish Monthly,* December 1972, p. 46.
15. Eugene Borowitz, "The Electoral Priorities for a Jew," *Sh'ma,* September 1, 1972, p. 122.
16. *The New York Times,* July 17, 1972, p. 11.
17. Michael Kramer, "Is Nixon Kosher?" *New York* magazine August 14, 1972, p. 33.
18. *Time,* August 21, 1972, p. 12.
19. See *Washington Post,* June 11, 1972, p. 1.
20. *Washington Post,* June 17, 1972, p. 10.
21. *New York Post,* June 16, 1972, p. 5.
22. Albert Arent, "The Partnership Between the Jewish Communities of Israel and the United States," *Papers from the Plenary Session,* National Jewish Community Relations Advisory Council, June 28, 1972, p. 9.
23. Borowitz, op. cit., p. 122.
24. Mark M. Krug, "Have American Jews Lost Their Political Clout?" *The Jewish Digest,* November 1971, p. 28.
25. Horowitz, op. cit., p. 31.
26. Reeves, op. cit., p. 26.
27. Ibid., 27.
28. Jerome H. Bakst, "Implications for the Jewish Community of Voting Patterns in the 1972 Elections," National Jewish Community Relations Advisory Council Memorandum, p. 6.
29. Ibid., p. 6.
30. Commission on Social Action of Reform Judaism, "Analysis of the 1972 Election including Jewish Vote," Memorandum, December 11, 1972.
31. Ibid.
32. Victor Lasky, "Satisfaction With a Job Well Done," *The National Jewish Monthly,* December 1972, p. 54.

CHAPTER VII
SURVIVAL IN AMERICA

1. Raul Hilberg, *The Destruction of the European Jews,* (Chicago: Quadrangle, 1961), pp. 5–6.
2. Robert Sherrill, "The Jew: The Endless Quest," *Lithopinion,* Spring 1970, p. 9.

3. Ibid., p. 9.
4. Loc. cit.
5. Earl Raab, "American Jewry in Ferment," *Israel,* October 1972, p. 10.
6. *The New York Times,* February 7, 1968, p. 35.
7. *The New York Times,* June 25, 1968, p. 37.
8. *The New York Times,* March 19, 1970, p. 22.
9. *The New York Times,* June 21, 1973, p. 32.
10. *The New York Times,* February 9, 1973, p. 24.
11. Jewish Telegraphic Agency, February 9, 1973.
12. Ibid.
13. Religious News Service, January 25, 1973.
14. See Erich Rosenthal, "Studies of Jewish Intermarriage in the United States," *American Jewish Yearbook,* Vol. 64, 1963.
15. See Milton Himmelfarb, *Commentary,* April 1971.
16. *The New York Times,* February 11, 1973, Sec. IV, p. 8.
17. For this and following quotes see Jewish Telegraphic Agency, June 8, 1973.
18. For this and following quotes see Jewish Telegraphic Agency, June 22, 1973.
19. Religious News Service, January 25, 1973.
20. Ibid.
21. Albert Jospe, "The Jewish Student Today: A Portrait," *Jewish Heritage,* Fall 1969, p. 23.
22. Dorothy Rabinowitz, "Are Jewish Students Different?" *Change,* Summer 1971, p. 47.
23. *The New York Times,* December 23, 1971, p. 22.
24. Grace Davidson, "Hasidic Activists," *Jewish Spectator,* December 1969, p. 18.
25. *The New York Times,* January 10, 1971, p. 69.
26. Jon Groner, "The 1973 Phenomenon: Jewish Residences," *Sh'ma,* May 11, 1973, p. 105.
27. Bill Novak, "The Havurah in New York City: Some Notes on the First Year," *Response,* Fall 1970, pp. 11–14.
28. Steve Robkin, "The Residence in Chapel Hill, N.C." *Sh'ma,* May 11, 1970, pp. 108–9.
29. Wolfe Kelman, "The American Synagogue, Present and Prospects," *Conservative Judaism,* Fall 1971, p. 16.
30. George Johnson, "The Long Range Significance of the New Jewish Consciousness on Campus," Synagogue Council of America, December 15, 1972, p. 3.
31. Novak, op. cit., p. 13.
32. Groner, op. cit., p. 106.
33. Johnson, op. cit., pp. 5–6.
34. Jon D. Levenson, "Life Without Jews is not yet Jewish Life," *Sh'ma,* May 11, 1973, p. 111.
35. Johnson, op. cit., p. 6.

36. Albert Jospe, "Jewish Studies in American Colleges and Universities," 2nd. rev. ed., B'nai B'rith Hillel Foundation, Washington, D.C.
37. *The New York Times,* January 14, 1973, Sec. IV, p. 8.
38. Jospe, op. cit., pp. 1–2.
39. *The New York Times,* June 25, 1972, p. 27.
40. Albert Jospe, *Free Jewish University: An Experiment in Jewish Study,* B'nai B'rith Hillel Foundation, Washington, D.C.
41. Ibid.
42. *American Jewish Yearbook,* 1972, p. 198.
43. See David Singer, "The Growth of the Jewish Day School," *Commentary,* August 1973, p. 56.
44. For much of my discussion of the Jewish Day Schools I am indebted to David Singer, *Commentary,* August 1973.
45. *The New York Times,* March 26, 1973, p. 12.
46. Ibid.
47. *The New York Times,* June 18, 1968, p. 41.
48. *The New York Times,* November 7, 1971, p. 30.
49. Michael P. Lerner, "Jewish New Leftism at Berkeley," *Judaism,* Fall 1969, pp. 474–75.
50. Hershel J. Matt, "Synagogue and Covenant People," *Conservative Judaism,* Fall 1968, p. 2.
51. *The New York Times,* November 17, 1968, p. 114.
52. *The New York Times,* March 31, 1973, p. 33.
53. *The New York Times,* December 3, 1972, p. 149.
54. Murray Saltzman, "Will Judaism Survive the 70's?" *Christian Century,* March 4, 1970, p. 264.
55. Matt, op. cit., p. 2.
56. *The New York Times,* March 5, 1972, Sec. VII, p. 1.
57. *The New York Times,* November 23, 1969, p. 65.
58. Harvey Swados, "A Visit with the Satmar Rebbe," *New York* magazine, January 19, 1964, p. 7.
59. *The New York Times,* November 23, 1969, p. 65.
60. Ibid.
61. *Jewish Post and Opinion,* April 21, 1972.
62. *The New York Times,* February 12, 1972, p. 31.
63. *The New York Times,* March 14, 1972, p. 18.
64. Jewish Telegraphic Agency, June 16, 1972.
65. *The New York Times,* June 12, 1972, p. 43.
66. *The New York Times,* September 11, 1973, p. 1.
67. *The New York Times,* April 4, 1972, p. 7.
68. *The New York Times,* May 27, 1968, p. 49.
69. Jewish Telegraphic Agency, January 30, 1970.
70. *The New York Times,* July 29, 1973, p. 54.
71. Ibid.
72. *The New York Times,* July 18, 1971, p. 48.
73. *Jewish Post and Opinion,* June 23, 1972.
74. *The New York Times,* March 4, 1972, p. 27.

75. Daniel J. Elazar, "A Note on the Structural Dynamics of the American Jewish Community," *Judaism,* Summer 1971, p. 337.

76. See *New York Times,* November 13, 1971, p. 37. See also *Brochure of Institute For Jewish Life.*

77. Daniel J. Elazar, "Building Citizenship in the Emerging Jewish Community," *Assembly Papers,* Council of Jewish Federations and Welfare Funds, November 1972, p. 13.

78. *The New York Times,* October 11, 1973, p. 19.

November 8, 1975

Temple Israel

Minneapolis, Minnesota

In honor of the Bar Mitzvah of
SCOTT ZACHARY BURNS
by
Marc Burns, Paula Berg and
Charles Berg